A MINORITY

IN

A CHANGING SOCIETY

First published in 1979 under the title Les Portugais du Québec.

This revised edition was translated by Margaret Butler *in collaboration with the authors*

© João António Alpalhão and Victor Manuel Pereira Da Rosa, 1980

All rights reserved by the authors
ISBN 2-7603-3056-7

RESEARCH MONOGRAPHS IN SOCIAL SCIENCES
TRAVAUX DE RECHERCHE EN SCIENCES SOCIALES
NO. 6

A MINORITY
IN
A CHANGING SOCIETY

The Portuguese Communities of Quebec

JOÃO ANTÓNIO ALPALHÃO

AND

VICTOR MANUEL PEREIRA DA ROSA

UNIVERSITY OF OTTAWA PRESS
OTTAWA, CANADA
1980

BRESCIA COLLEGE
LIBRARY
44663

CONTENTS

Foreward

This translation of the book *Les Portuguais du Québec* was prepared following suggestions coming initially from official circles and also in response to the urging of several friends and of groups engaged in social action.

The warm reception given the French edition was an incentive for us to bring out the present English version which also affords us the opportunity to update certain data and to add some new ones.

We wish at this time to extend our thanks to all those who have used their good offices to assist us. This publication was made possible thanks to a grant from the Secretary of State and to the support of the Faculty of Social Sciences of the University of Ottawa.

THE AUTHORS

Preface

When I first read A Minority in a Changing Society, *in its original French version, I was impressed by the serious and comprehensive ethnographic work that had been done by the authors both at the theoretical and at the empirical level. Thus, it is with great pleasure that I welcome this English translation which makes their study available to interested English-speaking persons.*

J. António Alpalhão and Victor M.P. Da Rosa have succeeded in organizing and presenting in a lucid and attention-captivating fashion an incredibly large number of facts and insights concerning the Portuguese of Quebec, their history, present situation, existential problems, their vulnerable points as well as their contribution to their host country. While remaining close to the human dimension and to the discursive language of vivid images, wit, and pun, the authors have produced a work of the highest scientific quality, precision, and objectivity, which informs as well as entertains, and describes as well as explains, the socio-cultural processes of adaptation, acculturation, and integration of an ethnic minority in the North American context. While focusing on the Portuguese communities of Quebec, this work, in my opinion, constitutes an indispensable tool for the proper understanding of anyone who is seriously concerned with the larger problems of immigration, sociocultural adaptation and integration, and social change of any ethnic minority in North America. From a sociological standpoint, particularly for those sociologists who have espoused a humanistic perspective, this work can be looked upon as a model for future studies from which serious methodological and theoretical insights and guide-lines can be gained.

Some two decades ago, I came to the United States as an immigrant who faced many difficulties and challenges. In reading

9

A Minority in a Changing Society, *I could easily identify my own situation, dilemmas, and perplexities with those of some of the persons described in this book and, more important, I could now understand and "put into a proper perspective" many situations and problems which had greatly baffled me and left me perplexed at the time when I lived them. Thus, I feel that any immigrant, as well as any person who is seeking to understand the problems and situations facing immigrants, and especially social scientists, psychotherapists, and concerned officials and laymen will find this work enlightening and well worth reading and discussing.*

Alpalhão and Da Rosa, writing in a precise, scientific, and exhaustive yet humane fashion, look at the history of the Portuguese in Quebec, then at the existing conditions pertaining to their family structure, working conditions, recreation and leisure, education, health, religion and to their community relations. Using the comparative method and an anthropological approach, they aptly contrast the lives and existential conditions of the Portuguese in their country of origin with those of their host country to provide a larger framework with which to understand their problems of acculturation and integration in North American society. After having uncovered and described, in a detective-like fashion, many facts and insights concerning the Portuguese communities in Quebec, they then proceed to analyze and interpret these facts and insights and to propose concrete and practical solutions for many of their current problems and perplexities.

The authors have also compiled a large and important inventory of existing community organizations and agencies dealing with the integration of the Portuguese in Quebec culture and daily life. This should certainly be emulated by other studies of different minorities. Finally, the authors conclude their work with a good theoretical and practical synthesis offering a larger, scientific, perspective for the understanding of the challenges and opportunities facing any ethnic minority which is settling and becoming acculturated in Canada as well as in the United States and, perhaps, elsewhere as well—for the fundamental principles here remain the same anywhere. Students of the Portuguese and concerned persons will also find, at the end of this book, a large and well researched bibliography which is a priceless instrument for other studies along the same lines.

At a time when ethnic minorities throughout North America are reawakening and feeling a rising need for getting back in touch with their family roots, their cultural heritage, and their distinctive life-styles as a way to achieve identity and to contribute to the cultural wealth and diversity of their host community, this work could not have been more timely and useful to scholar and layman alike. Today, moreover, with rapid social mobility and even more intense social change, when many are called to change repeatedly not only their physical residence but also their values, ideas, and cognitive perspectives, are we not all, to a greater or lesser extent, "immigrants" for whom sociocultural adaptation and integration is a most vital issue—an issue that is so timely and crucial that it may well make the difference between "surviving" at the sociocultural level or simply "vegetating" and reacting to external events and changes which we no longer understand and thus cannot control? If this hypothesis is correct, as I feel it is, then A Minority in a Changing Society *will cease to be "just another" ethnographic monograph, of good scholarly quality and an important reference work for social scientists, about another ethnic minority in North America, to become a store-house of insights and guide-lines of immediate and direct personal concern for all of us. While not being able to speak for others, I can at least say that this is what this work has become for me and is one of the main reasons why I rejoice at its timely English translation.*

January 1980 **Peter Roche de Coppens,** Ph.D.
Professor of Sociology
East Stroudsburg, Pennsylvania

Introduction

The Portuguese presence in Quebec, characterised in recent decades by an increase in numbers, has been arousing growing interest, which is not always devoid of concern.

This being an ethnic group whose members have almost all arrived very recently, the people and organisations responsible for their social integration are up against a lack of essential tools, especially in the area of socio-cultural analysis. Recognising this need, we are pleased to offer our contribution in response both to a suggestion and to the need to fill a gap.

Considering that Portugal has, in recent times, been one of chief suppliers of immigrant labour in Quebec, we can understand the growing interest shown in the culture of the Portuguese ethnic group. Its presence bespeaks a whole set of values which go beyond the question of simple manpower.

Our intention in writing this book has been to identify these values and situate them within their new context, so as to give responsible and interested parties the chance to know, promote and properly integrate the Portuguese culture within the context of Quebec society.

Given the general and fundamental character of this research, we first of all attempted the most thorough study possible of existing documentation relating directly or indirectly to the Portuguese ethnic group. The absence or scarcity of documents in several areas was partly offset by participant observation and informal interviews. In our concern for objectivity, we relied heavily on the vast documentation which supports this work. Consistent with this approach, we have preferred direct quotations to indirect narrative. Statistical data have been included to better document the text, although certain figures may soon be outdated.

Though our work is not essentially theoretical in approach, it was nevertheless deemed necessary to introduce certain theoretical concepts in order to have a point of reference. We shall limit ourselves to defining the basic terminology used in order to prevent the confusion and ambiguity to which certain expressions peculiar to the field of social science may give rise. Given the subject matter of this study, we are devoting special attention to the following terms: migration, ethnic group, assimilation, integration, acculturation, multiculturalism and culture.

We have taken the term migration in its broadest meaning which encompasses both the movement of individuals or groups from one region to another and their physical transfer to a different society. [1]

We consider an ethnic group to be a community situated within a larger society and characterised by cultural traits which differentiate it.

We define assimilation as the process of relinquishment of the values of a subordinate culture as a function of another dominant one. [2]

---

1. Brinley Thomas (1959) defines migrations as displacements of individuals or families to a different region and includes a change in permanent residence. Eisenstadt (1958) defines migrations as physical transfers from one society to another.

2. Mitchell (in *Dictionary of Sociology*, 1968, p. 9) considers the word assimilation to be a "term generally applied to an immigrant or to an ethnic minority in the process of being absorbed socially by the receiving society". Louis Wirth is thinking along the same lines when he describes assimilation as a phenomenon whereby minority groups are forced to meld with a dominant society, abandoning their cultural characteristics and adopting the values and the way of life of that society (cf. Schermerhorn, 1970, p. 78).

14

We see integration as the process of cultural symbiosis of different groups of individuals in more or less continuous contact. Assimilation leads to a sacrifice of the immigrants' culture to the goal of cultural uniformity; conversely, integration supposes unity in cultural diversity. [3]

For acculturation, we have adopted the definition of anthropologists Redfield, Linton and Herskovits: "Acculturation is the sum of the phenomena resulting from direct continuous contact between individuals or groups having different cultures and translates into a subsequent change affecting the cultural context of one or both the groups". [4]

Summarising the definitions just given, we shall say that assimilation implies the disappearance of the culture of one group as a function of another, that integration leads to mutual adaptation of several complementary cultures and that acculturation is the end result of adaptation, in other words, the unity and personal growth achieved within the integrated cultures.

The term multiculturalism has been applied particularly to the Canadian context, including Quebec, to designate the policy of integration of the different ethnic groups. At first blush, this word suggests cultural pluralism. However, following the example of official sources, we shall define Canadian multiculturalism as a policy of developing individual and collective awareness of the cultural values of the ethnic groups and of their ancestral roots, having as its aim to contribute to the creation of a new cultural entity. [5] According to Steve Paproski, former Minister of State for Multiculturalism: "Multiculturalism is basically a social programme; one of

3. We shall say with Eisenstadt that "it is only when someone has been fully accepted at the informal level that we can say total integration has taken place" (*cit. in* Thomas, 1961, p. 57).

4. Redfield, Linton and Herskovits, 1936, p. 149.

5. Canada. Canadian Advisory Committee on Multiculturalism. *First Annual Report to the Multiculturalism Committee,* 1975, p. 6.

its basic tenets is to ensure that Canada becomes a society in which everyone, irrespective of race, religion or ethnic origin, is in fact treated equally. It is a policy which is based on the philosophy of full participation of residents of Canada in the political, social, economic and cultural life of Canada''. [6]

Within the context of this study, the term culture is the keystone of the concepts which we wish to clarify. Among many possible definitions, we prefer the classical one of Sir Edward Tylor: "Culture is that complex whole which includes knowledge, belief, art, morals, custom, and any other capabilities and habits acquired by man as a member of society". [7] In the broad sense, we shall say that culture is made up of the sum of experiences transmitted by preceding generations and enhanced by the contribution of the present generation. [8]

*   *   *

To facilitate the socio-cultural analysis of the Portuguese community in Quebec, we must necessarily have a vaster framework to enable us to situate this particular case within the overall context of migrations. It should be noted that, although there is an infinite number of empirical works on special instances of the migratory phenomenon, this plethora of material must be contrasted with the scarcity of theoretical references on migrations. [9] In fact, it is only

---

6. Address to the Biennial Conference of the Canadian Ethnic Studies Association, Vancouver, October 13, 1979, p. 6.

7. Tylor, E., *Primitive Culture*. London, Murray, 1871.

8. We have declined to go into the complexities of the concepts evoked by the term culture and we refer the interested reader to the study of Kluckhohn, Clyde and Kroeber, Alfred: "Culture: A Critical Review of Concepts and Definitions" in *Papers of the Peabody Museum of Archaeology and Ethnology*, 1952, Vol. 47, No. 1, Cambridge, Mass., Peabody Museum.

9. This lack has been remarked by known authors, such as Lee (1969) Mangalam and Schwartzweller (1970), Nikolinakos (1975), Price (1969) and Tapinos (1974).

in recent years that some attention has been paid to conceptualisation and to the verification of pertinent hypotheses with a view to formulating a general theory of migrations. Despite the research conducted in this area, the materialisation of this effort to create a theoretical framework which is universally valid and applicable does not seem to be for the near future.

Since, in the present day, emigration is characteristic of less industrialised milieux, as is the case of Portugal, this has given rise to studies relating the phenomenon of emigration to underdevelopment and capitalism.[10] No analysis of contemporary migratory phenomena could dare to disregard the harsh reality of the exploitation of immigrant labour which accompanies these movements.

In considering the etiological factors which precede emigration, we find that it is rarely the result of a totally free choice. There are almost always factors beyond the individual's control which motivate the decision to emigrate.

Among the most frequent underlying causes of present-day migrations, economic reasons hold a prominent place. Immigration is closely linked to the world capitalist economy where labour is exported and imported like any other commodity, and bartered and exploited on the international market.[11] A knowledge of these factors and others of a general nature helps in understanding particular cases. However, their specific study is outside the scope of this work.

To answer an immediate need, we have concentrated, in this study of the Portuguese of Quebec, on elements serving to identify

---

10. We cite, by way of example, the works of Almeida and Barreto (1974), Cinanni (1975) and Nikolinakos (1971 and 1975).

11. As is pointed out by Sauvy (1970), the change from an agricultural economy to an industrial economy radically altered the laws which govern the migratory phenomenon.

their cultural values and to determine the concrete situations which must be taken into account in terms of the goals inherent in the acculturation process.

Since this is essentially a monographic work, intended for wide distribution, it was necessary to compromise, that is to say, to reconcile the requirements of critical analysis with the need to reach the public at large.

We hope that this work will be a useful tool in the hands of those who are dedicated to the well-being of the Portuguese ethnic group of Quebec. It is hoped that this research will facilitate and encourage further studies, which hopefully will elaborate on certain aspects that often we have barely been able to touch upon. We hope, too, that new research will be conducted on the Portuguese living in other Canadian provinces, to yield additional information which will help give a truly comprehensive picture of the Portuguese presence in Canada. [12]

---

12. As regards the Province of Ontario, valuable elements of socio-cultural analysis are already to be found in the study of Anderson and Higgs (1976). In their work and in that of Marques and Medeiros (1978), some data are also provided on the Portuguese living in other provinces of Canada. Special mention should also be made of the research of Grace M. Anderson (1974) on the Portuguese of Toronto.

PART ONE

PORTUGUESE EMIGRATION

I

AN OVERVIEW *

Emigration, which has always been one of the most marked traits of the Portuguese people, has become even more intense today. It is now both constant in time and universal in space.

From the 17th century onwards, it was Brazil that attracted the Portuguese. In the last quarter of the 19th century, it was Africa which offered them a new horizon. In the 20th century, South America, North America and even Europe became the lands of hope of Portuguese emigrants.

Up until the 19th century, Portuguese emigration had never been accompanied by any real political direction or suitable legislation. It had been governed up to then by more or less exceptional and sporadic provisions. [1] It is only in the last century that various decrees have been promulgated to regulate Portuguese emigration at the national level.

In 1919, the *Comissariado Geral dos Serviços de Emigração* (Commissariat General of Emigration Services) was established, which later came to be called *Inspecção Geral* (Inspectorate

---

* It is within the overall context of Portuguese migrations that we can better understand the particular case of the Portuguese in Quebec. This is the "raison d'être" of the two chapters which make up the first part of this study.

1. At the beginning of the 18th century, emigration to Brazil attained such proportions that the government of Portugal introduced a passport system in 1720 (cf. Franco, 1974, p. 8).

44663

General). On October 28, 1947, decree-law No. 36,558 was published, establishing the *Junta de Emigração* (Emigration Board) coming under the Ministry of the Interior.[2]

At a later date, the *Junta de Emigração* came to be called the *Secretaria Nacional da Emigração* (National Secretariat for Emigration) and today, it is called the *Secretaria de Estado da Emigração* (Secretary of State for Emigration).

These different agencies served mainly as bureaucratic institutions and never confronted the problem of Portuguese emigration in its socio-political dimensions. If we can speak of an emigration policy in Portugal, we must regard it as a wrong-way policy insofar as it has served to worsen a situation which is becoming more and more alarming. In effect, Portuguese emigration has ". . . above all starting in the 1960s, reached an intensity and a gravity without precedent in our history".[3]

Mass Portuguese emigration began far back in history. During the last hundred years, almost three million Portuguese have emigrated. This exodus has now been stepped up. Suffice it to say that two million individuals have left Portugal in the last twenty years, a million of them in the last decade.[4] The situation is that much more serious in that it is mainly the youngest and most active population that emigrates.

---

2. This board was made up of a chairman and eight members, one of them from the P.I.D.E. (political police)—who worked among other things to "ensure that emigrants sent money to Portugal or that a portion of their wages was paid to Portugal" (Para. C, Article 1, Law No. 36,558, *cit. in* Lima, 1974, p. 16). Police control of migratory movements was another of its functions. "When special circumstances require, the government, through the Ministry of the Interior, may order total or partial suspension of emigration to a certain country or a certain region" (Law No. 44,427 of June 29, 1962, *cit. in* Granotier, 1970, p. 161).

3. Serrão, 1974, p. 60.

4. Cf. Ferreira, 1976, p. 78; Lima, 1974, p. 29.

The political change which took place in Portugal in 1974 has not yet been able to stem the tide of emigration. It has diminished only as a result of the quotas imposed by the countries of immigration. On the other hand, the new political situation is far from persuading the emigrant masses to return to Portugal. With the exception of individuals having some connection with politics and the military, the number of Portuguese who have returned is statistically insignificant. No mass return of Portuguese is foreseeable in the immediate future, because they are unconvinced that an economic miracle will come about as a result of the new political situation alone.

Statistical data

Here below, we are presenting some statistical data which will serve to better situate emigration within the general context of the Portuguese exodus. First of all, some Portuguese population figures:

TABLE 1-1

Portugal: Population growth and decline, 1969-1978

Year	Total population
1969	9,074,700
1970	9,013,700
1971	8,967,200
1972	8,973,700
1973	8,978,200
1974a	9,218,400
1975a	9,633,100
1976a	9,698,800
1977a	9,773,000
1978a	9,819,600

Source: Portugal. Instituto Nacional de Estatística. *Anuário Estatístico*, 1979, p. 28.
    a. Tentative figures

23

TABLE 1-2

Portugal: Breakdown of population by age groups

Age Group	1960	1971	1975
0-14	2,586,600	2,507,600	2,603,600
15-19	750,600	759,400	845,100
20-29	1,379,400	1,367,300	1,374,400
30-39	1,222,300	1,111,700	1,069,300
40-49	1,008,600	1,038,700	1,150,800
50-59	881,700	868,500	982,900
60-69	593,300	725,900	835,100
70-	439,900	490,600	587,600
TOTAL	8,865,400	8,869,800	9,448,800

Source: cf. *Demographic Yearbook* (U.N.) 1978.

TABLE 1-3

Portugal: Performance of the main population indices, 1963-1976

Year	Natality %	Mortality %	Natural growth %
1963	23.5	10.8	12.7
1964	23.8	10.6	13.2
1965	22.9	10.3	12.6
1966	22.2	10.8	11.4
1967	21.5	10.2	11.3
1968	20.6	10.0	10.6
1969	19.8	10.6	9.2
1970	20.0	10.8	9.2
1971	21.9	11.4	10.5
1972	20.3	10.5	9.8
1973	20.1	11.1	9.0
1974	19.6	11.0	8.6
1975	19.0	10.4	8.6
1976	19.2	10.5	8.7

Source: *Demographic Yearbook* (U.N.) 1978.

The tables just presented indicate both a drop in the Portuguese population and an aging of same.

This phenomenon supports the statement of Karl Marx to the effect that capital has a growing need for young workers and a declining need for older workers. The following data can help us to better understand the Portuguese emigration of recent years and its impact on the population figures shown above.

TABLE 1-4

Portugal: Breakdown of emigrants by countries, 1977

Country	Emigrants
France	900,000
Brazil	620,000
South Africa	500,000
Canada	204,000
Venezuela	140,000
United States	122,300
West Germany	110,000
Argentina	40,000
Australia	30,800
Luxembourg	30,000
Spain	26,000
United Kingdom	25,000
Zaire	20,000
Belgium	12,000
Zimbabwe	11,600
Netherlands	10,000
Switzerland	6,800
Hong Kong	2,500
Bermuda	2,000
Sweden	2,000
Dutch West Indies	1,500
Italy	1,500
Others	735
TOTAL	2,818,735

Sources: Date compiled by Serrão (1979:8) from information provided by the Ministry of Foreign Affairs, the *Instituto Nacional de Estatística* (Portugal) and Report SOPEMI/OCED, 1978.

TABLE 1-5

Portugal: Legal emigration by decades, 1875-1974

1875-1884	142,919
1885-1894	221,903
1895-1904	251,104
1905-1914	483,501
1915-1924	308,083
1925-1934	218,798
1935-1944	92,688
1945-1954	239,961
1955-1964	354,205
1965-1974	746,243
TOTAL	3,059,405

Source: Data compiled by Serrão (1974, pp. 30-32) and statistics supplied by the *Secretaria Nacional da Emigração* (Lisbon).

Based on the foregoing tables, we must conclude that along with a population of nine and a half million Portuguese residing in Portugal, there are presently close to three million living abroad. This means that more than 20% or close to one quarter of all Portuguese, live in other countries, a phenomenon without precedent in the history of Portugal.

Emigration policy

Along with legal emigration, we must also take into account clandestine emigration to all countries. Particularly in the case of

TABLE 1—6

Portugal: Total emigration (legal and clandestine), 1960-1978

Years	Legal Emigration		Clandestine emigration		Total emigration	
	Emigrants	%	Emigrants	%	Emigrants	%
1960	32,318	98.7	414	1.3	32,732	100.0
1961	33,526	96.4	1,270	3.6	34,796	100.0
1962	33,539	87.8	4,671	12.2	38,210	100.0
1963	39,519	73.2	14,451	26.8	53,970	100.0
1964	55,646	64.5	30,636	35.5	86,282	100.0
1965	89,056	76.1	27,918	23.9	116,974	100.0
1966	120,239	90.5	12,595	9.5	152,834	100.0
1967	92,502	87.0	13,778	13.0	106,280	100.0
1968	80,452	77.2	23,697	22.8	104,149	100.0
1969	70,165	45.7	83,371	54.3	153,536	100.0
1970	66,360	38.3	106,907	61.7	173,267	100.0
1971	50,400	33.3	100,797	66.7	151,197	100.0
1972	54,084	51.5	50,892	48.5	104,976	100.0
1973	79,517	66.3	40,502	33.7	120,019	100.0
1974	43,397	61.8	26,876	38.2	70,273	100.0
1975	24,811	55.2	20,107	44.8	44,918	100.0
1976	17,454	52.6	15,753	47.4	33,207	100.0
1977*	16,995	59.1	11,763	40.9	28,758	100.0
1978*	18,651	76.0	5,802	24.0	24,453	100.0
TOTAL	1,018,631	63.2	592,200	36.8	1,610,831	100.0

* Tentative figures

Source: data provided by the *Secretaria Nacional da Emigração* (Lisbon).

27

Portugal, "[...] the clandestine emigration considered to be a scourge of modern times is really as old as emigration itself. During the 19th century, Portuguese workers left clandestinely for Brazil and even Spain. This "flight" did not begin yesterday. Oliveira Martins sounded the alarm as early as 1890, saying that very soon the number of clandestine emigrants would exceed the number of legal emigrants". [5]

Based on table 1-6, we may conclude that between 1960 and 1978, 592,200 or 36.8%, out of a total of 1,610,831 Portuguese emigrants, left the country illegally.

Young people are highly represented in these percentages. The colonial wars were one of the primary causes of the clandestine exodus of thousands of young Portuguese starting in 1961, when the wars began. According to Almeida and Barreto, the number of draft dodgers in 1967 totalled 14,000 young men of draft age, and, over a period of ten years, more than 415,000 young men under 30 apparently left the country. [6]

When we speak of illegal immigration, we run the risk of placing the entire blame on the immigrants involved. But when, as in the case of the Portuguese, we find that clandestine emigration accounts for 66.7% of the total annual figure, it becomes obvious that it is rather emigration legislation and policy which are responsible and not the refusal to submit to them. According to Ferreira, "it is not an accident that there are no official figures on illegal emigration. Either they are not known, or their volume and their significance are being concealed, because we do not want to put our finger on the source of the trouble, as if ignoring the symptoms could remedy the disease". [7]

---

5. Almeida and Barreto, 1974, pp. 171-172.

6. Cf. Almeida and Barreto, 1974, p. 207.

7. Ferreira, 1976, p. 73.

Whatever political interpretation we give to the phenomenon, the laws passed could never fully explain the reasons and the circumstances of this exodus. It seems to us that Portuguese legislation on clandestine emigration is an excuse rather that an attempt at control. [8]

Under all regimes, past and present, Portuguese emigration policy has been very ambiguous. Generally speaking, emigration is a personal or collective solution, adopted in a situation of extreme emergency. At the individual level, the decision to emigrate appears logical because it means choosing a lesser evil. However, at the collective level, the attitude of governments is paradoxical insofar as they bemoan the exodus of workers without doing anything to put an end to this situation.

If we analyse the attitude of the Portuguese government during the last decades and even up until very recently, it is difficult to argue with those who accuse it of employing a policy of repression and exploitation which disregards the interests of the less privileged social classes, who are thus forced to emigrate.

An economic policy whereby emigration is considered an "escape valve" for internal social tensions is perforce a policy which serves the interests of the dominant minority. While the national development requirements of the countries which receive this manpower permit such a policy to gain acceptance, it is harder to justify at the international level in the case of the less developed countries which export manpower.

Emigration is frequently justified by the claim that it is a logical, necessary consequence of population pressure. That is in effect a simplistic, superficially convincing way of masking the defects of a faulty system. "There is no population surplus except

---

8. Decree-law No. 39,749 of August 9, 1954 assigned the International State Security Police (PIDE) functions of emigration control. Decree-law No. 46,939 of 1966 established a penalty of two years imprisonment for all persons found to be involved in clandestine emigration.

when social conflicts, which cannot be resolved within existing structures and relations of production, bring about an expulsion of part of a population, generally workers". [9]

The defects which have resulted in a sick Portuguese social organisation go back a long way. Even today, this society is still suffering the consequences of a hierarchical system where the vertex is an oligarchy of the absolutist type encompassing political, religious, economic and military power. This situation underscored the marginalisation of the disadvantaged social strata, by exposing them to opportunistic exploitation. In a system which consciously exposes workers to the exploitation of man by man, we must recognise the complicity between governments which export their manpower and those which accept this manpower.

An analysis of the Portuguese migratory exodus of recent decades suggests that Portugal has had an emigration policy of the suicidal type. This policy has had very heavy consequences for the Portuguese people, who suffer and will suffer the effects of the exploitation to which they have been subjected.

Nevertheless, however serious these defects and however great the tragedy which has driven the Portuguese from their homeland, it seems to us that a good policy is not one which is limited to belabouring the errors of the past. It is more basic, more essential and more urgent to get rid of the old head-in-the-sand policy once and for all.

*   *   *

Some tens of thousands of Portuguese live in Quebec today. Their destiny is bound to two continents, two peoples and several governments. It is clear that the governments of Canada and Quebec have serious obligations to those whom they called upon when they experienced a shortage of manpower. This does not

---

9.   Almeida and Barreto, 1974, p. 252.

mean that the Portuguese government should lessen its interest in and its support for those who continue to serve it far from their homeland. The attitudes and decisions of immigrants vis-à-vis their country of origin depend on the political directions of the Portuguese government. According to Jorge de Sena, "Portugal, if it is to survive and assert itself as a free nation, needs all Portuguese, wherever they are. More than that, it must *regard* them and treat them *as Portuguese*. If we think of Portugal as a giant community spread throughout the globe, we must also consider the millions of Portuguese that a suicidal policy has scattered to the four winds in the sometimes bitter search for means of survival which an absurd system, institutionalised by an archaic regime, denied the majority of them". [10]

---

10.   Sena, Jorge de, "Reintegrar o emigrante" in *Voz de Portugal* (Montreal), June 7, 1974, p. 8.

II

CAUSES AND EFFECTS

While it is true that man is essentially a migrant being, this truth should not be an excuse for failing to examine the causes of emigration or doing nothing to solve the problems inherent in this emigration. When an individual decides to emigrate, it is often for reasons beyond his control. It is by looking at the socio-economic context of the future immigrant that we can better understand the reasons which prompt him to leave his country.

If we consider the causes and the effects of migratory movements in general, we can better situate the Portuguese example within the broader context. This chapter contains only a few elements of analysis, because migratory phenomena are so complex that we cannot hope to offer a synthesis of all their causes and effects.

The causes

It is our impression that the fundamental constant of emigration in our age has been the search for living conditions that are more compatible with human dignity. In modern times, we find factors of an economic nature among the principal causes of migrations. [1]

---

1. The survey of Kemp and Morisset (n.d., p. 1), conducted among the Portuguese of Hull, shows that 73% emigrated to seek a better life, 11.5% for socio-political reasons and 15.5% to join relatives already living in Canada.

Emigration is today more than ever linked to the labour market and dependant on this market at the international level. "Emigration, though it has multiple characteristics, is today one of the facets of the international division of labour, and is imposed by the dominant social organisations and by the most industrialised economies, that is to say, by imperialist capital and its production logic". [2] We can thus understand why the countries supplying manpower are countries whose economy is somewhat backward and whose political regimes are frequently totalitarian.

We cannot deny that a great deal of responsibility for the emigration phenomenon lies with capitalism. "Like a servant subject to orders, a slave of shameful exploitation [...] the people of each country carry the burden wherever and whenever capitalism decrees". [3]

In effect, it is not normally the rich who emigrate in a capitalist system. It is instead the victims of the system who are forced to undergo this trial by fire and to place themselves in the service of a similar system. Though it is wrong to generalise, we must nevertheless admit there is truth in Almeida and Baretto's statement that "hunger, misery, life's oppressions and total insecurity bring about emigration". [4]

Alexandre Herculano was already expressing the same idea when he said that: "some may have created their own misery, but when most members of a society live in miserable conditions, it is

---

2. Almeida and Barreto, 1974, p. 241.

3. Navarro, 1973, p. 15.

4. Almeida and Barreto, 1975, p. 251. The frequent use of these expressions might tend to suggest that immigrant populations are made up of indigents exported by the country of origin. Generally, this is not the case. Persons living in the most abject misery do not have the means to emigrate. Immigrants are generally persons who, refusing to resign themselves to the status quo, have had the initiative to seek to improve their lot.

either because the institutions of that society were badly designed to start with or because they were disrupted later on". [5]

A few years later, to better emphasise a drama which seems to have become the lot of the Portuguese, "Guerra Junqueiro, in his time, deplored the fate of emigrants, those living symbols of a poor homeland whose most deprived children are scattered throughout the world". [6]

To attribute the migratory phenomenon to the adventurous spirit of a people or to fatalistic theories of socio-economic equilibrium would clearly be evidence of naïveté or even of bad faith. Certain authors denounce this phenomenon as an offshoot of minority and capitalistic policies which exploit the working class and threaten its survival. Almeida and Barreto has this to say about Portuguese emigration: "it is not enough to speak of a drama; we are dealing with a veritable rape of the working classes, with one of the cruellest forms of exploitation to which they are subject, and which takes the form of the *expulsion* pure and simple of millions of workers in the course of time". [7]

The drama of emigration has always been a part of Portuguese history. The comment of Fernando Emídio da Silva, at the turn of this century, is very pointed" . . . it is from the emigration of the miserable that the Homeland gets the gold to settle the invoices of its economic confusion and its financial squandering". [8]

More recently, in their attempt at diagnosis, Almeida, Barreto, Krieger and Petitat had this to say: "the causes of emigration do not lie *in a sector in crisis* or in a *depressed region*, but in the struc-

---

5.   *Cit. in* Serrão, 1974, p. 117.

6.   Serrão, 1974, p. 27.

7.   Almeida and Barreto, 1974, p. 174.

8.   Silva, 1971, p. xi.

tures of Portuguese society, in the overall economy and in the economic policy pursued".[9]

The great social upheavals which have taken place since the middle of the last century have been accompanied by the characteristic migratory flows at the time of each event. In these flows, it is above all necessary to emphasise variables of the economic type, even though one does occasionally find political factors. We might recall here the polemics and the persecutions of the second half of the 19th century and the establishment of the First Republic under which "emigrants leaving continental Portugal were astonishingly numerous: 49,560 in 1911, 177,745 in 1912, 67,821 in 1913".[10] A similar phenomenon is presently taking place with the establishment of the Second Republic, although the flow of Portuguese emigrants shows particular features in terms of motivation and type of individual involved.[11]

Among the primary causes which contribute to making emigration an emergency solution, we might mention the following: deterioration of the Portuguese economy compared with industrialised countries; negative aspects of the social status of workers; lack of suitable housing; increase in the cost of living; inadequate school structures; high population density especially in the North of the country and on the islands, inequitable distribution of lands and improper utilisation of these lands; scarcity of jobs and inadequate wages.[12] Another cause of Portuguese emigration would appear to be the inability of the secondary and tertiary sectors to absorb the surplus workers from the primary sector. It is

9. *Cit. in* Serrão, 1974, p. 171.

10. Girão, *cit. in* Serrão, 1974, p. 164.

11. Beginning in 1974, the decolonisation of Portuguese Africa created a new flow of Portuguese emigrants having particular characteristics.

12. According to Martins (1972), 39% of arable Portuguese land is owned by 3% of the population, an imbalance which is unlikely to be found elsewhere to such a marked degree.

unquestionably the primary sector that is most directly affected by this imbalance, which explains why the majority of today's Portuguese immigrants come from the primary sector of the Portugueses economy and from peripheral geographical regions where the standard of living is low.

We cannot conclude, based on the context of emigration and its determining causes, that it is the most inept individuals who are forced to emigrate or who want to emigrate. We would even go so far as to say that such individuals cannot emigrate. Both the initiative to emigrate and the conditions imposed by the receiving country imply that prospective emigrants meet a certain number of basic requirements. Now, these required traits are not common in the more depressed areas. The rural exodus is in many cases the first step towards emigration abroad. In the case of the Portuguese, as Cutileiro remarks, numerous individuals from the rural areas of Alentejo move first to the urban centre of Lisbon, to later leave for France. [13] For a long time, the rural worker lived in subhuman conditions which even denied him access to emigration. [14] His lack of schooling and his low level of general knowledge, to which were added repression by local authorities who toadied to the interests of business, meant that he could not extricate himself from the obscurantism into which he was thrust. Karl Marx, in discussing this problem, spoke of the *reserve army of workers* who guarantee high profits for the ruling classes. [15] In addition, wages being very low, the idea of emigrating ran aground because of a lack of financial means. The mechanisation of agriculture and the rise in

---

13.   Cf. Cutileiro, 1971, pp. 66-67.

14.   The anthropologist Jorge Dias, in discussing this problem, has this to say: "It is not because he is attached to his land that the resident of Alentejo does not emigrate, but rather because financially speaking, he can't afford to" (Dias, 1961, p. 124).

15.   Already in 1845, Friedrich Engels had remarked: "The rapid development of British industry would not have been possible had England not had a reserve: the large miserable population of Ireland" (Engels, 1960, p. 134).

unemployment favoured an exodus towards the more industrialised urban areas, a move which helped to broaden the horizons of rural workers and to give them the financial means needed to go further in their search for better living conditions.

Though this decision is almost always a more or less direct, more or less conscious function of the milieu and of living conditions, if one studies individuals case by case, one finds that there are as many causes and reasons as there are migrants. Not all emigrants are victims of a system which exploits them, but emigration as a mass phenomenon is also a result of the economic systems which give rise to it and maintain it. "Sometimes exploitation begins in the country of origin. For certain countries, emigration represents a gain: it reduces unemployment, brings in foreign currency and makes possible a certain degree of professional training. Rather than concentrate all their efforts on the real development of their own economy, creating new jobs at whatever cost, these countries prefer to profit from migrants". [16]

To attribute Portuguese emigration solely to internal causes would be to consider only one part of the problem. The "push-pull" theory also applies to the Portuguese case. Foreign countries' utilisation of Portuguese manpower obeys economic and political criteria which are linked to their interests. The aim of those countries which import manpower is to increase their production potential, by using a labour force which can be requested at their own convenience.

In the specific case of Quebec, we would list as the main elements of the "pull" factor a high economic level, high wages, the advantages of social security, better prospects for education, and in general, greater potential for children's development. The choice of Quebec as a place of destination may also be attributed to the presence of and testimony by immigrants already established there, to its politico-social image and to advertising abroad.

---

16. Angel, 1973, p. 965.

The effects

Migrations do not just affect those who migrate; they also have repercussions, on the short or long term, on the receiving society and on the society of origin.

One of the immediate consequences, in the case of Portugal, is apparent in population factors. We must consider not only the reduction in the population of certain regions but also the imbalance found in the population pyramid and the inherent social consequences. [17] This imbalance manifests itself particularly in the low marriage rate and hence in a drop in the birth rate. The aging of the age pyramid is another obvious consequence, since the majority of Portuguese immigrants are in the twenty to thirty age group. Thus, we have both a reduction in the population of Portugal and an aging of this same population. [18] This phenomenon qualitatively and quantitatively alters the population structure. [19]

An immediate consequence of this population drop has been a gradual depopulation of rural areas. Another anomaly readily noted in these areas is the predominance of women and children over men and boys. The magnitude of male emigration affects particularly the socialisation of children. In the agricultural sector,

17. Portugal has one of the highest birth rates in Europe. Paradoxically, it is also one of the European countries in which the overall population growth is relatively insignificant. The explanation does not lie in the mortality rate but rather in the emigration drain, the consequences of which are becoming a cause for concern, especially on the long term. "If the sharp drop in the population of most Portuguese districts is not necessarily 'catastrophic' on the short term (because of the surplus of agricultural workers which existed), its consequences have been a cause of concern at the national level: sharp decline in the birth rate (from 24% to 19% in seven years), aging of the population and stagnation of the mortality rate (10.6% in 1969)" (Leloup, 1972, p. 73).

18. Cf. Ferreira, 1976, p. 91.

19. Because the emigration rate exceeds natural growth in several regions of Portugal, one notes an aging of the population due to the high percentage of young emigrants. Already in 1973, this population imbalance had reached disconcerting proportions (cf. Varão, 1973).

migration has caused either a reduction in or an almost total abandonment of traditional crops like olive trees, fig trees, cork-oak, etc.

As a manpower exporting country, Portugal suffers simultaneously from major dependance on international capital, from stagnation of its rural areas, in particular in the agrarian sector, from a reduction in qualified manpower, and from inflation and its effects on the cost of living. In the socio-cultural context, the factors which alter traditional institutions, for instance the family, merit particular consideration. Among the more direct consequences, we might mention the improvement in the family's standard of living, as reflected in more advanced, schooling for the children, and in diet, clothing and household appliances. The increase in buying power translates into the purchase of real estate. In the housing sector, one notes both a renovation of old houses and a building of new homes, which, in certain villages with a high emigration rate, have had an impact on the countryside and on urbanisation.

When we seek to pinpoint the positive results of emigration for the country of origin, we tend to speak of the transfer of foreign currency and the positive effect on employment and underemployment. [20] Some people also mention as positive factors technological advances and the experience acquired in the working world, which can eventually come to benefit the country of origin. However, this theory does not appear to hold up. [21] We must also consider what Tapinos calls the phenomenon of imitation whereby "humble families are led to purchase certain durable goods not produced by the

---

20. Transfers of money do not automatically translate into a real gain for the manpower exporting country. As Tapinos (1974, p. 191) points out: "In the country of origin, the revenue from emigrant workers creates a monetary wealth which remains artificial and precarious if the State does not take advantage of it to make productive investments".

21. Cf. Böhning, 1975; Rhoades, 1977.

national economy and, in so doing, increase the number of imports which are not directly productive".[22]

The reduction in surplus population is also taken to be a positive result for the country of origin.[23] However, resorting to emigration as the sole solution to overpopulation is perhaps a simplistic way of envisaging the problem. An effort in the direction of more rational economic development, based on the real interests of the people, would certainly have been a more effective solution and, on the long term, would have created acceptable conditions on the national territory, thus sparing a large portion of the population the sacrifice implied by the permanent emigration drain. Clearly, the intelligence and industriousness shown by the children of emigrants could have been used to benefit the country of origin.

There is a logical causality between emigration policies and their consequences. However, the arguments which attempt to place the blame on the immigrants are a form of sophism. The desire of Portuguese emigrants to achieve a standard of living compatible with human dignity, either by sending home funds to remodel or build houses, or by raising the educational level of their children, is well known.[24] It is true that these particular goals seem to conflict with the development of the national economy and to be obstacles to the goals of certain economists. Some say that "serving the interests of individual emigrants threatens the future of the global economy".[25]

---

22. Tapinos, 1974, p. 175.

23. We might mention, by way of example, the Azorean archipelago where emigration is so high that today there are more Azoreans (including their descendants) on the North-American continent than on the islands making up that archipelago, in spite of its high population density (cf. *Le Monde*, Paris, August 14, 1975, p. 4).

24. Cf. Trindade, 1973.

25. Ferreira, 1976, p. 141.

Armando Nogueira has this to say about the problem: "On the short term, emigration resolves the human problems of the emigrant, economically speaking [...]. But, on the long term, and at the national level, we are moving towards the creation of serious obstacles to the country's economic development. These obstacles have been downplayed or forgotten, to take second place to something considered essential to the Portuguese economy: the remittance of foreign currency by emigrants".[26] It would however be unjust to say that emigrants are directly responsible for the imminent cataclysm, and to deny their contribution to the growth of the national community.

Recent Portuguese emigration may be regarded as a historical phenomenon of which the repercussions are not yet entirely clear. Nevertheless, if we consider that a quarter of the Portuguese population today lives in foreign countries and that this is the most active segment of the population, we are forced to conclude, even now, that this phenomenon will have immediate negative repercussions on the future of the nation

The effects of immigration on the receiving country are generally the opposite of the effects on the country of origin, as negative factors become positive ones. In the case of Canada, for example, recourse to immigration is first of all an ideal solution to her population problems.[27] The Immigration Department is directly linked with the Labour portfolio, and admission of immigrants is authorised as a function of manpower shortages. It is obvious, therefore, that it is above all in the labour sector that the receiving country feels the benefits of immigration. While workers' education and specialisation must be provided by the country of origin,

26. Nogueira, 1969, pp. 50-51.

27. The sudden and continued drop in the fertility rate, which has been evident in Canada since 1960, has been offset and attenuated by immigration. Suffice it to say that in 1974, the population increased by 348,000 inhabitants, half of whom were immigrants (Bonavia, 1976, p. 11).

immigrant manpower is welcomed with open arms by the receiving country, which then has a select human reserve that it uses according to its needs.

Granotier, following Kindleberger and Zolotas, having studied the consequences for the receiving country, identifies the following advantages and disadvantages: [28]

Advantages	Disadvantages
—Filling of manpower needs	—Loss of currency [29]
—Greater utilisation of production capacity	—Technological stagnation
—Brake on the increase in salaries and wages, and therefore reduced inflation	—Increase in unemployment
—Increase in the rate of economic growth	—Risk of ethnic conflicts
—Advancement of national workers	

We must consider that "the introduction of foreign workers prevents the formation of bottlenecks and brings with it the creation of new jobs". [30] When we realise that contemporary migrations are based on economic interests, we should not be surprised that the manpower importing country sees its inflation rate drop.

---

28. Cf. Granotier, 1970, p. 262.

29. There is no exact correspondence between the European and Canadian contexts. In the case of Quebec, "the average immigrant family has $2,028 in its pockets at the time of its admission and plans to transfer another $3,552. This money largely compensates for the amount sent abroad, which is about $250 per family per year" (Françoise Côté, in Le Devoir, Montreal, December 8, 1978, p. 2).

30. Tapinos, 1974, p. 140.

Superficially speaking, it is as easy to praise migratory phenomena as it is to condemn them, based on their effects, without really doing anything about their causes. The criticism made of this attitude by Oliveira Martins seems quite apropos and constructive, in view of the situation which has prevailed for such a long time: "It is certainly good to oppose emigration, but it is as useless as it is good. To really prevent the population drain, we need actions rather than words and instead of taking coercive measures which prove counterproductive, we should rather revive the domestic economy of the kingdom".[31]

It appears evident that emigration, in certain extreme cases, has offered the most rapid solution to problems to which some kind of response could no longer be delayed. But emigration, as an ideal solution on the medium and long term, seems questionable. The principle which states that, instead of exporting men, countries should import factories, would be valid in a world whose ideal was development and socio-economic balance, because it would prevent needless displacements of manpower. However, in actual fact, the exportation of factories is almost always a somewhat more sophisticated means of exploiting foreign manpower in marginal countries.[32]

The traditional supposed dependence of less developed countries on the more developed ones is, in effect, closer to sophism than to reality. "We always find it hard to imagine that poor countries may be a source of wealth for others and that we may extract a profit from populations considered underdeveloped and which live in difficult material conditions".[33]

---

31. *Cit. in* Almeida and Barreto, 1974, p. 171.

32. Certain authors connected with the Catholic Church also emphasise that "the present migratory phenomenon represents a typical case of exploitation on the sociological level" (Angel, 1973, p. 965).

33. Meillassoux, 1975, p. 13.

In the Portuguese case, we must admit that emigration has, on the short term, clearly improved the material well-being of emigrants and their families in the country of origin. [34] The problem becomes more complex when we consider this phenomenon on the long term in its impact on the country of origin as a whole. The positive aspects attributed to emigration are normally temporary in nature or are even an illusion, because it is necessary to honestly consider the other side of the coin and realise the negative consequences, which are mainly long term and felt at the national level.

To treat emigration as the result of a free choice would, at least in the Portuguese case, imply a certain naïveté, for this emigration is obviously the result of unequal development. The impoverishment of regions and the lack of means to overcome the problem have led populations to explore new horizons, in the hope of finding better living conditions.

Admitting that emigration represents a real drain for the country of origin, how do we explain its form and its continuity? As certain technocrats claim, emigration occurs as a function of income in foreign currency; for many politicians, it is a means of postponing solutions which are beyond their possibilities; for the majority of emigrants, leaving for another country is an extreme solution in the struggle against misery. A country which survives thanks to emigration might be compared to an indigent dying man who is forced to sell his blood to pay for the medical care he needs.

---

34. This situation is described in the study of the village of Queiriga in the district of Viseu (Portugal), conducted by Maria Beatriz Rocha Trindade (cf. 1973a).

PART TWO

FROM ONE PEOPLE
TO
ANOTHER

III

HISTORICAL BACKGROUND

To better understand the historical links between Quebec and Portugal, we must go back to the era of maritime discoveries in the 15th and 16th centuries and situate the Quebec case within a very broad context, or at least within that of the North-American continent.

Discoveries and expansion

The history of Portuguese emigration is closely linked with maritime discoveries, which played a key role in the history of Portugal and which have had a determinant impact on the course of world history. The genius of Luís de Camões evokes and records these immortal exploits in *Os Lusíadas*.

From its foundation in 1143 up to the 15th century, Portugal lived in a corner of Europe, in its own little shell, mainly due to geo-political circumstances. If we look at a map of Europe, we see that Portugal is deeply marked by the sea. Given its geographical position and the fact that it could not increase its territory at the expense of Spain, a richer and stronger nation, the Atlantic remained its sole possible means of expansion. [1] The Atlantic Ocean was thus the route by which the Portuguese travelled to the four corners of the earth, to become a nation of navigators and emigrants.

After the 15th century, more precisely after the conquest of Ceuta in 1415, the Portuguese nation threw itself into the adventure of discovery, trade, evangelisation and colonisation. Bettencourt regards this adventure and the presence of the Portuguese in Africa "as a starting point for the great maritime trading and cultural movement of West European peoples from the 15th to the 17th century, which was to be the greatest spatial revolution in history". [2]

The period of discovery and the age of the Portuguese colonial empire began in the 15th century. When the Portuguese started to challenge the mysteries of the sea, we might say that Portugal discovered her historic mission and that the voyages and discoveries never ceased to multiply from that time on. In 1418, João Gonçalves Zarco discovered the islands of Porto Santo and Madeira; in 1432, Gonçalo Velho discovered the first Azorean islands; in 1445, the coasts of Guinea were visited; between 1477 and 1485, Diogo Cão reached the mouth of the Zaire River and Bartolomeu Dias found his way to the Indian Ocean and, lastly, in 1498, Vasco da Gama sailed along the east coast of Africa and arrived in India.

During this period, there were also Portuguese who went off to discover the western hemisphere. Thus, in 1472, João Vaz Corte-Real explored the coasts of Greenland and Newfoundland and

---

1.   Godinho (1969, pp. 40-41) mentions the following factors, among others, which have determined overseas discoveries and conquests: the thirst for gold due to the scarcity of circulating currency on the markets; currency devaluation pushed to the extreme; the lack of cereal grains and the inability to purchase them; the demand for slaves to fill manpower needs; the expansion of fisheries zones.

2.   Bettencourt, 1961, p. 30.

João Fernandes Lavrador and Pedro de Barcelos reached the Labrador Peninsula and the Bay of Hudson.[3] Almost simultaneously, in 1500, Pedro Alvares Cabral landed in Brazil and the fleet of D. Nuno Manuel explored the coasts of Uruguay and Argentina.[4]

Shortly afterwards, the Portuguese turned their attention to the Orient, sailing from the Indian Ocean to the Pacific Ocean. Thus, António de Abreu discovered and occupied some islands of Insulindia; Jorge de Meneses reached New Guinea (1526) and António da Mota landed in Japan in 1541. It was then that Portuguese expansion took on decisive significance for human history. "The effect of the discovery of a sea route to India on geography, on international trade and on relations among peoples, led the famous historian Toynbee to divide human history into two periods: before and after Gama".[5]

While it is true that Portuguese navigators usually came back to their country, it is also true that other Portuguese left with them, never to return. Navigators and traders, in their more or less sporadic contacts with new peoples, contributed only indirectly to the phenomenon of migrations. Those who accompanied them and who did not return were part of the first waves of Portuguese emigrants, made up of soldiers sent to guarantee Portuguese sovereignty, missionaries carrying the gospel to new peoples and simple settlers going to people and occupy the discovered lands.

In this mass movement, we must not forget the slaves who, against their will, formed a large contingent of migrants during the period of Portuguese expansion.

---

3. *Idem,* p. 33.

4. The Florentine Americo Vespucci was reputed to have been a member of this fleet in the service of the King of Portugal (cf. Patterson, 1890, p. 128).

5. Bettencourt, 1961, p. 53.

It is difficult to estimate the total number of Portuguese who emigrated during the period of discovery. Nevertheless, if we consider that the Portuguese population totalled almost two million at that time, and that military mobilisation was very considerable, we can safely say that the Portugal of that era suffered mass emigration. "We can estimate without risk of error that a million Portuguese emigrated during the 385 years from the conquest of Ceuta up to the end of the 18th century". [6]

The data compiled by Manuel Faria de Sousa are telling indeed. According to this author, between 1497 and 1612, 806 vessels, carrying an average of 500 persons including crews, left for India. Of a total of 400,000 emigrants, only 10% returned to the continent. [7] In the 18th century, with the decline in Portuguese influence in the Orient and in North Africa, Portuguese emigration was mainly in the direction of Brazil.

Contacts and settlement in North America

The first Portuguese contacts with North America date back to the middle of the 15th century, at the latest, around 1501, when Newfoundland and Labrador were discovered by Gaspar Corte-Real. In 1502, the coasts of New England were apparently explored by Miguel Corte-Real. [8]

---

6.   *Idem,* p. 37.

7.   *Idem,* p. 36.

8.   The inscription, still a subject of controversy, on "Dighton Rock" near Narragansett Bay, in the State of Massachusetts, as reconstructed and interpreted by the late Professor Delabarre, seems to read thus: "MIGUEL CORTEREAL V DEI HIC DUX IND 1511" (Miguel Corte-Real, by the grace of God, here chief of the Indians 1511). This interpretation is linked to the legend according to which Miguel Corte-Real survived a shipwreck, in which he was believed dead, took refuge in Narragansett Bay and became chief of the Indians among whom he had lived (cf. Pap, 1949).

The United States of America

It should be emphasised that Christopher Columbus lived in Portugal from 1470 to 1484, where he heard of the latest discoveries in maritime sciences and where he married Filipa, daughter of Bartolomeu Perestrelo, a Portuguese navigator and first governor of the island of Porto Santo.[9] It is also necessary to point out that a number of the seamen making up the crew of the caravels of Christopher Columbus were Portuguese.[10] The contacts which took place between Columbus and the Corte-Real brothers are also very revealing.[11] In addition, according to the testimony of Fra Bartolomé de Las Casas (1474-1566), the Portuguese had already visited the North-American continent towards the middle of the 15th century.[12] It is probable that Las Casas had in mind the voyage of Diogo de Teive which apparently took place in 1452.[13] A companion of Teive, Pero de Velasco, supposedly provided Columbus with information on this voyage.

Among the Portuguese who touched the present territory of the United States, we must mention Alvaro Fernandes, a noble from Elvas, who, with seven other Portuguese, accompanied Hernando de Soto in his exploration of the southern United States. It was also during that period, in 1542, that the Portuguese João Rodrigues Cabrilho, in the service of the Spanish Crown, discovered San Diego Bay to the south of California.

Portuguese contacts with North America were not limited to the period of discovery and continued with varying intensity

---

9. Patterson, 1890, p. 127.
10. There were also Portuguese among Samuel Champlain's crew (see note 51 of this chapter).
11. Gaffarel and Gariod, 1892, p. 11.
12. Cf. Anderson and Higgs, 1976, p. 4.
13. Cf. Brazão, 1964, p. 61.

throughout the centuries which followed, especially through fishermen. The first Portuguese to settle permanently in the United States of America were apparently a group of Jews who arrived in New York (New Amsterdam at that time) during the 18th century. A Portuguese Jew, Aarão Lopes, who had settled in New England, was the first to begin whaling there. [14] This activity attracted other Portuguese coming mainly from the Azorean archipelago. [15] According to Taft, trade relations between the Azores and the United States of America were established as early as 1830. These activities opened the way for a migratory flow to that country from the Azores. Towards the middle of the 19th century, there were already large concentrations of Portuguese in New England, more particularly in New Bedford and Fall River, and in some parts of California. [16]

The Portuguese presence also made itself felt for a long period on the Pacific coast, where they were engaged in whaling. "Before 1800, there were Portuguese in California. They came from Faial, Pico, São Jorge and Flores, to carry on whaling operations and they settled at Half Moon Bay, Pescadero, Monterey, Carmelo, San Simeon, Point Conception, Portuguese Cove, Portuguese Bend and San Diego. Their descendants are employed in the fishing and fish canning industries". [17]

According to statistical data provided by Joel Serrão, 379,130 Portuguese arrived in the United States of America between 1820 and 1872 to engage in whaling operations or to work as farmers. [18]

---

14. Cf. Santos, 1953.
15. Cf. Rogers, 1953.
16. Cf. Taft, 1923, pp. 88, 121 and 205.
17. Bettencourt, 1961, p. 55.
18. Serrão, 1974, p. 45.

Today, there are two regions in the United States with a large concentration of Portuguese immigrants: the eastern region which includes the states of Massachusetts, Connecticut, Rhode Island, New York and New Jersey and the western region including California.

In Portuguese migratory movements, there is a tradition which draws the natives of the Azores towards the North-American continent, because of certain features which recall their own family and social environment, and which offer them guarantees of welcome and employment by relatives and friends.

Among the other regions with a high concentration of Portuguese, we should mention Hawaii, where 21,000 Portuguese coming from the Atlantic islands settled at the beginning of the century. [19]

Canada—period of discovery

In prehistory, Canada was colonised by peoples who crossed the Bering Strait from Asia and who gave rise to the various Amerindian societies. Other peoples followed. The Vikings, under the command of Lief Erickson, were probably the first Europeans to settle on the Atlantic coast of Canada around the year 1000. [20] This presence is not however confirmed by satisfactory historical documents.

When we come to the era where the European presence in Canada is indeed documented historically, we are already at the end of the 15th century, right in the middle of the period of maritime discoveries. Numerous authors attribute the discovery of

---

19. Cf. Freitas, 1930.
20. Cf. Cornell *et al.,* 1968.

St.John's Land, today Prince Edward Island, to John Cabot, in the year 1497. [21]

According to Magnan, three years later, in 1500, the Portuguese Gaspar Corte-Real sailed along the Labrador Peninsula up to Hudson Strait. [22] He believed he had discovered the route to the East Indies. Vigneras, recalling the same historical event, says that "the territories discovered by Gaspar Corte-Real appear for the first time on Cantino's map (1502) under the name "Land of the King of Portugal". They are also shown on Kunstmann maps II and III, ('Land of Corte-Real')". [23]

However, it appears that the first official Portuguese presence on the territory of what is today Canada dates back only to 1501, that is to say, to the landing of Gaspar Corte-Real in Newfoundland, and his exploration of the coast up to Placentia Bay. [24] It was during this expedition that the navigator disappeared. The next year, Miguel Corte-Real organised a new expedition to search for his brother. He was unsuccessful, but he came to learn much about the coasts of North America. According to Edmund Delabarre, the first colony of Europeans was established on the North American continent at that time. [25] During the second half of the 16th century, Francisco da Sousa mentions the presence of the Portuguese in Newfoundland, in a book entitled: *Tratado das ilhas novas e dos descobrimentos dellas et outras . . . et dos Portugueses*

---

21. During a second voyage, Cabot was accompanied by the Portuguese João Fernandes Lavrador, who probably gave his name to the Labrador Peninsula. Vangilisti (1958, p. 18) is mistaken in considering this name to be of Spanish origin.

22. Magnan, 1919, p. 107.

23. Vigneras, 1967a, p. 242. See also Lanctôt, 1959, p. 70.

24. Canada. Secretary of State. Canadian Citizenship Division, 1967, p. 295. A statue was erected to the memory of this Portuguese navigator in 1965, in St. John's, Nfld.

25. Cf. Pap, 1949, p. 1.

que forao de Vianna, et das ilhas dos Açores a povoar a Terra nova do Bacalhao vae en 70 anos, deque sucedeu o que adiante se trata. Anno de Senhor 1570. [26] This peopling was particularly difficult because of the climate: "because they had found the country very cold, they left the East-West coast and settled along the Northeast-Southwest coast. Because their ships had been destroyed, there was no more word of them except through the Biscayans who go there, and who bring back news. These people ask that we tell of their life there and send them priests, because the savages are tamed and the land is good and generous". [27]

During the year 1506, King Manuel I ordered a certain Diogo Brandão to collect a duty on the fish coming from Newfoundland. [28] This same king, in a royal edict dated March 13, 1521, made João Alvares Fagundes Captain of the American coasts of New-foundland and Nova Scotia. This same document makes reference to Fagundes' discoveries on the territories entrusted to him. [29] In this same historical and geographical context, it is important to mention the discovery and official recognition of the Iles des Onze Mil Vierges, also called the Fagundes Islands, situated at the mouth of the St. Lawrence. [30]

---

26. The title might be translated as follows: "Treatise on the new islands, their discovery and other things . . . and on the Portuguese who, leaving from Viana and the Azores Islands, came 70 years ago to people the new Land of Bacalhao and what happened is now told to you. Year of Our Lord 1570"

27. Sousa, in Brazão, 1969, pp. 89-90.

28. Cf. Gaffarel and Gariod, 1969, p. 14.

29. "Posterity showed itself ungrateful: the name of Fagundes appeared for a time on the maps, then a new toponomy completely supplanted it. Nevertheless, Fagundes marks a crucial phase in the exploration of North America, and he should be elevated to the same rank as John Cabot and the Corte-Real brothers" (Trudel, 1963, p. 29).

30. Cf. Patterson, 1890, p. 148; Peres, 1960, pp. 571-572 and Trudel, 1963, pp. 28-29.

The theory of Jaime Cortesão, according to which the Newfoundland banks were discovered by Diogo de Teive, is questioned by the historian Morison.[31] This same author also disputes the historical authenticity of the voyage to Newfoundland, in 1472, of João Vaz Corte-Real, father of Gaspar and Miguel Corte-Real.[32] Contradicting Morison, Brazão cites the comment of Theo Layng to the effect that "for more than a century, a whole series of facts and opinions, established in favour of the Cabots, have tended to downplay the discoveries made by the Portuguese in the North Atlantic. It is unquestionably João Fernandes and Pedro de Barcelos from the Azores, and not John Cabot, who first rediscovered the Viking route to America".[33]

It must be emphasised that João Fernandes Lavrador and Pedro de Barcelos left from Bristol, as did John Cabot, in order to avoid any conflicts resulting from the Treaty of Tordesillas (June 7, 1494), and to avail themselves of the patronage of Henry VII of England, who was less affected by this treaty.[34] Given the presence of these Portuguese in Bristol, it is clear that Cabot may have obtained information essential to his expedition from these latter.[35]

31. Morison, 1940, pp. 22-23.

32. João Vaz Corte-Real served the Duke of Viseu, brother of Afonso V, as "chief bailiff". On April 2, 1474, he was named donee of the south of Terceira Island, where he died on July 2, 1496.

33. Brazão, 1964, p. 47.

34. In 1493, a bull issued by Pope Alexander VI awarded to the Spanish all the territories west of an imaginary line extending from pole to pole, and passing 100 leagues west of the Cape Verde Islands, and gave the Portuguese all territories to the east of this meridian. This decision, which disregarded the antipodes situated on this meridian, was contested by the Portuguese. The negotiations which followed ended in the Treaty of Tordesillas, by which the closing line was displaced 270 leagues further to the West.

35. As is pointed out by Anderson and Higgs (1976, p. 7), trade between Portugal and the port of Bristol dates back to the 12th century. The Bristol merchants loaded salt in Lisbon, took it to Iceland where they went to fish, and returned to Portugal, where they sold the fish and with the earnings, purchased wine, olive oil and salt which they took to England.

Brazão expresses his opinion thus: "It is tradition, and not the scarce existing documentation, which tells us of voyages like those of Diogo de Teive, in 1452, or of João Vaz Corte-Real, donee of Terceira Island and father of Corte-Real who disappeared in Newfoundland, or those of Martins Homem, in 1472, or of Fernão Teles, in 1476. I do not believe we need the support of these Portuguese voyages to the North Atlantic, prior to Fernandes and Cabot, to seriously conclude, given the scarce sources of information, that the "plowman" of Terceira preceded the Genoan Cabot and the sailors of Bristol in the discovery of the American coasts which today are part of Canada." [36]

This same Brazão, in another work on the Corte-Real family, says that: "Until substantial evidence demonstrates the contrary, we shall continue to believe that João Fernandes and Pedro de Barcelos were the real "discoverers" of North America, in particular of that vast region overlooking the Atlantic which today belongs to Canada". [37] While it is difficult to obtain a consensus on this matter, it is more readily agreed that Cabot stayed in Lisbon before leaving from Bristol for North America. During his stay in Portugal, he may have learned about previous voyages, specifically from João Fernandes Lavrador, and it was perhaps based on this information that the King of England approved his own proposed voyage.

Let us leave the historians to their research and their polemics concerning the identity of the first discoverers of Newfoundland, Labrador and Nova Scotia. We shall merely say that the Portuguese have their rightful place in the history of these discoveries and that they have maintained contacts with these territories up to our time. Even Morison, who is known for his tendency to downplay the role of the Portuguese, says: "Concerning the last

36. Brazão, 1964, pp. 61-62.
37. Brazão, 1965, p. 47.

voyage of Gaspar [Corte-Real], who left Lisbon with three ships towards the end of April or the beginning of May 1501, we have more precise knowledge, thanks to the letters of two Italians from Lisbon, Pietro Pasqualigo and Alberto Cantino. Two of these ships returned to Portugal, respectively in October and December, after having touched Labrador, Newfoundland, Nova Scotia and after naming some bays and promontories, which names still remain even though they have now been anglicised". [38]

In studying the history of Canada, and in particular its discovery, we must consider the role of the Portuguese within the historical context of the times. Unfortunately, the majority of Canadian historians ignore or are unaware of the historical presence of the Portuguese on the North Atlantic coasts. [39] This is why Eduardo Brazão, former ambassador of Portugal in Ottawa, felt obliged to add some new data to the main Canadian historiographies of the last two centuries. [40]

The historical Portuguese presence in Canada is demonstrated both by the maps dating to the time of the discoveries and by local place names. In effect, "the best proof of the frequency and continuity of Portuguese expeditions to North America is offered by the maps of that time. On most of these maps, we note names of Portuguese origin in the entire northeastern region [...]. The names of ports, rivers and capes from Labrador to the coast of the

38. Morison, 1940, p. 71.
   During the expedition of the Corte-Real brothers, some Indians were captured, several of whom were brought back to Portugal in 1501, in the vessel of Gaspar Corte-Real (cf. Patterson, 1890, p. 132). According to Lanctôt (1959, p. 68) "they captured fifty-seven men, women and children, who were destined for slavery".

39. An eminent historian of British origin made this comment to the authors: "What is painfully obvious is that the traditional, chauvinistic historiography of the English and French Canadians has systematically downplayed the contribution of the Portuguese and the Spanish, that is to say, the Basques, in the discoveries made in Canada".

40. Brazão, 1969.

present-day United States, are all Portuguese. The most astonishing thing is that even on the maps drawn up by the Spaniards, the French and the Italians in the first half of the 16th century, Portuguese names were carefully preserved: an obvious proof of the voyages undertaken and the discoveries made by the Portuguese in the area of the Northwest." [41]

We have compiled some examples of local place names considered to be of Portuguese origin:

TABLE 3—1

Place names of Portuguese origin on the northeastern coast of the Atlantic

Anticosti	Flowers Island
Bacallao	Fogo
Baccaro Point	Freyluis
Bay of Fundy	Labrador
Boa Ventura	Minas
Bona Vista	Mira
Brazil Rock	Porto Novo
Cape Razo	Portugal Cove
Conception Bay	Portuguese Shoal
D'Espera	Torbay
Fermuse	

Source: Data taken from Patterson, 1890, pp. 172-173.

Buchanan, too, demonstrated the historical presence of the Portuguese in Newfoundland in an interesting work on Portuguese names given to capes, bays, islands, etc. and their evolution over the centuries. [42]

---

41. Gaffarel and Gariod, 1892, pp. 15-16.

42. Buchanan, 1952.

Canada—contemporary period

At the time of their first contacts with what is today Canadian territory, the Portuguese were not immediately concerned with settling here. According to Brazão, João Alves Fagundes was "so far as we know, the only Portuguese who attempted to settle the southern part of these regions of Canada". [43]

Although few Portuguese settled in Canada during the age of discoveries, perhaps on account of the climate, Portuguese fishermen have been very numerous on the Newfoundland coasts during the last four centuries. It is logical to suppose that the Portuguese, along with the Bretons, the Normans and the Basques, periodically fished for cod off the Canadian coasts. It is therefore probable that the first Portuguese to settle in Canada were fishermen, similar to what occurred in New England and California. However, information on their origin and their numbers remains forever lost.

Prior to the Second World War, Canada was not the favourite country of immigration of the Portuguese. In effect, Portuguese emigration to Canada, although there was always some, did not take on importance until the present era. We obtained the following figures for the period July 1, 1904 to December 31, 1907:

TABLE 3-2

Canada: Portuguese immigration, 1904-1907

Period	Number
Fiscal year 1904-1905	1
Fiscal year 1905-1906	6
July 1906 to June 1907	3
June 1907 to December 1907	1
TOTAL	11

Source: Data taken from Woodsworth, 1972, pp. 23-25.

Statistical data thus confirm that the mass emigration of Portuguese to Canada is a fairly recent phenomenon. In 1926-1927, only 14 Portuguese entered Canada; in 1955, 1965 and 1974, the figures were respectively 1,427, 5,734 and 16,333. [44]

1953 is considered a milestone year for Portuguese immigration to Canada because of the bilateral agreements signed between the Portuguese and Canadian governments. It was in fact in 1953 that the first contingent of 555 Portuguese officially requested by the Canadian government arrived in Canada. [45] The results having been seen as positive, this quota was tripled the next year and in 1974, it reached 16,333 persons. [46]

We can say, therefore, that since the age of discoveries, Portuguese contacts with Canadian territory, however sporadic, have resulted in some of them settling in Canada. It is only during the last quarter century, however, that Portuguese emigration to Canada has reached significant proportions. Today, the Portuguese ethnic group is among the largest in Canada as may be seen from the figures in the following table:

---

44. Cf. Gonçalves, 1971, pp. 230-231; Canada. Ministère de la Citoyenneté et de l'Immigration, 1956; and Canada. Department of Manpower and Immigration, 1965, p. 8 and 1974, p. 5.

45. According to an immigrant of that period, the group accepted by the Canadian government in 1953 had to meet certain requirements including the posting of a bond. This bond was meant to cover the cost of a return trip to Portugal if the immigrant was unable to adapt. Although selection was made in rural areas, the poorest individuals were excluded, because of the required bond.

46. Cf. Canada. Ministère de la Citoyenneté et de l'Immigration, 1974, p. 5. We sometimes find discrepancies between Canadian statistics and Portuguese statistics. The admission to Canada of Portuguese immigrants coming directly from other countries such as France, Brazil and Venezuela may in some cases explain these differences.

TABLE 3-3

Canada: Population by mother tongue, most representative groups, 1976

Group	Population	Group	Population
British Isles	14,122,770	Chinese	132,560
French	5,887,205	Portuguese	126,535
Italian	484,050	Amerindian	117,105
German	476,715	Dutch	114,760
Ukranian	282,060	Polish	99,845

Source: Canadian census, 1976.

The Portuguese presence in Quebec

Quebec territory was the stage of great events when Canadian history was beginning. And precisely in the Province of Quebec, the Portuguese presence is historically certain and constant from the time of her foundation.

The age of discoveries

Portuguese contacts with Quebec certainly date back to the time of the discovery of the North-American continent. In the log books of the Corte-Reals and other Portuguese navigators, there is mention of locations on the coast of the present territories of Canada and the United States. It is logical that the Quebec seaboard and in particular, the mouth of the St. Lawrence, should be included. Certain legends on the origin of the word Canada thus find their explanation. The word Canada is supposedly a deformation of an old Portuguese word which means a passage between two walls. The term is said to have been used by Portuguese navigators to designate the St. Lawrence valley which is situated between two cliffs. [47]

---

47.   Cf. Descamps, 1959, p. 88.

According to another legend, the origin of the word Canada dates back to the initial contacts of Portuguese navigators with the country's coasts. These navigators, who had set out in search of El Dorado, disappointed in finding only snow, exclaimed: "Cá nada!" (there is nothing here). [48] The tradition according to which the word Canada comes from the native words *Kan-a-ta* or *Kan-a-da* which means "the place where people dwell" seems to us closer to history than to legend. The word seems to have appeared for the first time on the maps of Jacques Cartier in the 17th century. The use of the name Canada was first limited to the St. Lawrence region, but later it gradually came to be used to designate the surrounding areas. By the 19th century, the name Canada encompassed its present geographical dimensions.

The presence of Portuguese fishermen on the Quebec seaboard is even more clearly demonstrated. Codfishing in this area, which dates back to the age of the discoveries, is still carried on today. [49] According to some, Anticosti Island, situated at the mouth of the St. Lawrence, owes its name to a European source, and more precisely, is a deformation of the Portuguese names Anta Costa. [50]

---

48. Patterson (1890, p. 158) states that "there are good reasons for believing that the word Canada is of Portuguese origin". In effect, this word, common in the Portuguese spoken in the 15th century, is still used today in the Azorean archipelago to designate a passage, in particular when it is delimited by mountains". The St. Lawrence River, which is surrounded by cliffs along a good stretch of the way, supposedly inspired this name.

49. According to Taft (cf. Descamps, 1959, p. 150) there were restrictions in 1765 on the number of Portuguese fishermen allowed in the St. Lawrence. One notes a certain absence of Portuguese fishermen during the 17th century, due to the Spanish occupation of Portugal and the hostility of England in her attempt to eliminate all competitors.

50. Patterson (1890, p. 158) goes even further and speaks of the presence of Portuguese navigators who sailed up the St. Lawrence to what is presently the Montreal area. In his opinion, this name, too, is of Portuguese origin (Monte Real).

The genealogy of the founding peoples [51]

The Portuguese have been part of Quebec history since its beginnings. If we were to trace family trees back to their roots, we would certainly discover clues confirming the constant presence of numerous Portuguese in Quebec. The documents which we have been able to uncover make mention of some families descended from Portuguese settlers, at the time of the founding of Quebec, settlers whose surnames remain up to our time.

Here are some historical data concerning these families. [52]

---

51. If the entire territory of present-day Canada is considered, the first Portuguese to settle here, to our knowledge, was Mateus Da Costa. This free black man was Samuel Champlain's interpreter in his contacts with the Amerindians. In effect, Da Costa was part of the crew of the "Jonas", the ship which set sail from La Rochelle on May 13, 1606 and which arrived in Acadia under the command of Champlain. The fact that he knew the Amerindian languages proves that Mateus Da Costa had already lived in Canada prior to that date. Since he was Portuguese, there is good reason to believe that he was part of the crews of Portuguese ships, perhaps under the command of Corte-Real. Since languages are not learned from one day to the next, it is logical to assume that Mateus Da Costa lived in Canada earlier. The establishment of this Portuguese settler at that time was surely not an isolated case. This suggests to us that several Portuguese settled in Canada following their contacts with the territory, from the beginning of the 1500s, even before the arrival of Jacques Cartier.

    Da Costa is described hy historians as "well educated and a baptised Christian" and also as one of the founders of the "Order of Good Cheer". He died during the winter of 1606-1607 at Port Royal (cf. Bertley 1974 and 1977).

52. We have limited our historical research to the early Portuguese pioneers. Some reference is made to their descendants without exhausting the topic, which deserves a more in-depth study. To this end, we offer a certain number of sources in the notes which follow.

— *Pedro da Silva*[53] — Native of Lisbon, Portugal, son of Joseph and Marie François, he was baptized in the parish of São Julião (St. Julian) in 1647.[54] After he came to North America, he settled in Beauport, near Quebec City. His marriage to Jeanne Greslon, daughter of Jacques Greslon and Jeanne Vignau, took place in Quebec on May 16, 1677.[55] They raised a family of 15 children. He was interred in Quebec on August 2, 1717.[56]

Pedro da Silva appears from the outset as part of the bourgeoisie, that is to say, as a land-owner.[57] However, what makes him an exceptional, and even a historical figure, is his work in the area of communications. He was the first official mailman in Canada and carried the messages of the governor of New France between Quebec and Montreal.[58] We read the following reference

53. The surname *da Silva* is still common in Quebec, with several variations in spelling, such as *Dassylva, Dasilva* and *Da Silva*. As regards the first Pedro da Silva, we read in the old documents: "He signs Pedro Dasilva" (Tanguay, Vol. 1, p. 158); "He was educated and signed his name thus: *Pedro dasilva*" (Cf. Gagnon, 1909, p. 54). "The vendor was Pedro *Dassilva,* called the Portuguese, who in turn had received this property from the Quebec Seminary by a concession dated September 15, 1715". (Brother Odoric-M., p. 126). Cf. also Eloi-Gérard, 1941, p. 148 and *Dictionnaire national des Canadiens-français,* 1965, Vol. 1, p. 342.

54. Cf. Tanguay, Vol. 3, p. 243 and *Dictionnaire national des Canadiens-français,* 1965, Vol. 1, p. 342.

55. Jeanne Greslon was known by the name of Jolicoeur. Cf. Tanguay, *loc. cit.* and Eloi-Gérard, 1941, p. 148.

56. A few months later, on January 23, 1718, the widow Jeanne Greslon married Jacques Morand (Cf. Tanguay, Vol. 1, p. 158).

57. Cf. Tanguay, Vol. 3, p. 243; Brother Odoric-M., p. 126; Québec. Ministère des Affaires culturelles. *Rapport des archives nationales du Québec,* 1971, Vol. 49, pp. 67 and 91.

58. "The oldest courier known to us is Pierre Dasilva, called the Portuguese, and his name appears in the Montreal archives beginning in 1693. [...] To earn a living, this courier had to have a lot of irons in the fire. Since letter carrying could only be a means of supplementing his income from other sources, we suppose that Dasilva travelled by canoe or boat and that this permitted him to carry quite a few passengers and parcels and thus earn enough money to maintain himself and his numerous family" (Massicotte, 1921, pp. 211-212).

to him in the *Bulletin des recherches historiques:* "This Portuguese Canadian was a fine man and one day it was noticed that he was providing services. That is why, on December 23, 1705, Intendant Raudot appointed him messenger and we have the complete text of this appointment". [59]

The Canadian Commission on Historical Sites and Monuments, which recognised the importance of this historical figure, in 1938, had a bilingual plaque placed on the post office building in Montreal, situated on rue St-Jacques, at the corner of rue de la Cathédrale. It bears the following inscription: "Beginning in 1693, letters were carried by messenger between Quebec and Montreal. The first known courier was Pierre da Silva, called the Portuguese". [60] The surname "da Silva" appears in several historical documents, which could assist experts in reconstructing the history of this family of Portuguese origin, the first or one of the first in Quebec. [61]

59. Massicotte, 1921, p. 212. Here is an extract from the text cited: "It being essential to the King's service and the public weal to establish in this Colony a Messenger to carry orders to all parts of the country where required, and having been informed of the diligence and fidelity of Pierre Dasilva, called the Portuguese.

We, at His Majesty's good pleasure, have appointed and established the said Portuguese as an ordinary messenger to carry letters from the Governor General and ourselves, in the service of the King, throughout the length and breadth of this Colony, further permitting him to load those of private persons for delivery to their addressees, and bring back the replies [...]. In witness whereof, we have signed these presents, affixed with our coat of arms and countersigned by one of our secretaries, in our Hotel, in Quebec, on December 23, 1705, signed Raudot (Roy, Inv. des Ordres des intendants, I, p. 8 and provincial Archives)".

60. During a speech to the Montreal Historical Society on February 28, 1977, Julien Déziel, o.f.m., President of the French Canadian Genealogical Society, spoke of the Portuguese Pedro da Silva, describing him with humour as "The first *man of letters* in Quebec".

61. Cf. among others: Tanguay, 1887, pp. 243-245; Éloi-Gérard, 1941, pp. 61-62; *Rapport des archives nationales du Québec,* 1971, p. 438.

— *Martin Pire-Henne* (called the Portuguese)[62] — Son of Sebastien Pire-Henne and Anne Gonçalves, he came from São Martinho (St. Martin's) in Braga, Portugal, where he was apparently baptised in 1647. On October 15, 1674, in Quebec, he married Françoise du Faye, daughter of Jean du Faye and Marguerite Noury (from St-Hilaire, Reims), and he was the father of seven children. He became a widower on December 17, 1705, and died six years later. He was interred in Charlesbourg on December 9, 1711.[63] Available sources provide information on the descendants of Martin Henne down to the third generation.[64]

— *Jean Rodrigue* (João Rodrigues)[65] — Son of João Rodrigues and Suzana da Cruz, he was born in Lisbon in the parish of São João (St. John), where he was baptised in 1650.[66] On October 28, 1671, in Quebec, he married Anne LeRoy, daughter of François LeRoy and Anne Bourdais, a native of St-Germain-l'Auxerrois, Paris.[67] The records show the names of seven children issuing from this union.[68] Jean Rodrigue died at the age of 65 and was interred in Beauport on November 15, 1720.[69] We have not found any documents providing details of the life of this early Portuguese pioneer. However, today, the Rodrigue are to be found just about everywhere in Quebec. Brother Eloi-Gérard, in his work, presents the complete family tree, from 1650 up to the present.[70]

---

62. It occurs to us that the name Pire-Henne might be derived from Pires Enes (or Hennes). His descendants also go by the surnames *Piré, Pire* and *Lepire*. Cf. Tanguay, 1871, Vol. 1, pp. 304 and 384; *idem,* 1887, Vol. 4, p. 489.

63. Cf. Tanguay, 1871, Vol. 1, p. 304; *idem,* 1887, Vol. 4, p. 489.

64. Cf. Tanguay, 1887, Vol. 4, pp. 489-490.

65. Tanguay (1890, Vol. 7, p. 25) mentions the variation *Rodriguez.*

66. Cf. Tanguay, 1871, Vol. 1, p. 252; *idem,* 1890, Vol. 7, p. 25.

67. Cf. Éloi-Gérard, 1948, Vol. 9, p. 251.

68. Cf. Tanguay, 1871, Vol. 1, p. 525; *idem,* 1890, Vol. 7, p. 25.

69. Cf. Tanguay, 1890, Vol. 7, p. 25.

70. Éloi-Gérard, 1941, p. 148; *idem,* 1948, Vol. 9, pp. 251-278.

These are the first Portuguese pioneers in Quebec that we were able to identify. There are other documents which make reference to Quebec residents bearing the name "Portugais", but there is no direct reference to their origins. [71] At one point, there is mention of one Joseph Demourache (de Morais?) "called the Portuguese". [72] This suggests the presence of several Portuguese families in Quebec from the time of its foundation. [73] Some retained the nickname "Portugais" as a mark of their origin and their culture. Today, there are still a certain number of Québécois with this word as a family name. [74] There are also Quebec families that have had the surname "Portugal" for several centuries. [75]

Other documents attest to the presence of Portuguese in Quebec in recent centuries. Thus, in the 18th century, and more specifically in 1768, the first Jewish congregation, *Shearith Israel,* which observed the sephardic rite of the Spanish and Portuguese Jews, came into being in Montreal. [76]

---

71. Cf. Québec. Ministère des Affaires culturelles. *Rapport des archives nationales du Québec,* 1945-1946, p. 348; *idem,* 1971, p. 465.

72. Cf. *op. cit.,* 1971, p. 10.

73. Some Portuguese mercenaries may have served in Quebec under the French flag during the 17th century. They were entered in the regiment rosters with French names for reasons of a politico-military nature. Some of these mercenaries apparently chose to settle permanently in Quebec. We may assume that their assimilation has been total and that they have lost not only their original names but also their cultural identity.

74. In the Montreal telephone directory, (Nov. 1979, p. 1577), the surname *Portugais* appears 22 times.

75. This is the case of Mathurin Bideau, baptised in 1718, who went by the nickname *Portugal.* Cf. Tanguay, 1886, Vol. 2, p. 274.

76. This congregation initially met in a building on rue St-Jacques and later purchased a temple situated on rue Stanley, near rue Ste-Catherine (cf. Atherton, 1914, pp. 285-288). Today, the "Spanish and Portuguese Synagogue" is located at 4894, rue St-Kevin in Montreal.

The contemporary period

As we already mentioned, the arrival of large numbers of Portuguese in Canada and in Quebec is a recent phenomenon. The Portuguese community in Quebec is made up essentially of first generation immigrants. These immigrants come for the most part from rural, less economically developed areas. [77] Recently, above all following the political events occurring in Portugal in April 1974, we find a larger percentage of specialised persons coming from urban areas, which is also an offshoot of the migratory flows resulting from the decolonisation of Portuguese Africa. [78]

The majority of Portuguese immigrants to Quebec come from the Azorean archipelago. For Montreal, we have obtained the following percentages for 1974: 60% coming from the Azores, 38% from continental Portugal, 1% from Madeira and 1% from other Portuguese territories. [79] These percentages coincide more or less with those obtained by Henry-Nieves. [80] According to this latter, out of 91,583 Portuguese who arrived in Canada between 1953 and 1973, 61.2% came from the Azores, 37.7% from continental Portugal and 1.1% from Madeira. The extrapolation of these percentages to Quebec is certainly justified.

The following statistical table shows the percentage of Portuguese in Quebec compared with other Canadian provinces.

---

77. This is confirmed by statistics for the year 1972, according to which the Portuguese, who represented 7% of the total landed immigrants in Quebec, brought in only 1% of the total currency in the possession of immigrants (Data prepared on the basis of an internal document of the Federal Manpower Department).

78. According to the data provided by Marques and Medeiros (1978, p. 21), there are in Canada about 3,000 *retornados* (repatriates) from the former Portuguese colonies in Africa.

79. Anderson and Higgs, 1976, p. 64.

80. Henry-Nieves, 1975, pp. 51-52.

TABLE 3-4

Canada: Portuguese immigration by province, 1946-1978

	Nfld.	P.E.I.	N.S.	N.B.	Que.	Ont.	Man.	Sask.	Alta	B.C.	Yukon N.W.T.	Total
1946	—	—	1	1	18	15	—	1	—	2	—	38
1947	—	—	2	—	12	8	—	—	—	3	—	25
1948	—	—	1	1	19	25	1	—	1	3	—	51
1949	—	—	2	—	23	37	—	—	2	2	—	66
1950	—	—	—	1	28	50	1	—	1	6	—	87
1951	—	—	4	3	44	81	6	—	7	12	—	157
1952	1	—	5	1	92	133	3	—	7	14	—	256
1953	2	—	2	—	231	288	3	—	10	19	—	555
1954	1	—	5	4	639	653	2	—	5	15	—	1324
1955	4	1	115	1	464	701	18	—	6	117	—	1427
1956	2	14	27	22	656	969	10	—	5	266	—	1971
1957	3	—	31	23	1687	1746	104	85	236	833	—	4748
1958	4	—	1	3	512	1339	20	27	40	231	—	2177
1959	2	—	1	2	1035	2590	115	30	119	459	1	4354
1960	3	—	7	4	1338	2949	223	39	189	504	2	5258
1961	2	—	21	6	629	1780	122	14	90	311	1	2976
1962	5	—	13	7	734	1595	143	16	123	292	—	2928
1963	8	—	21	4	988	2133	227	19	104	496	—	4000
1964	9	—	18	1	1104	3280	244	29	119	504	1	5309
1965	25	—	54	7	1114	3627	223	31	127	526	—	5734
1966	30	—	84	38	1958	5885	355	39	247	882	7	9525
1967	20	—	94	22	1587	6514	381	52	181	645	4	9500
1968	18	—	19	1	1229	5415	295	41	163	549	8	7738
1969	23	—	12	12	1175	4900	301	4	262	489	4	7182
1970	12	—	18	8	1230	5330	498	23	237	545	1	7902
1971	16	—	15	4	1478	6059	657	16	258	652	2	9157
1972	9	—	6	1	1372	5895	509	13	288	644	—	8737
1973	3	—	12	5	1825	9892	623	18	394	711	—	13483
1974	32	—	20	8	1676	12864	637	18	357	719	2	16333
1975	94	—	8	89	1059	6361	318	10	172	432	4	8547
1976	11	—	100	98	892	3611	219	1	180	231	1	5344
1977	1	—	17	39	582	2344	214	11	168	202	1	3579
1978	10	2	4	3	549	2056	167	17	115	163	—	3086

Sources: Canada. Department of Citizenship and Immigration, Statistics Section, *Ethnic origin by province of destination: Calendar years, 1946-1955*, Ottawa, 1956;

Canada. Department of Citizenship and Immigration, Directorate of Technical Services, *Immigration*, 1956, 1957, 1958, 1959, 1960, 1961, 1962, 1963, 1964, 1965, 1966, 1967, 1968, 1969, 1970, 1971, 1972, 1973, 1974, 1975, 1976, 1977, 1978.

*   *   *

The growing interest in the Portuguese ethnic group seems justified in the light of the historical data reviewed here above. The history of Canada, and of Quebec in particular, would show serious gaps if it disregarded the action and the presence of the Portuguese.

It would be unjust to regard the Portuguese ethnic community simply as a group of recent immigrants. If we regard the Portuguese presence in Canada as dating solely from 1953, we run the risk of being overshadowed by a particular event and forgetting history in general. [81] In effect, the agreement signed by the Portuguese and Canadian governments in 1953 is historical insofar as it recognises and favours a migratory movement that already existed as is demonstrated by the figures cited above.

When we speak of the Portuguese in Quebec, we must not forget all those who, from the beginning of colonisation, integrated into the people who are today called Québécois. Whether or not they have lost their original names, the Portuguese shared in the founding and in the evolution of Quebec society. The Portuguese immigrants who arrive in this province today in larger numbers find not only another people, but also their own people, who have been there since the beginning of Canadian history.

---

81. Marques and Medeiros (1978, pp. 14 and 16) state that the first contingent of Portuguese immigrants officially requested by Canada arrived in Halifax on May 13, 1953, on board the S.S. "Saturnia". Halifax and Quebec City had in fact been the main ports of entry for Portuguese immigrants up to the end of the 1950s.

IV

PLACES OF SETTLEMENT

Next to Ontario, Quebec is the Canadian region with the highest concentration of Portuguese. This preference for Quebec as a place of settlement is explained chiefly by certain socio-economic factors held in common. When one moves from Portugal to Canada, Quebec is in fact a particularly ideal milieu where cultural and geographical similarities attenuate the immigrant's problems of adaptation. The presence of members of the same ethnic group becomes a "pull" factor facilitating the establishment of Portuguese on Quebec territory. Similar to what was found by Anderson (1974) for the Portuguese of Toronto, immigrants living in Quebec usually made the decision to emigrate as a result of networks created by friends or family members. [1]

Since the majority of the Portuguese coming to Quebec are from rural areas, it would seem logical for them to choose to settle in a milieu similar to that of their origins where their experience with farm work could be put to advantage. This was, moreover, one of the main considerations of the Canadian government when it called for Portuguese immigrants during the 1950s. In effect, the Canadian government wanted to fill a gap, that ever more disturb-

---

1. On a sample of Portuguese living in Hull studied by Kemp and Morisset (n.d., p. 2), 88.5% came to Quebec to join other members of their families.

ing gap created by the exodus of the rural population to urban areas. Thus, initially, the majority of these immigrants were sent to farming regions, either in Quebec or in the other provinces of Canada.[2]

However, paradoxically, it was found that, in a very short time, almost all the Portuguese who came from rural areas and who were expected to remain there, gradually left the country to settle in the large urban centres of Quebec. The reasons which prompted them to leave the country for the city had to do both with wages and with the poor working conditions and lack of security prevailing in the agricultural sector. These factors were perhaps more marked in Quebec.[3]

Serge (1970) tried to explain this apparently paradoxical displacement of Portuguese immigrants by the high degree of technology in Canadian agriculture for which they were not prepared, and by the high cost of farm land.[4] This high cost did

---

2. Cf. Hamilton, 1970.

3. At the time the first immigrants were recruited, one had to have the status of farm worker. At the beginning of the 1950s, a delegation of immigration officers coming under the jurisdiction of the Canadian Embassy in Lisbon set up offices in Ponta Delgada (Azores) for the selection of immigrants. To prove that one was a farmer, one had to show calloused hands. Once admitted, immigrants had to work for one year for the sponsoring farmers who had requested them. An immigrant whom we interviewed, and who has been in Quebec for 25 years, told us about the poor working conditions which he encountered in the farm region to which he was assigned. After settling in Grand-Mère, he was forced to look for another type of work. He then began to work in the lumber industry in northern Quebec. Later, because it was difficult to find employment, he came to live in Hull, where he found work on construction. This type of transition was normal among the immigrants of that period.

4. The opinion of Lenormand (1971, pp. 66-67) appears to contradict this assessment. He states : "The farmer in the province of Quebec is thirty years behind the times [...]. The immigrant farmer must not forget that since 1945, the Province of Quebec has received about seven hundred and fifty immigrant farmers, who have purchased farmland. Of this number, about three hundred have left the Province of Quebec since 1969".

prevent them from purchasing a piece of land where they could settle and receive their families, with some guarantee of subsistence and of education for their children.

The number of Portuguese living in Quebec today is estimated at more than 50,000. Almost all of them live and work in large urban centres, especially Montreal. However, written documents, personal observations, and verbal information enable us to affirm that the Portuguese are established, in more or less large numbers, in all regions of Quebec.[5] We shall first discuss their presence in the areas where they show the highest concentration and then deal briefly with the regions having a lower concentration and with the few dispersed groups that we were able to identify.[6]

High concentration areas

Montreal

The metropolitan region of Montreal is the main pole of attraction for immigrants settling in Quebec. The presence of large numbers of Portuguese in metropolitan Montreal has been evident since the beginning of 1950s. The number of Portuguese in the Montreal region is presently estimated at 40,000.[7] Almost 60% of them come from the Azores.[8]

---

5.   To determine the number of Portuguese immigrants, we sent a query to most Quebec municipalities. Unfortunately, several replies obtained do not provide concrete figures, given the absence of official data.

6.   The community organisations which came into being in the main centres of Portuguese immigrant concentration are dealt with a separate chapter of this book.

7.   In 1971, Canadian official statistics showed that there were 14,500 Portuguese immigrants in Montreal. However, according to the Consulate General of Portugal, the number of Portuguese established in this region in fact totalled 40,000 persons (cf. Santos, 1975, pp. 7-8). It is noted that this figure exceeds that of official statistics. Nevertheless, it must be emphasised that official statistics do not include children born in Canada, who obviously must be considered Portuguese in the case of the first generation.

8.   The percentage of natives of the Azores is lower in Montreal than anywhere else in Quebec.

Even though there are Portuguese in all the districts of greater Montreal, they are particularly numerous in the area bounded by Sherbrooke St. to the South, St-Joseph to the North, St-Denis to the East and Park Avenue to the West. In the heart of this area is the St-Louis district where almost 12,000 Portuguese live.[9] This district has for a long time been the gateway for successive waves of immigrants from several countries.[10] Up to the Second World War, it was a Jewish district. Later and sometimes simultaneously, immigrants of Polish, Ukranian, Yugoslavian, Italian, Greek and Portuguese origin settled there.[11] The passage of these different peoples has left traces which make the St-Louis district one of the most colourful, most densely populated and most varied in all of Montreal. In the same district and even on the same street, we find Portuguese, Greeks, Italians, Hungarians, Jews, Poles, Dutch, Germans, Czechs, Spaniards and South Americans, Russians, Chinese and native Canadians living side by side.[12]

The Portuguese of Montreal work in different sectors, and more particularly, in the hotel trade, service industries, workshops, building construction, manufacturing industries and commerce. On streets with a high concentration of Portuguese, such as boulevard St-Laurent and Bullion, Coloniale, Duluth, Hôtel de Ville, des Pins, Rachel and Roy, one finds shops, travel agencies,

---

9. Cf. Centre Portugais de Référence et de Promotion Sociale, 1976, p. 10.

10. Although it is located in the centre of Montreal, the St-Louis district is one of the poorest areas of the city, and one notes a lack of green spaces and most of the buildings are old and rundown. Formerly of a monotonous brick colour, they have been painted in bright colours by the Portuguese, who have helped give the district a more cheerful look (Cf. Beaupré, 1976).

11. The reason the Portuguese choose to live in the St-Louis district has to do with its socio-geographic location and the size of houses, since larger structures can accommodate larger families.

12. The Service d'Information Communautaire also offers an ethnic breakdown of the St-Louis district population, which includes a total of 41,427 persons: 50% were Francophones, 10% were Anglophones and 40% were Portuguese and Greeks (cit. in Santos, 1975, p. 176).

restaurants, banking establishments and associations which are typically Portuguese in name and in character. [13]

The different parts of the city in which Portuguese immigrants choose to settle may serve as a test of the socio-economic status achieved. We find that the most evolved strata tend to settle in the suburbs. This leaves room for the new arrivals, who are more deprived, to use the old St-Louis district as their "gateway". Among the new settlements with a high density of Portuguese residents is Longueuil, where their number totals about 500 at present. [14]

The Portuguese population of Montreal, which is becoming more and more highly represented in the mosaic of ethnic groups covering the city, is coming out of its former anonymity, thanks to a new group awareness and a political conscience which is beginning to manifest itself. The authorities and the local population today seem more attentive to this presence as certain recent attitudes attest. The awarding of the Prize of the Order of Architects of Quebec to the Portuguese and the name Parc du Portugal, given to

---

13. In Montreal, the number of businesses and other organisations with Portuguese names totals nearly two hundred. Fernández (1977, pp. 107-108) compiled the following statistical data which we are presenting in decreasing order of importance: grocery stores and butcher shops — 23; restaurants (including bars, cafés and taverns) — 12; volunteer organisations — 10; real estate and insurance companies — 10; garages and service stations — 9; travel agencies — 7; furniture and appliance stores — 7; barbershops and hairdressing salons — 6; hardware stores — 6; religious groups — 4; plumbing businesses — 4; clothing stores — 4; bakeries — 4; electrical repair shops — 4; banking agencies — 3; Portuguese language schools — 3; pharmacies — 3; importing companies — 3; radio programmes — 3; electronic repairs — 2; photographers — 2; medical centres — 2; schools of music — 2; upholsterers and drapers — 2; book stores and newspaper stands — 2; jewellers — 2; fish mongers — 2; tailors — 1; record shops — 1.

14. Estimate provided by the Municipality of Longueuil in 1978.

a green space situated in an area with a high Portuguese concentration, are examples of this. [15]

Hull

The second largest Portuguese settlement in Quebec is situated in Hull, the twin city of Ottawa, the federal capital, a privileged location which is particularly important within the context of Quebec and of Canada in general. For the purposes of this study, when we speak of Hull, we include the entire surrounding area situated on Quebec territory, and more specifically, Wrightville, Mont-Bleu, Gatineau, Touraine and Aylmer. Some of the first Portuguese to settle in Hull did so at the beginning of the 1950s, following their departure from the La Tuque region where they had worked in the lumber industry. Today, the Portuguese population of the Hull region is estimated at close to 3,000 persons, 70% of whom live in the centre of the city in what is called the island of Hull, 25% in Wrightville and the rest in the suburban areas mentioned above. Displacement towards these areas usually implies a rise on the socio-economic ladder.

We should emphasise the homogeneity of the Portuguese of Hull, in that 95% to 98% of them are natives of the Azores and more specifically come from the Parish of Maia on São Miguel Island.

Hull being a Francophone milieu, the Portuguese adapt easily, and show great stability once they settle. [16]

---

15. This name was given it on September 1, 1975 by the Place Names and Urban Development Committee of the City of Montreal. The opening ceremony was presided over by Jean Drapeau, Mayor of Montreal, and a speech was given by Maurice da Silva of the Montreal Historical Society, a descendant of Pedro da Silva (1647-1717), the first Portuguese immigrant in the history of Quebec.

16. On a sample of Portuguese in Hull studied by Kemp and Morisset (n.d., p. 2), 100% of the respondents indicated that they do not intend to leave Quebec. This attests to their desire to adapt to the receiving milieu. In reply to our questionnaire, the Municipality of Hull decided to add the following comment: "The Portuguese are excellent citizens who wish to integrate into the community life of the municipality".

The Portuguese of Hull work in several sectors, including construction in the case of the men. The women are employed mainly in the clothing industry, in bakeries and in cleaning services. Most of the Portuguese of Hull work in Ottawa.

Given the large size of the Portuguese group, some businesses are springing up in Hull to serve the Portuguese clientele. Sociocultural activities of some scope are carried on by the *Centro Comunitário Português Amigos Unidos.*

Laval

Under the name Laval, we include all the territory of Île Jésus. The Portuguese community scattered throughout the territory of this island is concentrated mainly in the area of Chomedey. Other Portuguese groups of lesser importance live in the vicinity of Laval, in particular in Fabreville, Vimont and Laval-des-Rapides.

The Portuguese began settling in Laval around 1953. The Portuguese population there presently totals 2,000. The vast majority of them are from the Azores. It should be pointed out that a certain number of families had emigrated to Brazil before coming to settle in Laval.

As regards sector of employment, we find that the men are employed chiefly on construction, and in gardening and paving; the women mainly in the clothing industry and in maintenance services.

Recently, a certain organisation has begun to take shape in the Portuguese community of Laval. Religious services in this community, which after 1965, were provided by the "Santa Cruz" Mission of Montreal, have been conducted full time since 1977 by the community's own priest.

The first Portuguese association in Laval, called *Associação dos Paroquianos de Nossa Senhora de Fátima,* came into being in

July 1974. Though its structures are still rudimentary, this association has begun to reflect the hopes and aspirations of the Portuguese community of Laval. At present, this association aims to establish its own Catholic mission and purchase a school to organise various community activities. Religious services are held in the church and at St. Martin's School situated in Chomedey. There, the Portuguese celebrate the feasts of Our Lady of Fatima, the Blessed Sacrament and the Holy Ghost. In the area of culture, folk dances are starting to be organised, reflecting a certain community spirit.

Quebec City

As we already mentioned, there were Portuguese in Quebec City from the beginning of colonisation. However, it was only in the 1950s that the Portuguese presence began to make itself felt. The Portuguese population of Quebec City and the surrounding area, which includes Beauport, Cap-Rouge, Charlesbourg, Giffard and Lévis, is estimated at about 750 persons. These are mainly Azoreans, who emigrated to Canada after the eruption of the Capelinhos volcano (Faial Island).

The Portuguese are employed in several sectors, and especially on construction. A certain segment of the community was quick to evidence concerns and initiatives of a socio-cultural nature. The *Associação Portuguesa de Quebec,* established in the 1970s with about 100 members, has been concerned with the organisation of cultural and recreational activities. Thus, it organised Portuguese language courses, which were discontinued a short time later because of the fears of certain parents who did not want to overload their children with too many school subjects. In this same city, Portuguese language courses are offered by the Faculty of Arts of Laval University. A Portuguese assistant professor is in charge of the Portuguese section of the "Cercle Cervantes-Camões". Thanks to a group of more culturally motivated Portuguese, exhibitions of Portuguese crafts have been

79

organised, which are also encouraged by the provincial government.

This Portuguese community has a reputation as a group of hardworking people who respect the social order. There are some, however, who see as negative the emphasis placed on economic concerns as opposed to the lesser interest shown in the culture of origin and in education. In general, young people tend to limit their schooling to the required minimum because they prefer to find jobs which can guarantee immediate earnings.

Even though there is evidence that the community is well accepted by the local population, their acculturation is slow because of their low level of schooling compared with the receiving culture. These differences also affect the process of complementarity of the two cultures.

Ste-Thérèse

The settlement of the first Portuguese immigrants in the Ste-Thérèse region dates back to the beginning of the 1950s. Initially destined for farm work in the outlying areas, they gradually moved to the urban centres where large industries are located. Today, it is in the urban region that almost all the area's Portuguese are to be found. According to the leaders of the Ste-Thérèse community, the first and second generation Portuguese population totals 2,500 persons. The centres with the highest concentration of Portuguese are Ste-Thérèse, Blainville and Boisbriand. The vast majority (90%) of these immigrants come from the Azores.

Because of the economic advantages and the better working conditions offered by the factories, immigrants quickly choose to become factory workers rather than remain farm hands. Today, the Portuguese community of Ste-Thérèse is essentially a community of industrial workers. The occupations chosen by the men are mainly construction, the automotive industry, furniture manufacturing and the aluminum industry. Women are mainly employed in clothing manufacturing and maintenance services.

The Portuguese community of Ste-Thérèse shows somewhat special characteristics, socio-culturally speaking. It is the only ethnic group which is highly represented in this region, and this facilitates its integration and helps it to earn the esteem of the local community. Close ongoing relations, both in the work place and in the place of residence, have created a process of spontaneous integration and mutual acceptance which goes beyond simple relations between neighbours. The percentage of marriages between Portuguese and native Canadians, which has been about 10% in recent years, is quite significant.

Areas with a lower concentration

The areas or localities where the Portuguese population is between 25 and 250 persons fall into this category. The data which we have assembled permit us to draw up the following table:

TABLE 4-1
Quebec: Areas with a low Portuguese population

Locality	Population (estimate)	Main Occupations
Joliette	35 to 45	Non-specialised workers [17]
Jonquière	40 to 50	Plant nurseries and miscellaneous
La Prairie	50 to 60	Dressmaking and miscellaneous
Nicolet	45 to 55	Furniture industry and dressmaking
Schefferville	25 to 30	Engineering, electricity and mechanics
Sept-Îles	150 to 200	Work on the docks, in hospitals and hotels. Others are employed mainly at the Iron Ore Company of Canada [18]
Sherbrooke	30 to 40	Miscellaneous occupations
Sorel	25 to 35	Naval dockyards, metallurgy and flour making.

17. The first Portuguese to settle in Joliette during the 1950s were employed in tobacco growing (cf. Anderson and Higgs, 1976, p. 37).

18. In Sept-Iles, there is a *Club Inter-Social,* in which the Portuguese participate very actively.

Small dispersed groups

All the groups spread throughout Quebec are included in this category even when they are very small in number. The presence of Portuguese immigrants has been reported in the following localities: Berthierville, Châteauguay, Clarke City, Gagnon, Lachute, La Sarre, La Tuque, Port-Cartier, St-Hyacinthe, St-Jean, St-Jérôme, Trois-Rivières and Victoriaville.[19] In all these places, the number of Portuguese is generally very low and very variable. In most cases, there are one to six families.

Concentration and dispersion

In the planning of immigrant settlement, geographical and psychological factors must be considered, along with historical and economic ones. We find that these factors, taken together, have influenced initial goals which, on the other hand, have not always been identical. In a democratic system, the distribution of immigrants seems to obey both government guidelines and personal initiative.

If we are to properly integrate the immigrant, the ideal distribution policy would seem to lie somewhere between the creation of areas with a large ethnic concentration and the dispersal of immigrants. While, in the first instance, we encourage the creation of "ghettos", in the second instance, a process of assimilation may be set in motion. In areas with a high concentration of Portuguese immigrants, there is a tendency to create an imaginary, bygone Portugal. Where numbers are small, isolation limits the possibilities of sharing and transmitting culture and easily leads to anomie, above all in the case of more deprived immigrants.

---

19. The list of places with Portuguese residents is not exhaustive. It is a list which has still to be completed. Concerning the number of Portuguese in different places, we sometimes relied on the figures provided by the municipalities and by persons in direct contact with the population in question.

The Portuguese immigrant population of Quebec comes mainly from the Azores, although other regions are also represented. In spite of regional differences, Portuguese from the islands and from the continent consider themselves members of the same group. However, the number of people from a given region is one of the factors which must be taken into account in assessing the degree of social participation or the rate of integration and acculturation.

Quebec little by little is beginning to take notice of the Portuguese. They are not destined to remain strangers or even just good neighbours. [20] Living side by side calls for acculturation, which implies acceptance of all the values of both parties and their promotion.

---

20. All the Quebecers whom we interviewed were unanimous in saying that the Portuguese are good neighbours and in praising their honesty and their capacity for hard work. In reply to our questionnaire on the presence of Portuguese on their territory, various Quebec municipalities sent the following comments: "To our knowledge, they are excellent citizens"; "They are very good citizens; well adjusted to their village and their community". One reply contained the following charming remark: "We have not the good fortune to have any Portuguese among us".

V

THE MILIEU OF ORIGIN

AND

THE RECEIVING MILIEU

In this chapter, we shall offer a summary comparative description of the physical and human chorography of Portugal and of Quebec. Since we cannot hope to be exhaustive, we shall mention only a few characteristic traits, to better illustrate the similarities and contrasts between the milieu of origin and the receiving milieu.

Although this study deals essentially with the Portuguese ethnic group, we nevertheless think it useful to briefly analyse the receiving milieu in order to assist mutual understanding. It is necessary to consider all the factors which condition integration policy so as to first of all eliminate the obstacle posed by ignorance. During our contacts with the two peoples, in several instances, we noted a mutual ignorance of certain basic facts which may be at the root of some poor relations. As Beattie said, "it is more important today than ever in the history of mankind that a people have an understanding of civilisations other than its own." [1]

---

1. Beattie, 1972, p. 7.

The geographical dimension

Geographically speaking, we can safely say that Portugal and Quebec are two linked regions. Turned towards the sea, they have between them the Atlantic Ocean, which is in fact a connecting link rather than a divider. The Cape of Roca, in Portugal, is the most westerly point of Europe, that is to say, it is one of the points on the European continent that are closest to Quebec.

Present Portuguese territory consists of a continental portion and an insular portion. The former is situated at the western extremity of Europe and is an integral part of the Iberian Peninsula. The latter is situated in the North Atlantic and is made of the archipelagos of Madeira and the Azores. The total area of Portugal is 92,082 km^2, 88,941 km^2 of which form the continental part and 3,141 km^2 the insular part. Generally speaking, Portuguese territory is very rugged and very diversified.

*

Quebec is one of the ten provinces of the Canadian Confederation. With its total area of 1,539,843 km^2, about 17 times the area of Portugal, Quebec is the largest province of Canada. [2] Almost 92% of the area of this province consists of plateaux and most of its territory lies at an altitude of 300 to 600 meters. The province of Quebec is situated in the eastern part of Canada, bounded by Ontario and Hudson Bay, Labrador, New Brunswick and the American states of Maine, New Hampshire, Vermont and New York.

---

2. The Canadian territory occupies a total area of 9,960,000 km^2 from the Atlantic Ocean to the Pacific and from the United States border to the glacial Arctic Ocean. The Canadian coat of arms bears the following motto: "A mari usque ad mare" (from sea to sea). In terms of area, it is the second largest country in the world.

85

Climate

Portugal has a temperate maritime climate. This climate is influenced by the Gulf Stream, which makes it relatively mild. The four seasons are quite well balanced. In Lisbon, average temperatures range from 11°C (52°F) in January to 20°C (68°F) in August. Average temperature variations on the island territory are very slight over the different seasons, ranging from 14°C to 22°C at Ponta Delgada (Azores).

*

The Quebec climate has all the characteristics of a continental climate: a hard winter with very low temperatures, a very short, hot, humid summer, a late, short-lived spring and an autumn which is well-defined in terms of weather and flora. In winter, heavy snowfalls cover the ground for 5 to 6 months of the year. In the Quebec region, average temperatures in January are —12.4°C. On the other hand, in summer, the average temperature is 18.7°C.

Historical factors

Portugal is one of the oldest countries of Europe and its borders have remained practically unchanged since the expulsion of the Arabs from Algarve in 1250. The existence of Portugal as an independent country dates back to 1143 and thus it covers more than eight centuries of history. [3] During the latter part of this period, that is to say, during the last four centuries, the history of Portugal has been deeply marked by colonial expansion.

*

Quebec entered history at a time when Portugal was at the height of her expansion. It was on the present territory of Quebec

---

3. The kingdom of Portugal was officially recognised by Pope Alexander III, through his bull *Manifestis Probatum*, May 23rd, 1179 (see *L'Osservatore Romano*, French Edition, June 5th, 1979, p. 4).

that the events which are the cornerstone of Canadian history took place. In 1791, this territory was given the name of Lower Canada. Quebec is one of the four provinces that signed the Act of Confederation in 1867.

Ethnic composition

In the beginning, the Portuguese, who today are culturally homogeneous, were an amalgamation of cultures and peoples who fought one another and finally settled on the Iberian Peninsula. "Total Portuguese unity is the result of the union of several peoples: Iberians, Celts, Romans, Germans, Jews, Berbers and Arabs with Phoenician, Greek, Carthaginian and Norman influences on the coastal populations. Our unity was born of a common culture which fed an ideal, the equality of all men. The diversity of landscapes and climates which characterises our country made our people exceptionally adaptable to other lands. All this explains the extreme flexibility which we demonstrate in settling anywhere in the world and tolerating all climates, sometimes under particularly difficult conditions". [4]

*

In Quebec, the Francophones and Anglophones are the largest ethnic groups. Nevertheless, immigrants from most countries of the world are represented within the ethnic kaleidoscope of this province. The Amerindians and Inuit are the only groups of non-immigrants insofar as they have been established on their territory since prehistoric times. Today, these peoples are claiming the status of founding peoples on the same basis as the French and English. [5]

---

4. Dias, 1961, p. 154.
5. The Inuit (or Eskimos), who live mainly in the Ungava Peninsula or New Quebec, have shown marked population growth, rising from 2,053 in 1951 to 3,206 in 1969 and 3,900 in 1974 (cf. *Annuaire du Québec,* 1974, pp. 255 and 259). The Amerindians are scattered throughout Quebec, forming about 40 groups. According to the 1971 census, the Indian population of Quebec totalled 32,840 (cf. *Annuaire du Québec,* 1974, p. 261). We may therefore conclude that the Portuguese population of Montreal exceeds the total population of Indians and Eskimos in all of Quebec.

From 1871 to 1971, the ethnic composition of Quebec showed the following picture:

TABLE 5-1

Quebec: Ethnic composition, 1871-1971

Year	Ethnic group			
	French %	English %	Other %	Total %
1871	78.0	20.4	1.6	100.0
1901	80.2	17.6	2.2	100.0
1931	79.0	15.0	6.0	100.0
1951	82.0	12.1	5.9	100.0
1961	80.6	10.8	8.6	100.0
1971	79.0	10.6	10.4	100.0

Source: *Annuaire du Québec*, 1977/78, p. 232.

Most of the inhabitants of the province of Quebec belong to ethnic groups coming from Europe and the Mediterranean Basin.

Population figures

According to the official census of 1970, the population of Portugal was 8,545,120.[6] The *Instituto Nacional de Estatística* estimates the population of Portugal at 9,448,800 for the year 1975.[7] Population density on the continent and the islands combined is estimated at 93.5 inhabitants/km^2, while in the Azores it is 124 inhabitants/km^2 and in Madeira, 218 inhabitants/km^2.[8]

*

6. Cf. Portugal. Secretariado Nacional da Emigração, *Boletim Anual*, 1972, p. 3.

7. Cf. Portugal. Instituto Nacional de Estatística, *Estatísticas Demográficas*, 1975, p. xxiii.

8. Cf. *Europa Year Book*, 1977, Vol. 1, p. 1030.

The population of Quebec, which totalled 3,600,000 in 1946, had risen to 5,780,845 in 1966, to 6,027,765 in 1971 and to 6,081,000 in 1973. This progression represents an annual growth rate of about 2.3%. [9] Today, the average population density of Quebec is 3.9 inhabitants per km [2]. [10] In 1871, Quebec had a birth rate of 46 per 1,000, which was one of the highest in the world. In 1951, this rate had dropped to 31 per 1,000 and in 1961, it was only 15.2 per 1,000. [11]

The following table, which covers the period 1962-1974, is self-explanatory in terms of the changes in certain population indices:

TABLE 5-2

Quebec: Summary of the main population indices, 1962-1974

Year	Births	Deaths	Nat. Growth	Immigration	Population
1962	135,000	37,142	97,858	19,132	5,366,000
1963	133,640	28,217	95,423	23,264	5,468,000
1964	130,845	37,552	93,293	25,973	5,562,000
1965	120,607	38,534	82,073	30,346	5,685,000
1966	109,818	38,680	71,198	39,198	5,781,000
1967	105,185	38,329	66,856	45,717	5,868,000
1968	96,622	39,537	57,085	35,481	5,962,000
1969	95,610	40,103	55,507	28,230	6,004,000
1970	91,757	40,392	51,365	23,261	6,017,000
1971	91,841	41,192	50,649	19,222	6,040,000
1972	84,921	42,525	42,396	18,592	6,068,000
1973	86,161	43,052	43,109	26,871	6,112,000
1974	87,177	43,337	43,840	33,458	6,165,000

Source: *Annuaire du Québec,* 1977/78, p. 362.

9. Cf. Québec. Ministère de l'Immigration, 1974, p. 10; *Annuaire du Québec,* 1974, pp. 256 and 1156.

10. The total population of Canada is 21,000,000, which implies a very low population density (2.2 persons per km²).

11. Québec. Ministère de l'Immigration, 1974, p. 9.

In Quebec, as in Portugal, population aging is becoming more and more marked due to demographic stagnation. The members of the 0 to 40 age group formed 13.4% in 1951, while in 1973, they made up only 7.2%. [12] The following statistical table speaks for itself:

TABLE 5-3

Quebec: Average age of the population

Year	Average
1941	27.9
1951	27.9
1956	27.8
1961	27.9
1966	28.5
1971	29.6
1976	30.0
1981	30.3

Source: Data and forecasts provided by the *Service de développement économique, Bureau de recherches économiques.*

Language

Portuguese belongs to the family of Neo-Latin languages, but it has felt the influence of Celtic, Greek, German, Arabic, French, Spanish, Italian, English and other idioms of Africa and the Americas. These influences may be attributed both to the historical presence of different peoples on Portuguese territory and to Portuguese contacts with other peoples in the course of discoveries and colonisation.

There is no official second language in Portugal. Nevertheless, official curricula encourage the teaching of French, English, and

---

12. Partly because of emigration, the aging of the Portuguese population pyramid has become more marked (a fact already alluded to in a preceding chapter). Cf. Nazareth, 1979.

German. It is a unilingual nation and Portuguese is spoken over its entire territory. From region to region, one notes certain phonetic differences — more marked between the continent and the islands — which does not mean that there are dialects. Portuguese, which is today spoken by more than one hundred and fifty million people, is the official language of the following seven countries: Portugal, Brazil, Angola, Mozambique, Guinea-Bissau, Cape Verde, São Tomé and Prince.

*

In Quebec, a multitude of languages are spoken, because of the many different ethnic groups in the province. Several of these languages are taught within the corresponding ethnic communities and used in ethnic programmes, in the press and on radio. Up until recently, French and English were the two official languages of Quebec and of all of Canada in general. In the last few years, Quebec's separatist-leaning policy has sought to impose French as the only official language of that province. This goal has been achieved recently with the approval of provincial government bill 101.

Type of society

Portuguese society may be regarded as a traditional type society, characterised by a valuing of the extended family and by social relations of the "face to face" type. Even though today the rural and the urban populations tend to be about equal on Portuguese continental territory, it is not very long since the rural population exceeded the urban population. On the islands, inhabitants of rural areas make up most of the population even today. Present Portuguese society as a whole may be described as a pre-industrial one.

*

Quebec society, though more diversified by virtue of its ethnic pluralism, is socially less stratified than Portuguese society. Quebec was up until recently an essentially rural and traditional society.

91

The 1971 census indicates a predominance of the urban population (4,861,245) over the rural population (1,166,520); the urban population makes up 80% of the total population of Quebec. [13]

The family

Since we discuss the Portuguese family in one of the chapters which follow, here we shall only mention a few aspects which will permit us to continue the comparison between the two peoples. While in the north of the continental territory and the adjacent islands, the extended family of the patriarchal type prevails, in the south of Portuguese continental territory, the nuclear type family predominates. Up until recently, above all in the rural milieu and more particularly in the north of the continental territory and the islands, families typically have had large numbers of children. In general, each family is highly cohesive, and contacts among members are frequent. However, there is no great concern with their historical origins.

Even though by marriage, a woman can take the husband's name, she is only rarely identified by this name. In fact, individuals are generally identified by their Christian names, rather than by their family names. The children, in the majority of cases, take two family names: that of the mother followed by that of the father. Sometimes, children are registered with a whole series of surnames, especially in more snobbish circles.

The Portuguese family, as the nucleus of social organisation, is further united by its common ideal of production and consumption. Fictive kinship is particularly significant, with the creation of almost familial bonds similar to those of blood relatives.

*

13. Cf. *Annuaire du Québec,* 1974, p. 354.

In Quebec, above all among French speakers, the traditional family has numerous points in common with the Portuguese family. In the rural area, the extended family predominates. However, large scale urbanisation has made the nuclear family the most common type in Quebec. French Canadian families were distinguished by their large number of children. [14] The Francophone population has been deeply marked by the principles and teachings of the Catholic religion, as witness the high birth rate, the low divorce rate and the reinforcement of the patriarchal type family. [15]

Even if the Quebec mother is traditionally without authority, she has had considerable power in several areas, such as household tasks and the upbringing of the children. [16] The Quebec wife generally takes her husband's name and society identifies her by this name. This is also the case of the children, who are given only the father's surname.

Religion and beliefs

Catholicism has always been the religion of the majority of Portuguese. Even very recently, 95.8% of the population stated that they belonged to the Catholic Church. However, Portugal is the West European country with the lowest number of clergymen per inhabitant: 1/2,000. [17] The other religious groups, both because of tradition and because of their small numbers, have been victims of a certain ostracism on the part of the population and authorities in general.

---

14. Cf. Vattier, 1928, p. 222.
15. It is important to mention the traditional New Year's Day rite, in which the entire family, including the wife, kneels before the head of the family to receive the paternal blessing.
16. Cf. Elkin, 1971, p. 101.
17. Cf. Silva, 1972, pp. 36 and 123.

93

Based on statistical data, we would be led to assume that the Portuguese people are very religious. However, belonging to the Church sometimes seems to be more the result of a tradition than of a mature choice, which on the other hand explains certain religious behaviours based largely on magic and superstition.

*

In Quebec, as in Portugal, Catholics are in the vast majority. According to the 1971 census, 86.7% of the inhabitants of Quebec are Catholic.

In the course of Quebec history, French culture has been closely identified with the Catholic religion, so much so that the French language and Catholicism are almost inseparable. Christian hagiography is largely visible in the province's place names, as witness the names of lakes and mountains, villages and towns, rivers and streets.

In addition to Catholicism, the most important religions of Quebec include the Anglican religion, the United Church and Judaism.

The following table gives an overall view of the different religious confessions in Quebec:

TABLE 5-4

Quebec: Population and religious confession, 1971

Roman Catholic	5,226,150	Mormon	885
Anglican	181,875	Adventist	750
United Church	176,825	Brothers in Christ	740
Jewish	110,885	Mennonite	658
Greek Orthodox	59,910	Free Methodist	570
Presbyterian	51,785	Reformed Christian	435
Baptist	37,820	Confucianism	365
Ukranian Catholic	24,930	Church of the Nazarene	245
Lutheran	23,845	Doukhobor	220
Jehovah's Witnesses	17,130	Christian Alliance	195
Pentecostal	8,535	Hutterite	175
Salvation Army	4,030	Disciples of Christ	135
Unitarian	2,715	Plymouth Brothers	93
Buddhist	1,130	Others	18,020
		No religion	76,685

Source: *Annuaire du Québec,* 1977/78, p. 280.

Since the beginning of colonisation, clericalism has deeply marked Quebec society which, up until recently, was governed by a theocratic system. The habit of "cursing", which is very common among Québécois, finds its explanation in the reaction against this system. [18]

---

18. "A curious fault which is extremely common among country people and manual workers in the city, is the habit of swearing in a vulgar manner and, something extremely strange for such a religious people, generally using words which designate what they otherwise consider sacred [...]. Is it not a fact that, in times past, they organised swearing contests on Sunday? This vulgarity, which has continued in spite of all the remonstrances of the clergy and the progress of education, shocks foreigners and with just cause" (Vattier, 1928, pp. 166-167).

Dominant traits

For many outsiders, the typical image of the Portuguese evokes the melancholy of the fado or the taste of fish, particularly codfish. Even if these stereotypes reflect an easily observable reality, we must fight the temptation to generalise as a result of partial observation or badly directed propaganda. Quebec runs a similar risk. Influenced by propaganda, some Portuguese who arrive in Quebec expect to find the territory peopled by gangsters and cowboys.

The fado, associated loosely with the Portuguese spirit, does seem to reflect one of its characteristic traits. In effect, the fado almost always sings the tragedies of a past which is relived in a medley of nostalgia, passion, resignation and inability to oppose a fatal destiny.

The "saudade", more than the fado, translates the richness and the complexity of the Portuguese soul. The "saudade" is more than a word. It is at the same time a way of being and a philosophy of life. The Portuguese word "saudade" does not have an equivalent in any other language. [19] The "saudade" is a mixture of sentiments where we find simultaneously memories, nostalgia, tragedy, resignation, solitude and hope in which joy and sorrow mingle. It reflects a lyrical rather than a dramatic sentiment. It expresses the sorrow that sings and the joy that dreams. According to Jorge Dias, "the saudade is a strange feeling of anxiety which seems to combine three different types of emotion: the lyrical dreaming type — reminiscent of the Celtic temperament —, the Faustian type which is characteristically German and the fatalistic type common to the Orientals." [20]

---

19. The words *morriña* (Galician) and *Sehnsucht* (German) seem closest to the meaning of the term *saudade*.

20. Dias, 1961, p. 107.

It is not easy to define the character of an individual and even less so that of a people, because psychological reality is hard to define. It is however useful to mention some characteristic traits of the Portuguese people. According to a French author, "the Portuguese mind is generally superficial. It is a sentimental mind without logic; a poetic mind without philosophy; a curious mind which does not criticise, with an Oriental tendency to fatalism." [21]

This is what a Portuguese immigrant to Canada says of the Portuguese soul: "The Portuguese is joyful. He dresses gloomily but his soul is brightly coloured. He weeps easily but he loves to laugh, talk and fraternise. He is quick-tempered but he forgives offenses. He is good! It is only outside his country, surrounded by other peoples, that he is appreciated at his true worth. He has his faults, but who doesn't?" [22]

The Portuguese people rarely adopt attitudes which could be construed as a "superiority complex". Their simplicity unquestionably explains the favourable reception that they give strangers. "The Portuguese does not need to assert himself by negation, quite the contrary, he asserts himself through love, moved by an ideal of fraternity [...]; unlike most other peoples, he loves foreigners, listens to what they have to say, takes pleasure in speaking other languages and can show so much amiability that he sometimes gives the impression of having an inferiority complex vis-à-vis these foreigners. Clearly, this attitude is the most telling proof of the absence of any marked degree of ethnocentrism [...]. It is true that, sometimes, because of loving other people, we Portuguese undervalue what is ours to the point of showing the fault which is the opposite of ethnocentrism. This ability of ours to see outside ourselves, to put ourselves in the place of others and to be our own best

---

21. Reynold, 1936, p. 139.
22. Rodrigues, 1976, p. 215.

critics, inclines us to downgrade ourselves and to become our own worst enemies".[23]

What we say about a people in general does not, of course, apply to each individual in particular. It is also necessary to take into account regional differences and characteristics.[24]

*

The Québécois may be regarded as a young people, the legatees of very old civilisations. As is demonstrated by the large percentage of Francophones, their roots lie in the history and culture of the French people. The French ethnic group in Quebec, which was the first on this territory at the time of colonisation, in fact maintains its ties with the culture of origin. "The French Canadians were pure French in the beginning and were able to remain so, marrying one another and mixing only in a very small percentage with the natives of the country, the Anglo-Saxons or with other peoples of different races who emigrated to their land".[25]

Up until the middle of this century, Francophone Quebec was a society of the closed type: "Nationalist thought revolved around a society to be preserved rather than a society to be built. It was necessary at all costs to preserve this Catholic, French, rural society from the onslaught of industrialisation, from the onslaught of majority English governments, from the onslaught of France which was largely viewed as atheistic. It is not surprising then that this French-Canadian nationalism was highly xenophobic. In order to preserve the purity of the ethnic heritage, it was necessary at all costs to prevent contacts with any other nation or any other group.

---

23. Dias, 1961, pp. 147-148.

24. In the specific case of the Portuguese from the continent and from the islands, regional characteristics are evident. Close ethnic bonds and a common historical experience have reconciled these regional differences into a single united people.

25. Vattier, 1928, p. 13.

Any outside power or society threatened not only the language, but the very type of society which it was desired to preserve". [26]

In the 17th century, Quebec experienced a veritable "invasion" of settlers coming from different provinces of France. Let us mention, in order of importance, those which furnished the largest contingents at that time: Normandy, Ile de France, Poitou, Aunis, Saintonge, Perche, Brittany, Anjou, Champagne, Guyenne, Maine, Beauce, Charente, Touraine, Limousin, Burgundy, Orléanais, Gascony, Languedoc and Berry.

In spite of their French origin, it is a mistake to confound the inhabitants of Quebec with the French people. There are numerous factors which distinguish them: "The winter and more particularly the monotony of the snow-covered landscape have inevitably altered the character of the inhabitants". [27]

As marked characteristics of French Canadians, one might mention their sociability, their delicacy, their courtesy and their desire to please. According to Delacour: "their politeness, which is excessive, is not obsequious but their pride is not without a touch of vanity. They in effect have a taste for honours, distinctions, decorations, they are rebellious to the point of impertinence when an attempt is made to downgrade them; they are independent to the point of insubordination when they believe they will be coerced". [28] Vanity and pride are in fact words frequently used to describe French Canadians. According to La Hontan, "they are pretentious people who are full of themselves; they consider themselves superior to all the nations of the earth". [29] Nevertheless, the comments made to us suggest that today the Québécois are generally

---

26. Fortin, *cit. in* Cappon, 1974, pp. 35-36.

27. Vattier, 1928, p. 37.

28. Delacour, 1929, p. 412.

29. Vattier, 1928, p. 161.

liked by the Portuguese, who appreciate their good breeding, their hospitality and their democratic spirit.

In describing these few characteristic traits of the French Canadian group, we would repeat what we said before, in connection with the Portuguese, to the effect that we must avoid the dangers of generalisation.

Habitat and festivities

Even if the Portuguese people are scattered throughout the globe, it would be a mistake to consider them a nomadic or wandering nation. They are a people who love nature and who live in close contact with it.

For the Portuguese, the house is the ideal means of situating himself in space. There is a certain harmony among houses, people and the surrounding environment. Cleanliness and the good state of repair of one's home are a way of gaining esteem within the society. These houses stand out by reason of their solidity. Because of the materials used in their construction (stone, brick, cement), they are very resistant and last a long time. Central heating is practically non-existent because of economic conditions and the mildness of the climate.

The home and those who inhabit it are normally identified by the same word. Life's great events are simultaneously situated in time and in space. The house is the point of reference, the meeting point in space. Attachment to the home and love of life are deeply rooted in the Portuguese spirit.

The rites of passage are celebrated as all-important events. The significance accorded to the celebration of baptisms and marriages and the evolution which these celebrations have undergone are quite characteristic. In villages, these festivities last several days; in the cities, they are limited to the liturgical rite followed by a reception for relatives and friends. Just as baptisms and marriages take place in an atmosphere of overflowing joy, the death of close relatives deeply marks the Portuguese soul, and the dead are always honoured in religious manifestations and through outward signs of mourning. This mourning is continued for a shorter or longer period depending on the degree of kinship and, in the case of widows, it is total and perpetual. For a son or a brother, the period of mourning lasts a year. This practice reflects the grief felt and the interest shown in deceased close relatives. It is also imposed by traditional social norms, the transgression of which is an immediate source of criticism, especially in the milieu of origin.

Like all peoples, the Portuguese have their special holidays and feastdays, which may be historical, political, religious, folkloric or familial. Today, the main historical and political anniversaries are the following: April 25, commemorating the establishment of the Second Republic; May 1, international workers' day; June 10, Camões Day, honouring Portugal's great epic poet; October 5, which commemorates the establishment of the First Republic and December 1, which celebrates the return to national independence following the end of Spanish domination which lasted from 1580 to 1640.

The most important religious feasts are: January 1, New Year's; January 6 (Epiphany); Mardi Gras, Easter and the Feast of the Assumption (movable feasts), the Feast of the Holy Ghost, Corpus Christi, and the popular saints (St. Anthony, June 13; St. John the Baptist, June 24; St. Peter, June 29); August 15 (Our Lady of the Assumption); November 1 (All Saints); December 8 (Immaculate Conception) and December 25 (Christmas).

Some of these feasts, because of their tradition and their significance, are official national holidays. Others, like Epiphany, Mardi Gras and the popular saints are deeply imbued with folklore. This is especially true of Mardi Gras, which is celebrated throughout the country, and which today no longer has any religious significance. Regional folklore also has an important place in the celebrations for the patron saints of the different towns and villages.

We should also mention the national, regional and local fairs. These fairs, which are held just about everywhere in the country at regular intervals, though secular in character, also have many religious elements mixed in (St. Martin's Fair, St. Iria's Fair, St. John's Fair, etc.).

The feasts of Christmas and New Year's are generally spent with one's family, with the occasional visit to other families. Some festivities are typical of certain regions; this is the case of the feasts of the "Senhor Santo Cristo" (Holy Lord Christ) in the Azores. [30] The different regions of the continent and the islands also have a characteristic folklore. Some musical examples are the "vira" of Minho, the "fandango" of Ribatejo, the "corridinho" of Algarve, the "bailinho" of Madeira and the "chamarritas" of the Azores.

The bullfight is a typical spectacle in Portuguese milieux. The Portuguese corrida is distinguished from the Spanish and Mexican ones by the manner in which the bull is fought and by the fact that at the end of the corrida, the bull is traditionally subdued and not killed as in Spain or in Mexico. Fighting the bull on horseback is also a typical characteristic of the Portuguese corrida. In the Azores, especially in Terceira, there is a tradition of bull-fighting with a rope. These corridas are generally associated with religious feasts.

*

In Quebec, the home seems to have less importance. The wood used in the construction of houses in bygone years has today been replaced by other construction materials which guarantee the im-

---

30. The feasts of the Holy Ghost, originating in continental Portugal, which were first intended as charitable works, were particularly well received by the people of the Azores, who transplanted them to the North American continent.

proved insulation required by the climate. Stone was also used at one time, offering guarantees of resistance and durability. Today, most homes are built with prefabricated synthetic materials available in a whole series of standardised models, which leave little scope for creativity and variety. Solidity and durability are usually lacking. These houses are normally quite comfortable and functional. There is central heating in all buildings because of the climate.

Celebrations of certain rites of passage such as baptisms and marriages differ very little from Portuguese celebrations. On the other hand, funerals are radically different. In Quebec, the arrangements are entrusted to specialised funeral homes where the deceased is exposed for several days and where all the ceremonies are of a formal nature. The mourning period which was respected in bygone years has completely disappeared and mourning clothes are not even worn during interments. It is interesting to note that a meal is sometimes offered after the funeral for those who have attended, in a climate which we would describe as almost festive.

Among the main holidays on the Quebec calendar, the following hold an important place: New Year's, St. Joseph, Feast of Dollard, St. John the Baptist, Confederation Day, Labour Day, Thanksgiving, All Saints and Christmas.

Quebec folklore, the old traditions of which have essentially French roots, is very widespread. It is also necessary to take into account the typical folklore of the peoples established in Quebec, in particular the Amerindians and the Inuit.

Economic conditions

Portugal is traditionally an agricultural country. Close to 30% of its working population, two thirds of whom are small landowners, are still engaged in agriculture today.[31] In the North of

31. Cf. Collin, 1975, p. 382.

the continental territory, small family properties (*minifundia*) are predominant. Properties in Minho have an average area of 2 acres, which is an obstacle to the introduction of modern farming methods. In the South, until very recently, the situation was the direct opposite: large rural estates belonging to a few dozen landowners living in the urban centres were worked by hired help.

A situation similar to that of the continental territory is found on the islands. On São Miguel Island, for example, the land is owned by a handful of families and is worked by hired help, while on the other islands, lands are divided up into small properties. As the following table shows, the imbalance in the distribution of lands was still considerable in 1975:

TABLE 5-5

Portugal: Distribution of properties, 1975

Number of properties	Area	% of agricultural land
187,640	less than 0.5 ha	0.8%
126,380	from 0.5 to 1 ha	1.7%
317,060	from 1 to 4 ha	12.5%
155,480	from 4 to 20 ha	23.7%
17,716	from 20 to 50 ha	10.0%
4,494	from 50 to 100 ha	6.0%
3,599	from 100 to 500 ha	15.0%
652	from 500 to 1,000 ha	9.0%
488	more than 1,000 ha	21.3%

Source: Data compiled from Collin, 1975, pp. 383-384.

This imbalance is largely responsible for the country's low farm production. In effect, "one of the essential features of Portuguese agriculture is its low degree of productivity. In 1972, for example, the yield of wheat per hectare did not exceed 1,200 kg on the average, while during the same period, it reached 2,470 kg in Italy; the yield of corn was 1,330 kg per hectare in Portugal compared to 5,390 kg in Italy". [32] This low productivity is reflected in the poverty of the agricultural sector. As is pointed out by the same author, in 1974, the average income of each Portuguese living directly from farming was one third lower than that of other sectors of the economy. [33]

Fishing, though it is one of the country's traditional occupations, employs only a small percentage of the population and tends to diminish from year to year.

The Portuguese working population is broken down by sector of employment as follows:

TABLE 5-6

Portugal: Working population by sectors, 1976

Primary sector	789,100	28.0%
Secondary sector	768,700	27.2%
Tertiary sector	1,262,700	44.7%

Source: *Le Monde,* December 12-13, 1976, p. 9.

Within the European economy, Portugal holds last place. [34] Statistical indices relating to socio-economic conditions even today

---

32. Collin, 1975, p. 382.

33. Cf. Collin, 1975, p. 382.

34. We might cite here the findings of Sedas Nunes. Speaking of Portugal, he writes: "Among sixteen countries of Europe, we are second last in energy consumption per capita: only Turkey comes after us. We are in fourteenth place in steel consumption per capita: only Greece and Turkey rank lower. We are second last in level of schooling: only Turkey's is lower. We are last in terms of number of students in higher education out of the overall population; no one is below us. We are second last in meat consumption per capita: only Turkey comes after us. We are last in milk consumption per capita and daily protein ration (in Rosa, 1974, p. 20).

reveal a level of development lower than that of some countries of the Third World. In effect, Portugal is one of the least industrialised countries of Europe, with a per capita income of $1,250 in 1973.[35]

During recent decades, it is the tourism and emigration sectors of the Portuguese economy that have contributed most to the entry of foreign currency. Now that Portugal has renounced its colonial ambitions, its only remaining road to development lies in industrialisation. This development must however confront basic problems, which are already complex and which are aggravated by the world economic situation.

*

Quebec is an important agricultural province, though only one tenth of its lands are arable. Forage crops intended for cattle predominate, meat and milk being among the most important products of Quebec agriculture.

Commercial fishing is highly developed, above all in the Gaspé region. Some thousands of lakes spread throughout Quebec also make non-commercial sports fishing a very popular pastime.

The Quebec subsoil is very rich in minerals, in particular copper, gold, asbestos and iron. Forest and hydroelectric resources are also quite considerable. Pulp production is one of the highest in the world.

The working population of Quebec, which totalled 2,542,000 persons in 1972, consists of 76.5% men.[36] In 1973, this working population was broken down as follows, by sector of employment:

---

35.   Cf. Poinard and Roux, 1977, p. 53.

36.   Cf. *Annuaire du Québec,* 1974, p. 1156.

TABLE 5-7

Quebec: Jobs by sector of employment, 1973

Sectors of employment	Percentage %	Sub-total %
Primary:		
— Agriculture	3.7	
— Others	2.0	5.7
Secondary:		
— Processing	25.9	
— Construction	5.5	31.4
Tertiary:		
— Transportation and other public services	8.8	
— Trade	16.3	
— Finance, insurance and real estate	4.7	
— Social services and others	26.6	
— Public administration	6.5	62.9

Source: Quebec. Ministère de l'Immigration. *Une problématique des ressources humaines au Québec,* 1974, p. 61.

Canada is one of the most industrialised countries in the world. Quebec, for its part, is one of the richest provinces in Canada. In 1973, the average income of Quebec families was $11,581 compared to $12,532 which was the national average. [37] The main Quebec industries lie in the following sectors: food, textiles, leather, clothing, millinery, lumber, furniture, pulp, chemical products, etc.

In 1975, per capita income in the different Canadian provinces and territories was as follows.

---

37.   Québec. Ministère de l'Immigration, 1974, p. 31.

TABLE 5-8

Canada: Per capita income by provinces, 1975

Ontario	$6,431
British Columbia	6,272
Alberta	6,064
Saskatchewan	5,971
Yukon and Northwest Territories	5,678
Manitoba	5,635
Quebec	5,312
Nova Scotia	4,625
New Brunswick	4,498
Newfoundland	4,027
Prince Edward Island	4,008

Source: *Annuaire du Québec*, 1977/78, p. 1360.

Development indices

While economic level is one of the key elements in development indices, it is necessary to consider other equally important factors such as level of schooling.

In Portugal, under a law passed in 1899 and which remained in effect up to 1960, compulsory schooling was limited to 3 years. The situation was further aggravated by the fact that this law had been often ignored, particularly in rural areas and in the case of girls. In 1960, compulsory schooling was raised to 4 years and in 1967 to 6 years. Up until recently, formal education at the post-primary levels was more or less reserved for the privileged classes. Moreover, the rate of illiteracy is among the highest in Europe. According to data supplied by Silva, the percentage of illiterates among Portuguese 7 years of age and older was 24.1% in 1970. [38] More recent statistical data indicate an illiteracy rate of 35%. [39]

---

38. Silva, 1976, p. 38.

39. Cf. *Europa Year Book,* 1971, Vol. 1, p. 1030.

The health and social service sector is traditionally the responsibility of religious institutions and charitable organisations rather than of government. Given the deficiencies and limitations of these groups, it would be more correct to speak of amateurism than of professional services. The wide gaps in health care and social security, with which the Portuguese people are accustomed to living, have marked them deeply and have aroused in them a special preoccupation with illness and old age. In general, it may be said that the Portuguese live each day with an eye to the future, so that they will be able to cope with the problems of getting ill and growing old. Recently, the situation has improved, but the most basic needs are still far from being met.

*

Illiteracy in Quebec is very low compared to Portugal. According to the 1961 census, 53.3% of the population of Quebec had attended school below the secondary level, 40.9% had reached this level and 5.8% had attended university. Of these latter, 3% had obtained a university degree. [40]

Health services are very advanced, especially in the following sectors: prenatal care, school health care, psychosocial problems, maladjusted children, protection of children, rehabilitation of adults, senior citizens and specialised services. The Health Insurance Act passed on July 17, 1970 guarantees the Quebec population medical care in almost all health sectors, whatever the financial situation of the individual. [41] In 1974, Quebec had 9,374 health professionals, of whom close to half (49.1%) were specialised doctors and 40.2% general practitioners. [42]

---

40. Cf. Québec. Ministère de l'Immigration, 1974, p. 50.

41. L.Q., 1970, c. 37.

42. Cf. *Annuaire du Québec,* 1974, p. 350.

Political evolution

From its foundation (1143) up to the 20th century (1910), the political regime in Portugal was a monarchy. In 1910, the First Republic was established. From 1926 to 1974, the country was governed by a dictatorship backed by the military. In 1974, the armed forces established the Second Republic which, this time, plans to lead the country towards democracy. This regime is still marked by a climate of political instability. [43]

*

Quebec was a French colony from the beginning of the 16th century up to the first half of the 18th century, when it came under the British Crown. Since the 19th century (1867), Quebec has been a province of the Canadian Confederation.

Within Confederation, Quebec, like all the other provinces of Canada, has its own legislature. At the executive level, each province has a Lieutenant Governor appointed by the Governor General on the recommendation of the provincial government. The Lieutenant Governor is appointed for a period of five years. His functions consist in practice of a certain protocol and official representation, under the control of the province. In theory, he has certain powers vested in him, but "as in the case of the Governor General or the Queen of England, the Lieutenant Governors of the provinces *reign but do not govern*". [44]

The Executive Council or Council of Ministers is in fact the supreme body of government. The Prime Minister is at the same

---

43. In February 1980, the following parties, in decreasing order of importance, were represented in the National Assembly: Social Democrat Party (P.S.D.), Socialist Party (P.S.), Portuguese Communist Party (P.C.P.), Party of the Social Democratic Centre (C.D.S.), Popular Monarchist Party (P.P.M.), Portuguese Democratic Movement (M.D.P.), and Popular Democratic Union (U.P.D.). The present Constitution was promulgated on April 2, 1976.

44. *Annuaire du Québec,* 1974, p. 106.

time head of the government and head of the Executive Council. He belongs to the party with the largest number of deputies in Parliament, but he may also be the head of a coalition of deputies from different political parties. [45]

Conflicts between the French and English populations have marked Quebec's history. Among the former group, there has always been an undercurrent of two opposing political factions: those who are fighting for Quebec independence and those who wish to keep Quebec within the Canadian Confederation. These two trends are today in open confrontation in a climate of tension which could decide once and for all the history of Canada in general and that of Quebec in particular. "For some years now, the Province of Quebec has been living in a state of perpetual crisis. We have a nation in search of itself which is trying to lose itself at the same time. The left and the right are organising irreconcilably, and we cannot discard the possibility of temporary violence, the goal of which (however tragic) will be mainly to test the strength of the adversary, and above all to discover his weaknesses and take advantage of them". [46]

The migratory movement

In Portugal, emigration is a centuries-old tradition which is more marked in the islands and in the provinces in the north of continental Portugal. Most Portuguese immigrants in Canada come from these areas. The Portuguese migratory movement has been extensively discussed in the first chapter — "An Overview". Besides emigration abroad, it is necessary to consider the internal migrations caused by urbanisation. At present, one third of the

---

45. The main parties with seats in the National Assembly of the Province of Quebec are, at the present time: Parti Québécois, Liberal Party, Union Nationale and Social Credit Party. Since November 15, 1976, the Parti Québécois has been the government of Quebec.

46. Lenormand, 1971, pp. 14-15.

Portuguese population is concentrated in the cities of Lisbon and
Oporto.

*

While Portugal may be considered a country of emigration,
Quebec is at the same time an area of immigration and one of
emigration. [47] In 1871, the immigrant population represented 1.6%
of the total population of Quebec, while in 1971, this percentage
had risen to 15.8%. [48] Contrary to popular belief, Quebec is not
just a territory of immigration but also a region which exports manpower. We have only to consider the emigration of Quebecers and
the departure of immigrants having originally settled in that province. From 1891 to 1946, Quebec had a net emigration of more
than 300,000 persons. [49]

As may be seen from the following table, 46.9% of immigrants
to Quebec left that province between 1946 and 1971:

---

47. Side by side with the federal department of manpower and immigration, the
Province of Quebec also has a ministry of immigration. This ministry was
created in 1968 from the old Directorate General of Immigration, which in
turn was set up in 1966 under the Ministry of Cultural Affairs (Cf. *Annuaire
du Québec,* 1974, p. 276).

48. Cf. Humblet, 1976, p. 129.

49. Quebec. Ministry of Immigration, 1974, p. 90.

TABLE 5-9

Quebec: Length of stay of immigrants from 1946 to 1971 [50]

Period of Immigration	(1) Landed Immigrants	(2) Immigrants according to census	(3) Index of permanence $\frac{(2) \times 100}{(1)}$	(4) Index of absence $100 - (3)$
1946-1950	74,251	29,570	39.8	60.2
1951-1955	166,181	72,365	43.5	56.5
1956-1960	163,502	82,720	50.6	49.4
1961-1964	85,289	50,435	59.1	40.9
1965-1971*	210,534	136,455	64.8	35.2
Total	699,757	371,545	53.1	46.9

* Includes only the first 5 months of 1971

Source: Quebec. Ministère de l'Immigration. *Une problématique des ressources humaines au Québec*, 1974, p. 67.

The emigration of French Canadians to New England was particularly marked between 1870 and 1910, as may be seen from the study of Paquet. [51] Today, the number of inhabitants of Quebec origin scattered throughout the American states of Maine, Vermont, New Hampshire, Massachusetts, and New York is estimated at 3,500,000 persons. [52] This flow of emigrants, which has reached substantial proportions, continues up to this day. Suffice it to say that between 1961 and 1971, 680,000 persons left Quebec. [53]

---

50. In 1971, Quebec, which was home to 28% of the population of Canada, received 15.8% of immigrants, while Ontario, which counted 35.7% of the Canadian population, received 52,8% of all immigrants (cf. Quebec. Ministry of Immigration, 1974, p. 67).

51. Paquet, 1964.

52. Cf. Humblet, 1976, p. 129.

53. Cf. *Québec-Monde*, September 1977, p. 5.

The exodus taking place in Quebec would seem to favour neither a solution of her population problems nor the goal of maintaining certain socio-political ideals.

*   *   *

These few traits which we have just described in comparing the milieu of origin and the receiving milieu, enable us to identify those factors which are favourable or unfavourable to the integration of individuals and the mutual adaptation of the two peoples.

We consider as favourable the following:

— Geographically, the new milieu has a low population density;
— The varied ethnic population, above all in the large urban centres, which means that newcomers can more easily gain acceptance;
— The type of society, which is presently open to new contacts and new lifestyles;
— The fact that both French and Portuguese are Latin languages;
— The families are of the patriarchial type in both milieux;
— The Catholic religion is predominant among the two peoples;

As unfavourable factors, we would mention the following:

— History, insofar as the past plays a preponderant role in the present (this is what happens to peoples with a long history and ancient traditions); [54]
— The climate of the receiving milieu, which is of the continental type and characterised by extreme temperatures;

---

54. When William C. Atkinson, speaking of the history of Spain and Portugal, says "Happy the people that have no history", his thought is penetrating in the extreme.

— The traditionally closed Quebec society with its tendency towards xenophobia;
— The present political instability which results in a climate of insecurity.

Based on the data which have just been presented, we may conclude that the peoples of Portugal and of Quebec are sufficiently different to be distinguishable one from the other and similar enough to be able to live together.

VI

FACTORS IN ADAPTATION

Based on what was said in the preceding chapter about the similarities and differences between the two peoples, it is possible to determine the milieux in which the Portuguese living in Quebec are best adapted. In this chapter, we shall consider mainly socio-cultural aspects of this adaptation.

In analysing immigrant adaptation, a distinction must be made between the public milieu and the private milieu. This distinction has already been analysed at the theoretical level by Harald Eidheim and Constance Cronin. According to the latter, the change in immigrant behaviour is more marked in the public milieu occupation, place of residence, language fluency, participation in club and association activities) than in the private milieu (family relations, friends, language spoken at home, diet). [1]

The large-scale entry of Portuguese into Quebec began at a particularly important time in Quebec history, during what is called the "quiet revolution". Today, when Quebec is strongly asserting her socio-cultural identity, it would be a betrayal of the immigrant to refuse him full participation in the struggle toward this common ideal.

---

1. Cf. Cronin, C., *The Sting of Change*. Chicago, University of Chicago Press, 1970.

In the case of the Portuguese established in Quebec, we run the risk, both in theory and in practice, of encouraging this and other minority groups to adapt wholesale to the majority. Adaptation should be a mutual process (a two-way street) where similarities and differences are taken into account, however without any underlying suggestion that these differences are an obstacle; such differences may indeed be a source of mutual enrichment. In the pursuit of the ideal which sees the Québécois as both united and diverse, those who are already there and those who later arrive both have a role to play. In the history of all the groups established in Quebec we shall find that, at some point, each has known the adventure of immigration.

In effect, Quebec, like the rest of Canada, was peopled by immigrants. Suffice it to say that four and a half million Canadians were born elsewhere: one Canadian out of seven entered the country after 1946. [2] Consequently, if we exclude the Amerindian and Inuit minorities, all the other groups have historical roots in other continents, more especially in Europe.

Comparing the Portuguese culture with the French culture predominant in Quebec, we find some common features which seem to greatly facilitate the process of mutual adaptation.

Among the common traits of the Portuguese and Québécois peoples, the following in particular are deserving of mention: a cultural heritage rooted in the Latin civilisation and language, an Atlantic tradition and a belief in Catholicism. [3] Anthropologically speaking, we might emphasise the frequency of the same phenotype which, in most cases, makes any distinction between the two peoples difficult.

---

2.   Cf. George, 1976, p. 40.

3.   We should mention that the establishment of Portugal as a nation is directly linked to the House of Burgundy, since the first Portuguese king, Afonso Henriques (12th century) was of French origin.

Ethnic heterogeneity once characterised the newly founded Portuguese nation; it is now the prevailing situation in Quebec. The Latin type predominates among the Portuguese people, which does not change the fact that they are an ethnically heterogeneous people. As already mentioned in the preceding chapter, the Celts, the Iberians, the Phoenicians, the Jews, the Sueves, the Visigoths, the Alans, the Vandals, the Romans, the Greeks and the Arabs all contributed to the make-up of today's Portuguese population.

The ethnic mosaic which characterises Canadian society and which is becoming more and more evident in the province of Quebec, especially in Montreal, is giving birth to a society which could one day show a homogeneity similar to that of present day Portuguese society, thus proving once again that it is possible to reconcile unity and diversity. The different parties involved all act simultaneously on the adaptation process.

Mutual adaptation

Based on the history of Quebec, one might logically be led to conclude that her people are willing to welcome other peoples. However, in spite of contacts with immigrants and minority groups, complaints about some Quebecers' grudging welcome are quite common. In this regard, we might mention again the distinction made between public milieu and private milieu.

At the public level, immigrants are protected by legislation and standards of acceptance which are not readily found in other countries. Unfortunately, those who oversee the application of these laws are not always up to the task. "Officially, immigrants are both sought after and welcome, but in day to day life, they are not always well received."[4] As was remarked by former Immigration Minister Bryce Mackasey, it is sometimes the immigration officers

---

4.   Elkin, 1964, pp. 46-47.

themselves who detest immigrants and who oppose the open-door policy of the government. [5]

As proof of the concern shown for the acceptance and integration of immigrants, we might mention some agencies, programmes and publications devoted to these ends. In Quebec, the following agencies and programmes operate with the integration of immigrants in mind: C.O.F.I. (Centre d'orientation et formation des immigrants); O.V.A.L. (Opération vacances-loisirs); L.A.G.E. (Liaison avec les groupes ethniques); V.I.V.A.Q. (Vivre au Québec), F.O.R.M.I. (Projet formation de la main-d'oeuvre immigrante).

As regards the attitude of Francophone Quebecers in the private milieu, it would be unjust to deny their ideal of acceptance, but their difficulty in realising this ideal is considerable. The people of Quebec are in fact marked by a tradition and by an experience which can easily lead them to take a hostile, defensive stance. As was noted by Cappon: "During the long reign of Duplessis, the welcome given to new Canadians by Francophones was already cold. Following the recent development, among French Canadians, of a socio-political movement aimed at overcoming their inferiority vis-à-vis the Quebec Anglophones, relations between the French Canadian community and the immigrant population have deteriorated even more". [6]

The comment of Léger is in the same vein: "There is among French Canadians a long-standing and tenacious tradition of opposition to immigration, [...] a defensive reaction by a community which feels threatened [...]. In the situation in which we find ourselves, any immigration of a certain magnitude works against us. But where the thing exceeds all bounds is when this opposition

---

5. See in this regard the article published in the newspaper *Le Soleil* (Quebec) of June 19, 1972.

6. Cappon, 1974, p. 1.

to immigration translates into a hostility towards the immigrant himself." [7]

To better understand this attitude, we must consider what has been the socio-cultural context of Quebec for several centuries: "Living in a rural and clerical setting, the traditional French Canadian is hostile to the stranger, whether this stranger be the English occupant or someone of another origin." [8]

There are some who generalise and who say: "Segregation of immigrants is a day to day occurrence in the Province of Quebec." [9] As is pointed out by official sources: "immigrants and members of ethnic communities have unfortunately been long cast aside and forgotten by our society . . .". [10]

In contacts between different peoples, some initial impact and cultural shock are normal. However, the capacity for adaptation and acceptance seems to vary from people to people. According to a survey conducted by Brazeau and Carlos in 1971, 78.7% of Francophone Quebecers oppose the admission of new immigrants, while only 60.1% of Anglophone Quebecers held this view. [11]

Several attestations and studies confirm the difficulty or the inability of the Francophone population to achieve an optimum degree of intimacy with other groups. "French Canadians have a low capacity for assimilating outsiders. Certain studies have shown that in their relations with immigrants, they let themselves be guided by negative attitudes." [12]

---

7. *Cit. in* Humblet, 1976, p. 129.
8. Humblet, 1976, p. 128.
9. Lenormand, 1971, p. 73.
10. Québec. Ministère de l'Immigration, 1977, Annex 2, p. 7.
11. *Cit. in* Humblet, 1976, p. 130.
12. Larouche, 1973, p. 203.

A national survey has demonstrated that French-speaking Canadians have been "more inclined to have antisemitic attitudes and to express other types of prejudices against ethnic groups. On the other hand, English-speaking Canadians as well as immigrants of Italian, Portuguese, Greek and Polish origin tend to obtain more points than average on the Bogardus scale." [13]

The aggressivity which is sometimes shown towards immigrants seems usually to be linked either to the political system or to employment. As Wilson points out: "In general, the receiving community feels more threatened when the minority groups settle in electoral ridings where the election of members of their own groups to political posts becomes a possibility." [14]

As regards employment, it often happens that immigrants are seen as and accused of being "job snatchers". [15] This accusation and others like it, which are sometimes the fruit of ignorance and simplistic reasoning, serve to create a social climate which is unfavourable to acceptance. [16] It is by no means rare to hear certain Canadians say of immigrants: "If they are not happy, they should leave; we didn't ask them here, they came of their own accord." These statements are the logical conclusion from the generally accepted premises, but the sophism thus revealed is that much more lamentable in that it issues from an environment with a so-called Christian tradition and a democratic ideology.

The immigrants' own insecurity makes them particularly sensitive to any adverse manifestation coming from the society which

---

13. Richmond, 1974, p. 8.

14. Breton, Armstrong and Kennedy, 1974, p. 20.

15. Cf. Béliveau, *cit. in* Mvilongo *et al.*, 1972, p. 19.

16. "As regards immigration, the Quebecer's ignorance has given rise, in public opinion, to serious prejudices which work to the detriment of immigrants (Québec. Ministère de l'Immigration. *L'Immigration québécoise et les communautés ethniques,* 1977, p. 31).

receives them. While they are proud of any attentions received, they are hurt by indifference and sickened by rejection. "The low assimilating capacity of the Francophone group makes it aggressive towards immigrants to begin with and it will be found that the immigrant's reaction is often no more than a response to this aggressivity." [17]

Joviality and hospitality

For the immigrant, it is nevertheless important to avoid generalisation and the prejudices which prevent him from seeing the other side of the coin. Today as in begone days, the Portuguese can attest to the welcome accorded them by the Quebec people, including the Francophone group. At the end of the 18th century, in 1799, António Carlos Ribeiro de Andrada published a book in Lisbon dealing with living conditions in Eastern Canada, where the author described the French Canadians as "jovial and hospitable and particularly happy and sociable." [18]

It is important, too, to consider the reaction of the Portuguese ethnic group to integration and to the welcome received. We can say that Portuguese immigrants make the most, not just of the welcome which is accorded them, but also of the opportunity to welcome other people into their midst. They have practically no prejudices against other ethnic groups and their capacity for adaptation is remarkable. "There is among the Portuguese an extraordinary capacity for adaptation to any thing, person or idea, without this implying a lack of character". [19]

The common factors already mentioned: origin, language and religion, help to make the Portuguese generally feel culturally close to the Francophone group. As Anderson and Higgs point out,

---

17. Cappon, 1974, p. 7.
18. Cf. Anderson and Higgs, 1976, p. 12.
19. Dias, 1961, p. 179.

". . . it is possible that the Portuguese family is closer to the French Canadian family than to the English Canadian family in lifestyle".[20]

Certain opinions which tend to see the Portuguese communities of Quebec as marginal groups participating minimally in the receiving society are perhaps only generalisations of an occasional occurrence which then comes to be regarded as typical. It is normal that there should be difficulties of adaptation, particularly among first generation immigrants, but in that case we should speak of a transitory phenomenon and not of an attitude of "self-marginalisation".[21] Difficulties of adaptation seem to be correlated with the age of individuals and with their educational level. "Middle-aged or elderly immigrants show greater difficulties of adaptation, especially if their educational level is low".[22]

A large percentage of Portuguese residing in Quebec want to settle there permanently, which, in itself, is a factor favouring their integration.[23] However, neither in the case of this group nor in that of the majority group is goodwill enough to achieve the intended goals. In spite of what we have just said, it appears certain that the social psychology of the Portuguese group does not always favour adaptation or integration into a new environment. Attachment to traditional values and customs, while it can offer a contribution to the new society, may also become an obstacle to integration when these values are defended in a climate of opposition or intransigence.

---

20. Anderson and Higgs, 1976, p. 188.

21. The film "Les Borges" (directed by Marilu Mallet and produced by the National Film Board of Canada, 1978) portrays a typical case within the Portuguese ethnic group.

22. Richmond, 1974, p. 17.

23. Among the Portuguese immigrants in Quebec, the percentage who return permanently to their milieu of origin is very low. The percentage of definitive returns to Portugal is estimated at 5%.

123

The high number of Portuguese who take out Canadian citizenship is evidence of the good conditions offered by the receiving country. [24] Factors relating to the country of origin are not extraneous to the choice of a new citizenship. In taking out a new nationality, one does not implicity renounce one's mother country or one's culture of origin. However, according to some persons, certain unfortunate experiences and the abuse of bureaucratic requirements by representatives of the Portuguese government have been determinant in the decision to apply for a new citizenship. [25] The increased flow of Portuguese immigrants to the province of Quebec and the corresponding growth of this same ethnic group helps new arrivals during the initial period, but may also make their integration into the new society more difficult on the long term.

Even though the Portuguese of Quebec form a fully identifiable and distinct ethnic group, they try to maintain a certain closeness to other ethnic groups, and especially to the dominant groups. We cannot therefore conclude that the Portuguese communities live isolated, given their ongoing contact with other groups at work and study, in mass transport systems and at play.

Helps and hindrances

Since mutual adaptation with an exchange of cultural values is an ideal and a goal both for the Portuguese group and for the other groups in Quebec, it becomes important to identify the different factors which help or hinder this process.

---

24. The Canadian law on citizenship, nationality and naturalisation, and on the status of aliens, went into force on January 1, 1947. Up to that date, British citizenship was the only one recognised in Canada.

25. Canadian citizenship is granted to any immigrant who requests it provided he meets the following requirements: he is a permanent resident, he has resided in Canada for at least 3 years, he speaks at least one of the official languages, is of good conduct and impeccable morality, knows the rights and duties attached to Canadian citizenship, intends to remain in Canada and takes the oath of allegiance.

Some of these factors have already been dealt with either implictly or explicitly. We have mentioned the Latin origin of French and Portuguese and of some other languages spoken in Quebec as a factor favouring mutual adaptation. The Judeo-Christian tradition shared by the French group and the majority of immigrants living in Quebec also becomes a catalyst. Work is both an essential and an ideal means of coming into contact and getting to know one another. The mass media have a key influence on contacts and rapprochement between different cultures.

Several factors seem, to varying degrees, to hinder mutual adaptation of the different groups in Quebec. We refer in particular to the lack of preparation which precedes contacts among the different communities: this translates into an ignorance of the respective cultures, which is understandable when we consider geographical distances, but which is incompatible with the ideal of coexistence. The numerical disparities among the different groups and their more or less lengthy historic presence on Quebec territory help to create rivalries and encourage the dominance of the strong. The existence of areas with a strong ethnic concentration creates situations favouring socio-cultural isolation, which apparently is an obstacle to intercultural communication.

To live together happily, people must know and accept one another. Lack of knowledge is an obstacle to unity and becomes a source of prejudices which undermine the ideals of coexistence. One obstacle to mutual understanding is in fact the facility with which people passively accept stereotypes.

Another obstacle which it is important to recognise is the ethnocentric tendency characteristic of all groups. As John Beattie says: "There are serious misunderstandings which have arisen and continue to arise because individuals have tried to understand the institutions of other societies which were alien to them using familiar, unexamined models from their own cultures". [26]

Any immigration and integration policy, however good it may be, must rely on the capacity of adaptation and acceptance of the interested parties. In this regard, here is the testimony and the warning of Claude Ryan: ". . . the immigrant is not just someone we receive into our home, he is also and above all someone who brings a lot with him. We must earn his trust, if we want him to stay with us, above all at a time where we need him more than he needs us". [27]

The presence of the Portuguese in Quebec calls for a process of adaptation and not one of assimilation. The Quebec people, in welcoming their immigrants, can call on their own experience as an immigrant people and on the values of a society which sees itself as pluralistic, democratic and humane.

---

26.   Beattie, 1972, p. 8.

27.   In *Le Devoir* (Montréal), of November 19, 1976.

PART THREE

THE PORTUGUESE
OF
QUEBEC

VII

FAMILY LIFE

Although the family has persisted throughout time, it is not a static institution. Today, more than ever, the fast pace of modern life is altering the pattern and the visage of the traditional family. World scale industrialisation and resulting urbanisation have in general had a determinant impact on the family, and this is particularly evident in migratory phenomena, both national and international.

In examining the particular problems of the Portuguese family in Quebec, we shall deal at some length with the milieu of origin, since this migratory movement is very recent.

The traditional milieu

In Portugal, the family is uncontestably the foundation on which the social structure rests. As an institution, it is in fact one of the characteristics of Portuguese culture.

The traditional Portuguese family has a hierarchical structure. In this hierarchy, the father occupies the top rung, the wife is subject to her husband and the children come under the parents' authority. Traditionally, the Portuguese family is a compact unit, in which each member has specific responsibilities. The father makes the important decisions. It is the mother, however, who attends directly to the discipline of the children and the daily running of the home.

Economically speaking, the Portuguese family is also a unit of production and consumption, generally with a central administration to which all its members are subject. The children remain under this administration until their emancipation is recognised, almost always through the fact of marriage. The extended family of the patriarchal type is predominant mainly in the North of Portugal and in the Azores and Madeira. In the South of Portugal, on the other hand, it is the nuclear type family which predominates. Nevertheless, the trend towards the nuclear family is becoming more marked due to a number of factors, not the least of which is emigration.

Along with blood relationships and relationships by marriage, one must not forget the fictive kinship typical of Catholic Latin countries and which is readily observable in Portugal. These are the sponsors at baptism, marriage and even confirmation, who become an integral part of the family even when they are not relatives at all. As Jorge Dias points out, "the bonds with godparents are often stronger and more sacred then the bonds which unite distant relatives". [1] It should be emphasised that the words "compadre" and "comadre" are particularly common in rural areas. [2]

In the receiving country

The goal of almost all Portuguese immigrants is to reunite their families in Quebec. More noteworthy is the fact that both the

---

1. Dias, 1961, p. 125.

2. The circle of intimate friends is normally more restricted in Quebec than in the milieu of origin. Intimate friends sometimes visit daily and frequently partake of meals. More formal type visits or visits between acquaintances generally take place during the weekend.

130

husband and the wife bring their extended families. There are even cases where the extended families are almost completely re-established in the new milieu. The Canadian Parliamentary Committee charged with studying immigration policy expressed the opinion that ''relatives are usually helpful to new immigrants and support them both emotionally and materially in their initial period of settlement and integration into an unfamiliar culture''.[3]

It is rare, however, for the entire extended family to emigrate. Visiting the family that has stayed behind thus becomes the primary purpose of any trip to Portugal. Such trips result in a strengthening of bonds and a renewing of friendships which are an incentive for more trips. This explains the frequency with which Portuguese immigrants go to Portugal on holidays, often as a whole family.

When the immigrant arrives in the receiving country, the bonds with the family left behind are necessarily somewhat overshadowed by the interests of the nuclear family. Nevertheless, contact is maintained with the extended family through regular correspondence and frequent visits to Portugal. A study of the Portuguese of Montreal shows that ''more than half of immigrants exchange letters with their family twice monthly or weekly.''[4]

Generally speaking, the traditional Quebec family resembles the Portuguese family. Among both peoples, the extended family prodominates in the rural areas and the nuclear family in the urban areas.

The adaptation process

The Portuguese family in Quebec is not the end product of a simple transplantation. Between their *modus vivendi* in Portugal

---

3. Canada. Special Joint Committee of the Senate and the House of Commons on Immigration Policy, 1975, p. 30.
4. Romão, 1972, pp. 162 and 182.

and their adaptation to the new milieu, husbands, wives and children all undergo a period of very radical change. Most families emigrate in stages. First the husband emigrates and sometimes remains separated from his wife and children for a few years. Then it becomes the turn of the wife and children. Sometimes these latter remain in Portugal, mainly because of their studies. These various events reflect on each member of the family. In the beginning, the husband is forced to live as a "bachelor"; the wife has to assume responsibility for the home and develop a certain independence; the children are subjected to an authority of the matrifocal type. These factors will have brought about an evolution of the family even before its establishment in the new milieu. This evolution plays a positive role in integration into the new society, where family values of the patriarchal type are in sharp decline.

The Portuguese family in Quebec, despite this evolution which is hastened by cultural shock, clearly retains the traits of its origins. Men's and women's roles, as well as the upbringing and emancipation of the children and the family's housing conditions, deserve special attention. In the analysis of these factors, it is important not to overlook the problems inherent in them.

The male role

The man's role as family head is all-important within the traditional Portuguese family. Socially speaking, the honour of the Portuguese male is directly linked to his ability to improve his family's financial status and to ensure its good reputation. Because of his awareness of this role, it is he, generally, who is the first to emigrate, to make contact with the new milieu, to look at working conditions and to prepare a home for his loved ones. The Portuguese male, particularly when he perpetuates the mentality of his country, has a tendency to regard himself as the uncontested head of the family, with the wife and children being automatically placed in a situation of dependence. While this attitude may be considered general and regarded as characteristic of the Portuguese male, this does not mean that he is less sensitive to his family or that he loves them less. [5]

In spite of the evolution imposed by modern ideas and by the new milieu, the phenomenon commonly known as "machismo" seems to be deeply ingrained and reveals itself in common expressions indicative of a male-dominated hierarchy. Thus, for example, some husbands say: "At home, I'm the boss". More revealing still is the corresponding claim by the wife: "He's the boss". [6] While these remarks and others of a like type do not always reflect a reasoned opinion, they do nevertheless reflect the strength of the socialisation process. The strength of this phenomenon seems to show a direct correlation with social class. "While in the lower classes, the social and cultural differences between the man and the woman are negligible, in the middle class, this difference is considerable. One might even justifiably speak of a male culture and a female culture". [7]

Sharing household tasks is not in the habits of the Portuguese male. Nevertheless, the fact that the men (married or single) lived separated from their wives during their initial period as immigrants and were forced to do their own shopping and cooking encourages a sharing of household tasks after the wife arrives. It should however be pointed out that Portuguese tradition tends to be maintained in Quebec, since women do the cooking and the husbands, especially when there are family reunions, rarely take part in

---

5. The report of journalist Scott Young on a group of Portuguese immigrants working on the railway in Northern Ontario is worthy of mention. According to this journalist, the foremen had decided to give out the mail after supper because the Portuguese who receive mail do not come to supper until they have read it (in *Globe and Mail,* Toronto, June 4, 1957).

6. According to the study of Kemp and Morisset on the Portuguese of Hull, 37 persons out of 58 thought that the man should be "the only master of the house" (n.d., p. 4).

7. Dias, 1961, p. 141.

culinary activities and are vexed when they are "accused" of sharing tasks which, in their minds, are the exclusive domain of the female sex.[8] But we are witnessing an evolution in this respect, which appears to be directly proportional to the level of schooling and inversely proportional to age.

Woman's role

Beside the traditional image of the Portuguese male as master of the house, there is the image of the woman as the heart of the family and the reins which hold this family together. This may be easily verified during the prolonged absence of the man or the woman. While in the first case, we can say that the home is threatened, when it is the woman who is absent, it is not an exaggeration to say that the home has been broken up.

The honour of the Portuguese family rests mainly on the behaviour of the wife. The dignity demanded of the wife is not always accompanied by an explicit recognition of her equal social status.[9] In the rural areas, where a large percentage of Portuguese immigrants had their origins, the wife is rarely aware of her rights and she is passively resigned to her traditional status. This has not always favoured real equality or a recognition of women's rights. This is not just true from a legal standpoint. It is a situation inherent in the culture and which was born of a specific historical and economic evolution. The exclamation of a Portuguese midwife reported by anthropologist José Cutileiro is more than telling: "It is a beautiful child. What a pity she is a girl".[10] This statement may

---

8. In Montreal, eleven of the seventeen married Portuguese men interviewed by Romão (1972, p. 164) stated that they nèver help with household chores, while the other six help their wives.

9. We frequently note that the Portuguese have several surnames. It should be pointed out that the surnames of both parents are used simultaneously. In the case of the woman, the legal custom is to assume the surnames of her husband while retaining her own.

10. Cutileiro, 1971, p. 111.

sound somewhat less outrageous when we situate it within the socio-economic context which persists to some extent even today and where woman's work is less highly valued and her position less secure.

The Portuguese wife's acceptance of the decision to emigrate has a very significant impact. By agreeing to let her husband go off alone and assuming very heavy responsibilities herself, the Portuguese woman becomes an extremely positive factor in the modernisation and evolution of Portuguese society. Emigration affects the occupational status of women more than that of men. While it is true that the man must sometimes learn a new skill, the woman, for her part, frequently goes from being strictly a housewife to becoming a salaried worker.

The process of the wife's emancipation from her husband begins gradually when this latter leaves Portugal. Her new status as a salaried worker speeds up this process. The Portuguese immigrant woman generally adapts well to the working world, and feels a greater sense of self-worth because of her financial contribution to the family, despite the disgraceful exploitation of which she is frequently victim. Even if this fact places her on an equal footing with her co-workers from the new milieu, her status remains for all practical purposes unchanged, for within her family and in the Portuguese community, she re-encounters the conditions and the constraints of her milieu of origin.

But the Portuguese immigrant woman does not passively accept just any status which society may wish to impose on her. It would be wrong to believe that the sacrifices which she endures have been imposed on her in all cases. Personal motivation and her own ideals do play a role. On the other hand, the fact that the Portuguese immigrant woman, in addition to her household chores, performs others in the factory or in the service sector, including work as a cleaning woman, does not in itself imply a loss of prestige or of worth. As regards the job of cleaning woman, "many women who in Portugal could not accept the idea of doing this type of work, do it . . . without any trace of embarrassment. Having for most of their lives been part of a very traditional society where the status of women is tacitly accepted as inferior to that of men, when they discover their ability to earn money, they feel freed of this prejudice and able to fulfill themselves as women." [11] This remark made about Portuguese women who had emigrated to France applies largely to Portuguese women living in Quebec.

Emigration seems to have improved the social status of the Portuguese woman, for we find that in Canada her social relations are generally broader and her household tasks performed less individualistically. By way of example, we might mention the frequency with which Portuguese immigrant women do their shopping together, and the general use of the telephone as a means of daily contact. The Portuguese woman's emancipation is earned through her own merits. Though some factors inherent in emigration favour this process, we must however take into account the factors which work against it. According to Lenormand: "Legislation is rarely favourable to female people; we are still very far, in the Province of Quebec, from achieving equal wages for men and women". [12] In support of what he says, the author cites provincial legislation, which in 1970 permitted salary differences of more than 25% between men and women for equal work. [13] Although the growing autonomy of the Portuguese woman in Quebec goes hand in hand with a normal, desirable promotion, husbands do not always seem to approve.

The fact that the role of the Portuguese immigrant woman is sometimes a behind-the-scenes one does not necessarily mean that

---

11. Trindade, 1973, pp. 90-91.
12. Lenormand, 1971, p. 12.
13. *Idem*, p. 13.

it should be attributed secondary importance. Contrary to what was the case in Portugal, the role of the immigrant woman has important consequences, socially speaking. Through her contacts with the working world, her telephone conversations with her friends, her attendance at church, the interest which she takes in her children's schooling, her responsibility for household finances, the Portuguese immigrant woman expands her radius of action and becomes an important link in communications networks, providing information on jobs and lodging and serving to welcome and assist new immigrants. [14]

Upbringing of the children

The Portuguese immigrant generally lives the immigration adventure thinking more of his children than of himself. His children have first place in his dreams, in his work and in his plans, and the education and well-being of the children are among the factors which lie behind the decision to emigrate. Portuguese parents rarely settle in the new milieu without the entire family nucleus. The children, above all the younger ones, are treated with very special affection by their parents, their elder brothers and sisters and adults in general. Parents are rarely separated from their children because they frequently take them to social, religious and recreational events, often without any concern for the hour or for the children's interests. Children are thus in constant contact with their parents and especially with their mothers. [15]

The child holds a privileged position within the Portuguese family, where he is surrounded with affection. He is rarely entrusted to strangers. Whenever possible, he is entrusted to family

---

14. Cf. Smith, 1976.

15. José Cutileiro, referring to Alentejo province, notes that "children are the focus of attention and during their first years of life, are in constant contact with their mothers. They are breast-fed, sometimes until they are three years old" (1971, pp. 109-110).

members and learns to value discipline and to respect his elders, including his sisters and brothers. A hierarchy is established among these latter as a function of age. The tradition of entrusting the child to close relatives is generally maintained by Portuguese immigrants. A survey carried out in the Portuguese community of Montreal showed that 42.4% of the sample entrusted their children to relatives and that only 3.1% of this same sample took them to day care centres.[16]

The traditional hierarchy of father, mother and children makes itself felt in the upbringing and discipline of the children. "A father rarely beats his children. He spends much less time with them then does the mother, and, in matters of discipline, is regarded as a kind of supreme court: 'If you do that again I will tell your father', is a frequent threat heard from mothers. From very early childhood, the authority of the father is emphasised and the mother plays the role of an intermediary between father and children in matters that need his sanction; she seldom fails to obtain a favourable response."[17] Recourse to corporal punishment in the upbringing of children is rarely a sign of ill treatment. On the contrary, it is a manifestation of the parents' interest in their children even though it might be considered a questionable disciplinary method. Socially speaking, the behaviour and the appearance of the children reflect the image of their home. Being very aware of this, parents take great pains to ensure that their children are clean and well dressed.

In the country of origin, especially in the rural areas, adolescence was practically unknown as a stage in individual development. The child leaves school, sometimes very early, to go right out into the world, to work side by side with adults with whom he compares himself in terms of responsibilities and concerns.

---

16. Cf. *Statistique sur la communauté portugaise (Quartier Saint-Louis)*, n.d., p. 35.

17. Cutileiro, 1971, pp. 110-111.

In the receiving country, adolescence holds an important place in the life of the child and in the home itself. The reactions which characterise this phase of life may take on a particular form or intensity in the sons and daughters of newly arrived immigrants, who, during their childhood, are imbued with ethnic cultural values in a passive but perhaps more intense manner than in the country of origin. This is due almost entirely to the influence of the parents, who try to assert their identity by communicating their own cultural values to their children. Thus, these children may show a more or less marked ignorance of the new cultural milieu into which they must integrate.

It is during adolescence, following contact with the new milieu, that the children experience cultural shock and end up comparing the two sets of values, which often leads to their choosing the values of the new milieu and abandoning those communicated to them by their families. Pardoxically, this is due, among other things, to the higher level of schooling attained, which sometimes causes these children to feel superior to their parents. During adolescence, children not infrequently show a certain inferiority complex or embarrassment about their culture of origin. This attitude may be explained by a faulty transmission and assimilation of the cultural values in question.

Very young children can assimilate and reconcile several cultures without much difficulty. Once they reach adolescence, they are readily prone to compare their culture of origin with that of the new country, often, admittedly, to the advantage of the latter, even if this becomes a source of friction within the family.

Courtship and marriage

Portuguese parents continue to have a strong say in their children's marriages as regards the choice of the future spouse and his or her acceptance and, in the case of girls, also in the choice of boyfriends. This interest and this arbitration on the part of parents are normally looked at askance by the children and regarded as an attack on their liberty and as a form of overprotection.

Traditionally, the greater freedom given to boys favours their more rapid integration into the new society and has as a consequence a greater degree of exogamy. Conversely, the girls, who are subjected to greater vigilance, are conditioned to make their choice within the Portuguese community. On the other hand, it is normal among the Portuguese, and indeed seems to be characteristic of Mediterranean cultures, that the family exercise a certain authority over daughters' dating and courtship.

In Quebec, we find that the age of Portuguese fiancés usually exceeds the mean for the country of origin, which is perhaps explained by the fact that a certain percentage of Portuguese immigrants are single upon arrival. It is only after they are well established that they get married, sometimes to the fiancée who has been waiting in Portugal for her man to send for her. This explanation applies to first generation couples, but is probably no longer valid for the second generation, because circumstances lead the children of immigrants to seek early emancipation through marriage. [18]

While girls are denied all freedom as regards questionable company keeping, parents are more tolerant with boys. Unfaithfulness is unforgivable in a married woman and any husband who has been cheated regards it as an attack on his honour. [19] Cases of single

18. The study of Kemp and Morisset on the Portuguese of Hull (n.d., p. 3) shows that 37.1% of women were married between the ages of 15 and 20 and that 40% of men married between the ages of 21 and 25 years. These high marriage rates among the young seem to jibe with the thinking of the parents, 45.7% of whom thought that girls should marry between the ages of 18 and 20, while 85.7% hoped that their sons would marry between the ages of 21 and 25.

19. In the new milieu as well as in Portugal, "the risk of his wife's adultery (and even the most carefully chosen wife may err) is a risk of perpetual dishonour: if it happens he will be forever a *cabrão* or *corno* ('cuckold') (Cutileiro, 1971, p. 102).

mothers are rare within the Portuguese ethnic group. They are criticised and ostracised by their own group and are marked to such a degree that their social standing suffers a fatal blow. On the other hand, children born in these situations are considered innocent by the community and accepted as such.

In assessing the evolution and the adaptation of the Portuguese family to the new milieu, it is useful to consider the number of endogamous and exogamous marriages. Given the high percentage of men among the initial immigrants, it would seem normal for marriages to be exogamous. However, it is not certain that this is the case, since they generally remain very attached to their culture of origin. The increase in the size of the Portuguese ethnic group due to family reunification and the birth of the second generation may lead to a larger number of endogamous marriages. In fact, it appears logical that endogamy should increase in proportion to the density of ethnic concentration. [20]

The elderly

In any discussion of the immigrant family, it would be unforgivable to forget the elderly. Since the mass immigration of Portuguese to Quebec is relatively recent, we do not find any senior citizens among these pioneer immigrants. It must however be pointed out that the dependant parents of immigrants do come to join them and thus re-establish the extended family.

The most serious problems of the elderly are solitude and the great difficulty of adapting to the new milieu. In most cases, when aged parents come to join their children, this means leaving behind their other children who have remained in Portugal and the milieu in which they have spent their lives. With no prospects for the future, they feel even more isolated and dependant in the new

20. The case of the Portuguese of Hull, where almost all marriages are endogamous, may be cited as a typical example.

milieu. Shut up in their homes most of the time, their activities are limited to babysitting their grandchildren in the absence of the parents. Contacts with the outside world are impossible, given their inability to speak the language. The climate is another obstacle to their adaptation. Accustomed in most cases to living in the freedom of the fields, in the new country, they feel dependant in everything and on everyone.

Housing

We cannot conceive of the Portuguese family without a house, because it holds so important a place in family life. For the Portuguese, the purchase of a house and its maintenance are traditional virtues.

In spite of the relative poverty of some, most Portuguese own their own homes, however modest. This explains largely why the purchase of a house becomes the first goal of the immigrant, once he is settled in the new milieu. To achieve this goal, in the initial period after his arrival, he rents only one room, works overtime, spends less on clothing and eats very economically. [21]

To buy a house, he will go so far as to accept mortgages which are too high for his wages, and sometimes appeals to friends to obtain the funds needed for the down payment. Once he has bought the house, he sometimes uses one part of it and rents the other part to relatives or friends. [22]

---

21. "As regards lodging, it is common to begin by renting part of a house or a small apartment and to wait three or four years before buying a house. The "dream" of buying a house is a real obsession, the realisation of which is facilitated in this country by the availability of long term credit. Real estate agents claim that the Portuguese are among the principal buyers" (Martins, 1971, p. 23).

22. The study of Kemp and Morisset (n.d., p. 4) on the Portuguese of Hull showed that 97% of these latter found housing through the help of relatives or friends and that 50% are home owners. Among these home owners, 82% have Portuguese tenants.

For the Portuguese, the purchase of a house is not merely ownership of a real estate property; it is also an assertion of their independence. Recent studies on the Portuguese of the St-Louis district of Montreal have shown that prior to 1963, they did not buy houses. Between 1963 and 1970, they made up 36% of the home buyers in that district and this figure had attained 75% in 1970. [23] The fact that the Portuguese live in their own homes explains the care which they lavish on their upkeep and adornment. It is found that in the St-Louis district of Montreal, 54.5% of Portuguese own their own homes, which also adds to the value of the houses in question. [24]

In 1975, the Order of Architects of Montreal awarded its annual prize to the residents of the Portuguese community of the St-Louis district, in recognition of their architectural innovations in that district. Homage was rendered them for the renovations to their own homes, and to the district in general. An official publication of the Ministry of Immigration of Quebec pays tribute to them in the following words: "Thanks to their determination, the Portuguese of the St-Louis district have succeeded in rebuilding an urban area which is not only viable, but pleasant as well [...]. The modernised façades, which are discreet suggestions of more elaborate interior renovations, do not however give a true picture of those radical changes that have brought about the social restructuring of a neighbourhood which only yesterday was threatened with annihilation." [25]

The Portuguese of Montreal deserve praise, not only for having done this work but also for the methods and means by which it was accomplished. There was much reliance on co-operation

23. *Statistique sur la communauté portugaise (Quartier Saint-Louis)* n.d., p. 11.

24. Cf. *Statistique sur la communauté portugaise (Quartier Saint-Louis),* n.d., p. 20.

25. *Québec-Monde,* 1976, No. 13, p. 1.

among relatives and friends and the use of volunteer specialised labour, enabling them to perform works which would not have been financially possible had it been necessary to hire labour outside the community. This type of co-operation which characterises the Portuguese has been studied and described by the sociologist Roger Krohn who calls it "the local economy" as opposed to the "public commercial economy" which is essentially speculative. [26]

Strange as this may seem, in Quebec one often finds a lack of sufficiently large houses for a normal family. This problem affects immigrants more than anyone else, especially in the beginning, in view of their very limited financial means. A large, respectable home permits family reunions and gatherings of friends.

The desire and the need to have a small garden or a farm plot next to the house are generally associated in the immigrant's mind with the idea of owning his own home. Unfortunately, the Portuguese immigrants who can afford this are few, especially in the urban areas. When they are able to realise their dream, they devote their energy to growing vegetables and traditional flowers, which enables them to recreate a Portuguese atmosphere, while saving money and providing ingredients for their typical cuisine.

The underlying problems

Most Portuguese who settled in Quebec did so in the hope of improving their financial, family and general situation. However, their success should not be a reason for forgetting the other side of the coin. Portuguese families in Quebec generally encounter the problems common to all families, in addition to those which are peculiar to their status as immigrants. In the very beginning, the departure of the head of the family meant a more or less lengthy separation, which is at the source of certain mental and physical

---

26. Krohn, Fleming and Manzer, 1976.

traumas experienced by himself and by those he left behind. The lack of moral support, the division of responsibilities, financial difficulties and the children's upbringing are factors contributing to these troubles.

When he comes into contact with the more sophisticated Canadian environment, the Portuguese immigrant suffers a shock, which may result in a certain inferiority complex that is simultaneously economic, social, cultural and familial. This reaction is perhaps most evident in the children who, perceiving the contrasts between the culture of origin and the culture of the new milieu, are ashamed of their origins and their language, which in their minds become synonymous with a subculture.

In the parents, the difficulties of adapting to the new milieu translate into a more or less intransigent, more or less exclusivist attachment to the values of origin. Thus, first generation families have a conception of their rights and duties which leads them to attach more importance to a certain integrity of traditions than to adapting to the new milieu. This attachment to Portuguese values may, in extreme cases, lead to ethnocentrism and prevent interaction with other groups.

The generation conflict of our contemporary societies sometimes takes on dramatic proportions for immigrant parents, who feel left out of the mainstream and separated from their children by a cultural abyss. These parents, sometimes against their conscience, feel forced to accept moral standards or standards of human relations which are alien to them.

Though it is true that the majority of immigrants, whatever their cultural level, are exemplary parents, we must admit, and they themselves recognise, that they do not have the preparation needed to guarantee their children a good education and integration into this new milieu.

Material security, which is generally assured, is not accompanied by psychological security or any guarantee of the family's unity and stability. Parents are often trapped between two worlds: the past in Portugal and the present in the new country, the belongings that they left behind and those that they have purchased here, the desire to return and the need to stay, the family they left behind and the family they brought with them. On the other hand, the children, who are more attached to their new homeland, feel torn between their own tastes and those of their parents and suffer from a certain insecurity and an uncertainty about their destiny and their future.

To use the terminology proposed by Anderson and Higgs, we might say that the first generation undergoes a centripetal force in the direction of the family unity which is essential to the survival of its members in the new setting. The second generation instead experiences a centrifugal force which reflects new living conditions, a new mentality and a psychological need for greater independence. [27] This opposition of forces is not just the result of a confrontation between different ages or different mentalities, but also of a conflict between two separate worlds and two Weltanschauungen which are sometimes irreconcilable.

Immigrant parents, as well as their children, find themselves, so to speak, sitting uncomfortably between two chairs. Parents have difficulty accepting new values without relinquishing the values of origin; their children are convinced that there is no alternative, but are aware of the risk they run in rejecting their parents' option. In both cases, parents and children feel cut off from their society of origin and prevented from becoming full-fledged members of the new society.

The proximity, both emotional and physical, of family members prevents a chasm from developing between the different

---

27. Anderson and Higgs, 1976, p. 131.

generations. On the other hand, traditional child rearing practices create a certain distance between parents and children in their intimate relations, even if this distance is a sign of deference.[28]

The new living conditions, because they impose incompatible time-tables, prevent or hinder closeness within the family, despite the good will and the efforts of the parents to bring it about. These difficulties only make the efforts of Portuguese immigrant parents more commendable, in that they are able to maintain a certain togetherness in the family, as the good conduct of their children attests. The level of delinquency among young Portuguese is in fact relatively low. However, the number of young people in the different Portuguese agglomerations is increasing, and there is an absence of places for these young people to socialise and spend their time. The result is that a large number of young Portuguese hang about and frequent questionable places and companions. Partly responsible for this is the parents' employment, which deprives the young people of their presence when it is most needed.[29]

These differences in adaptation between parents and children are also found in some cases between spouses. Integration into the new milieu is normally easier for the man because he has been in the country longer and in contact with the working world. This contrast is even more marked in the case of non-working women, in

---

28. Referring to Alentejo province, José Cutileiro (1971, p. 115), notes that "young men often address their fathers as *Senhor*. They very rarely sit with them in the same groups in taverns or cafés, and they often avoid them even at home. They are shy of discussing personal problems with them and, when the father's intervention is needed, it is sought through the mother. The father-daughter relationship is of an even more distant nature than the father-son relationship". One encounters the same phenomenon in other regions of Portugal, especially in the Azores.

29. In the St-Louis district of Montreal, it was found that there were more Portuguese mothers than French Canadian mothers working outside the home (Santos 1975, p. x).

that they may limit their activities to the Portuguese milieu without ever having to come into contact with other ethnic groups, or to speak a foreign language.

Although in the new milieu, the Portuguese family continues to respect the indissolubility of marriage, divorce or the equivalent may be seen as a solution or as a threat by many families. Some of the causes are the financial level attained, the emancipation of the wife through outside work, the influence of the new milieu and conflicting values.

In spite of its traditional unity, the Portuguese family is not automatically immune from certain pressures which may undermine its integrity. Once again, we might mention the mother who works, the fact that the husband arrives in the country alone, which almost always results in prolonged separation from the nuclear family and aggravates the problems of adaptation to the new cultural milieu, once the family does arrive in the new country. The wife who works outside the home comes to feel equal to her husband. In addition, the children's more ready integration reverses the situation of dependence and we see parents either depending on their children, or growing away from them in the process of adaptation to the new society. The emergence of new types of relations within the family, between spouses and between parents and children, is one of the immediate consequences of this change. [30]

Any adaptation implies a certain evolution. In the case of Portuguese families in Quebec, the changes and contrasts which they

---

30. The circle of friends is also extended in the urban areas. While the rural family was a unit of production and consumption, the urban family adopts a new economic strategy and bases its security on collective organisations. According to the distinction of Tönnies, relations move from the "gemeinschaft" type to the "gesellschaft" type. While the former are characterised by "face to face" relations, the latter take on a functional and formal character and involve a certain anonymity not typical of the former.

experience may act as a positive stimulus, but may also force them into a violent transition. This may be a factor in disintegration, above all when their capacity for adaptation is exceeded or their optimum rate of evolution is surpassed.

VIII

EDUCATION AND CULTURE

Within the Quebec cultural context, the Portuguese ethnic group has today come to constitute a complementary factor. On the other hand, Quebec, since its foundation, has been made up of different cultures that constantly fought one another to survive. As we look at the evolution and the complexity of the Quebec milieu, we may conclude that her culture is still in a process of becoming and has not yet stabilised.

We shall simultaneously discuss education and culture, given the close connection between these two concepts. One of the main functions of education is in fact the transmission of culture. To separate the Portuguese ethnic group from its culture of origin would be to deprive it of its identity. It is safe to say that even the Quebec identity would be affected.

In considering the cultural traits most characteristic of the Portuguese ethnic group, it would clearly be a mistake to suppose an attitude of confrontation between Québécois and Portuguese cultures, given their complementarity.

In the search for or in the affirmation of a Quebec identity, it would be wrong to confuse multiculturalism with assimilation. These two things are incompatible. Neither would it be reasonable to regard each of the cultures present in Quebec as exclusive or self-sufficient. The multiculturalism policy encouraged by the federal government clearly does not aim at consolidating each ethnic group in a ghetto-like narcissism, but aims rather to recognise the unique values of each culture and to create an open-mindedness conducive to complementarity.

In the case of Quebec, education is particularly important in that it does not transmit a single culture but several. Unfortunately, the different ethnic groups represented in Quebec have not always had an educational level conducive to a cultural dialogue leading to an identification of their own values and those of others. According to Robin Williams, it may be said that ethnocentrism in its most varied expressions is a universal phenomenon common to all human groups. [1] This behaviour however appears more marked among isolated peoples and within social classes which are materially or psychologically insecure. Nevertheless, the opposite attitude, defined by the concept of cultural relativism, is the only possible route for a multicultural policy. [2]

Portuguese culture

It would be well to ask ourselves if there is in fact a Portuguese culture in Quebec. Viewed in a sociological context, the reply will obviously be in the affirmative, since the Portuguese community reflects the values, standards, traditions and behaviours

1. Williams, 1964, p. 17.
2. Goldschmidt, 1977, p. 350.

151

characteristic of the society of origin.[3] If, however, we regard culture as an artistic or literary heritage, an affirmative reply may be premature. Speaking of cultural identity will not make this identity exist or even subsist. And the existence of a Portuguese culture in Quebec does not guarantee its survival. Contact with a new milieu generally results in cultural shock of an intensity which is directly proportional to the conflict of values.

The Portuguese culture in Quebec, still not totally implanted and still adapting, is threatened by a conflict of values which in turn reflects a confrontation of cultures and which is also due to a certain element of cultural shock. The sudden transition from a rural to an urban milieu, from a milieu with a low level of schooling to a highly educated one, from a society of the traditional, authoritarian type to a liberal and secular society, is a rude jolt for most Portuguese immigrants. This new situation may give rise to the state of anomie referred to by Emile Durkheim, where traditional standards and values are found to be inadequate but their replacements have not yet been culturally integrated.

Another danger inherent in the transmission of culture is that culture will be regarded as non-dynamic. Immigrants, when they transmit their culture, may forget its natural evolution and the

---

3. The Portuguese Pavilion at "Man and his World" is a recent initiative which has a very important role to play in introducing Canadians to Portuguese culture. "Man and his World", which has inherited the premises and the facilities of Montreal's EXPO 67, is a recreational and cultural exhibition of which the aim is to promote understanding among peoples and among men. Since its inauguration in 1968, "Man and his World" every year has attracted millions of visitors during its normal season, which runs from June 21 to September 3. In the 1978 season, Portugal was among the participating countries for the first time and it was again represented at "Man and his World" in 1979. In 1978, the Portuguese Pavilion welcomed 157,000 visitors and in 1979, with considerably larger facilities that included a restaurant, it welcomed 207,000. The Portuguese community of Montreal and other parts of Canada co-operated in and contributed actively to the decoration and the activities of the two Portuguese Pavilions at "Man and his World". (Data supplied by the Consulate General of Portugal in Montreal).

historical events which hastened this evolution. Thus, in settling in Quebec, the Portuguese run the risk of retaining a frozen image of their own culture and of identifying today with the Portugal of yesteryear.

Portuguese language

In the transmission and communication of culture, language takes on primordial importance. "Language is not only the medium for social contacts, social expression, and social experience, but [...] it is likewise a symbol of nationality and of social status around which are wrapped many intimate memories and innermost emotions. It is the vehicle for cultural contacts and cultural interactions; by it also the history, the traditions, and the memories of peoples and ages long vanished become a part of the living present." [4]

The Portuguese language is common to all Portuguese, whether they come from the continent or the islands. Between the former and the latter, there is however a distinct difference in accent which is of secondary importance, because we cannot say that the islanders speak a dialect.

It is normally the parents who decide what language will be spoken within the family circle. In the case of the first generation, the choice normally falls to the Portuguese language. Generally it is taught to and imposed on children, pretending reasons of a cultural nature. But the truth is that psychological reasons are not alien to this wish, either because it is the parents' language or because these latter feel ill at ease with the official languages in which their children are more fluent.

For the children of immigrants, the most important part of Portuguese language learning takes place within the family and the community through a spontaneous process and in an informal way.

---

4.   Covello, *cit. in* Pap 1949, p. 19.

Sometimes, they are conditioned to perpetuate the use of the mother tongue in order to communicate with their parents or grandparents who do not know other languages. These factors in part explain the grammatical mistakes and deformations as well as the tendency to avoid the use of Portuguese once they are aware of their limitations.

In general, the parents feel more at ease in the Portuguese language while the children, after attending school, come to feel more familiar with the language of the school which they attend. Because of their children's difficulty in mastering the mother tongue, a certain percentage of parents in Hull, Montreal and Ste-Thérèse, enroll them in Portuguese schools which hold classes on Saturday.

The Portuguese language is regularly spoken by the majority of adult Portuguese in Quebec within their own ethnic group. In addition, Portuguese continues to be used within Portuguese ethnic associations, during religious ceremonies and partly in business transactions between Portuguese speakers. Portuguese being the language generally spoken within the family, we sometimes note that the older children speak Portuguese relatively well while the younger ones, who are growing up under different conditions, make less use of their mother tongue and speak it less fluently. With the rapid development of the mass media, the influence of French and English is felt more and more keenly by the Portuguese family in Quebec, especially by the younger generation. Among Portuguese children living in the areas with the highest concentration of Portuguese speakers, the mother tongue is the preferred language in contacts with playmates and neighbours.

The Church and volunteer associations are other centres where the Portuguese language is widely used and promoted, by reason of the number of people who participate and the emergence of "leaders" who are generally more proficient in the art of speaking.

In the main Quebec centres where Portuguese immigrants are concentrated, the existence of their own communication media, the religious and social services provided by members of the same ethnic group and the development of Portuguese business permit a large percentage of the community to live as if they were still in the milieu of origin, thus making the speaking of a foreign language dispensable. Hence, in religious rites and community information services, in visiting and daily shopping, in leisure activities and in the workplace, it is becoming possible for a great number living in large agglomerations to use only their native tongue.

While recognising the facilities which the immigrant finds within his own group and which permit him to use his mother tongue, we must also admit that its systematic use may engender a "ghetto" situation and deepen a certain marginalisation with respect to the larger society. Faced with this danger, we might see as logical a policy of acculturation favouring the use of the official languages, without taking into account the native language. Such an attitude would border on sophism. In language policy, it is essential to remember that immigrants are admitted according to the needs of the labour market, and that their ultimate integration into the receiving country is neither implicit nor clearly foreseeable. Thus any abandonment of the mother tongue creates a problem of no small magnitude for all those who must return to the country of origin.

The teaching of Portuguese seems to be justified and indispensable, not only as a vehicle of the culture which it represents, but also as an essential factor in the identity and survival of this culture.

Teaching of Portuguese

The following beginning and advanced courses having as their aim improved knowledge and promotion of the Portuguese language, were operating in Quebec in 1978:

TABLE 8-1

Quebec: Portuguese language courses, 1977-78

Types	Promotors	Locations	Students
Adult education	Associação Portuguesa de Ste-Thérèse	Ste-Thérèse	16
Adult education	Centro Português de Referência e Promoção Social	Montreal	12
Adult education	Movimento Democrático Português	Montreal	48
Primary level	Associação Portuguesa de Ste-Thérèse	Ste-Thérèse	40
Primary level	Banco "Português do Atlântico"	Montreal	355
Primary level	Centro Comunitário Português Amigos Unidos	Hull	60
Primary level	Mission "Santa Cruz"	Montreal	615
Secondary level	Escola Secundária Lusitana	Montreal	66
University level	Concordia University (Sir George Williams Campus)	Montreal	15
University level	Laval University	Quebec City	32
University level	McGill University	Montreal	45
University level	University of Montreal	Montreal	18
University level	University of Quebec	Trois-Rivières	70

Considering the aims of Portuguese schools abroad, there is certainly no need to emphasise the care which must be exercised in the selection of teaching staff, which must take into account their training and teaching skills and also their diction and knowledge of the language itself.

In primary schools, attendance by immigrant children is quite high and the parents' initiative in enrolling their children in these schools is due either to their desire to perpetuate their own culture in their children or to the prospect of a definitive return to Portugal.[5]

Official Languages

In Canada, French and English are the two official languages.[6] Though it is true that in Quebec in particular, the French language is necessary for optimum adaptation, it is important to recognise that, in the other provinces, only English is essential. This additional requirement, while it implies cultural enrichment, does make the acculturation process more difficult in Quebec than in other provinces.

The rate and the degree of integration into the new milieu are directly correlated with knowledge of the official languages. Since each of these vehicles a particular culture, the immigrant ends up identifying more with one than with the other depending on the degree of familiarity with the corresponding language. The opposite is equally true: lack of knowledge of a language accentuates isolation from the corresponding culture.

---

5. Just recently, the provincial government approved as an experimental project the "Projet d'enseignement de langue d'origine" (P.E.L.O.). The experiment was begun just at the end of 1978, by the Catholic School Board of Montreal, and was designed for a certain number of children aged 6. In all, there are about 70 Portuguese speaking pupils divided into four groups.

6. After the election of the Parti Québécois as the provincial government and reflecting its political philosophy, a new law was approved establishing French as the only official language of Quebec.

In any policy aimed at promoting the study and adoption of the official languages, a distinction must be made between language and culture. While the latter is linked to tradition and taste, the former represents an immediate means of survival and reflects primarily a need. In the case of the Portuguese, since theirs is a Latin language, preference for the French language option makes sense. However, one does note a certain tendency to favour English.[7] This tendency may be due either to the conditions of the labour market, or to the idea of possibly moving to other provinces of Canada, or again to the prospect of settling in the United States of America, which is conceivable since the majority of the Portuguese in Quebec have relatives and friends who live south of the border.[8]

It is frequently claimed that learning a new language is particularly difficult in the case of adults. It is in fact common to attribute the growing inability to master languages to advancing age. We must however reconsider this idea, which andragogic science denounces as a flimsy excuse and as something of a myth. It would seem that this difficulty may be explained by the low level of schooling of the majority of Portuguese immigrants, by the fatigue due to hard and sometimes alienating working conditions and also frequently to the lack of suitable methods for teaching adults.

Quite aside from individual facility and motivation, the learning of a language is conditioned both by the milieu where the immigrant lives and by the means available to him. Among these latter, the school becomes the most important factor.

7. In the sample of thirty Portuguese from Montreal interviewed by Romão, the percentage of those who prefer English as the language of ordinary reading is higher than the percentage of those who regularly read French magazines and newspapers.

8. Léger (1956, p. 8) made the following comment about the French Canadians: "Our minority situation, our low participation in the Canadian economy, the nearness of the powerful United States, all these things invite the immigrant to opt for the other language".

In Quebec, unfortunately, the choice of the language of study has become a political issue which opposes Francophones and Anglophones and which implicates ethnic minorities, who feel they are being used as pawns in a game. This is not a passing problem, but rather a never-ending conflict. The incompatibility of the Francophone and Anglophone groups in Quebec is more than proverbial, "this ethnic conflict seems indeed to be perpetual; it is a sort of chronic disease from which Canada suffers and which, every once in awhile, under the pressure of a particular situation, erupts into a major crisis".[9] As early as 1928, Vattier described Quebec's eternal language problem in the following terms: "Of all the difficulties which the French Canadians had to face, it was the question of French language rights which led to the longest struggle, for indeed this struggle is not yet over today."[10]

Despite the incongruities of language legislation, the negative consequences of which particulary affect immigrants, it is important to recognise the theoretical value of the provisions designed to facilitate learning of the official languages for the immigrant. Thus, every immigrant is entitled on arrival to receive courses in the official languages to facilitate his integration. In practice, these courses may or may not be accessible, because of criteria which fail to take into account the real needs of the individuals in question, but which aim exclusively at placing them on the labour market as quickly as possible. The choice of a French or English school for the children is a difficult problem for many Portuguese parents, both because of the dilemma with which they are faced and because of the legal constraints.

---

9.   Vattier, 1928, p. 327.

10.   Idem, p. 112.

Even when official language courses are available and relatively accessible, attendance and results are sometimes less than heartening. There are two basic reasons for this: first of all, there is the policy of the Department of Manpower and Immigration, which tries to rapidly integrate immigrants into the labour market; secondly, the immigrants themselves are inclined to renounce or delay this opportunity for self-improvement, pretending fatigue due to work and family responsibilities. To the adult's lack of experience with learning is added the inability to ascertain what his rights are or to stand up for them.

The working environment may be an opportunity and a stimulus for learning the official languages. What often happens, though, is that a large percentage of co-workers are immigrants speaking diverse languages, which runs counter to this ideal.

From a statistical study based on 272 Portuguese residing in the Saint-Louis district of Montreal, we obtained the following percentages for the ethnic origin of co-workers:

TABLE 8-2

Co-workers: ethnic origin

Ethnic group	%
Portuguese	36.6
French	28.7
English	11.8
Jewish	1.0
Other	21.5

Source: *Statistique sur la Communauté portugaise (Quartier St-Louis),* no date, p. 23.

From the analysis of this sample, we obtained the following figures for the use of the Portuguese language in the work place:

TABLE 8-3

Portuguese language at work

Used exclusively	9.7%
Used part of the time	69.4%
Never used	20.8%

Source: *Statistique sur la Communauté portugaise (Quartier St-Louis)*, no date, p. 22.

In Quebec, most Portuguese work in places where the French language predominates, and they do find French easier. But they have a tendendy to choose English schools for their children, because they have their eye on the labour market. This means that in some homes, three languages are spoken with the problems of communication and understanding which sometimes result. [11]

The Portuguese generally show a quite remarkable ability for learning languages. Examples of trilingual parents and children, who speak English, French and Portuguese, are numerous.

The following table, which is based on the sample mentioned above, though relatively incomplete as regards the level of proficiency in each language, nevertheless gives us a clear picture of the situation.

TABLE 8-4
Knowledge of languages

Languages	Spoken	Written
Portuguese, French and English	38.1%	11.9%
Portuguese and French	25.8%	14.2%
Portuguese and English	15.2%	7.1%
Portuguese only	19.1%	66.8%

Source: *Statistique sur la Communauté portugaise (Quartier St-Louis)*, undated, p. 36-37.

11. Recent Quebec legislation, which superficially should simplify the problem of the multiplicity of languages, may also place limitations on freedom of choice and on the legitimate goals underlying certain choices.

161

In the majority of cases, the Portuguese immigrants of Quebec learned the official languages after their arrival. The following table confirms that the percentage of Portuguese with a knowledge of French or English or both on arrival is minimal.

TABLE 8-5

Portuguese citizens with a knowledge of French and/or English admitted to Quebec between 1969 and 1974

Year	French	French and English	English	Neither French nor English	Total
1969	106	18	46	1,160	1,330
1970	109	25	53	1,166	1,353
1971	143	21	45	1,391	1,600
1972	101	33	30	1,291	1,455
1973	203	26	51	1,693	1,973
1974	257	31	41	1,576	1,905
1969-74	919	154	266	8,277	9,616

Source: Quebec. Ministère de l'Immigration. Direction de la Recherche, *Québec Immigration-Langues 1969-74; Bulletin spécial No. 4,* 1975, p. 22. Data compiled from table 6.

Though we agree that a knowledge of several languages is a plus and though we would not wish to denigrate the individuals who possess this ability, we must however admit that it is rare for a person to have a thorough mastery of several languages, especially if these are languages learned after childhood.

Sometimes quality is sacrificed to quantity. It frequently happens that the language normally spoken becomes in fact a mixture of languages, in which both vocabulary and structure are deformed. In the local Portuguese ethnic press, we often see notices and advertising in which the terminology is a linguistic hodge-podge.

When immigration is to a milieu where a different language is spoken, the problem of cultural integration takes on particular significance in the acculturation process. In the specific case of Quebec, the fact that the Portuguese and French languages have common roots helps the integration process. In the minds of those who opt for English, the cosmopolitan character of this language appears to be a determining factor.

Up to now, very few Portuguese immigrants have had sufficient language skills upon entering Quebec to be able to integrate immediately into the labour market, barring that of their ethnic group. In the beginning, there are a certain number of adults who attend French or English courses, with the intention of studying and mastering the official languages. Many, however, never took advantage of this opportunity, either because they did not feel motivated, or because of their immediate entry onto the labour market and the obligations which they had to assume. Out of a sample of 272 Portuguese immigrants living in the Saint-Louis district in Montreal, it was found that 78.3% of this sample had not attended any formal courses since their arrival in the province of Quebec. [12]

School and cultural integration

The school is the keystone of any policy aimed at the sociocultural integration of the Portuguese in Quebec. Therein lie the main problems which the society must confront. While other sectors may sometimes pass unnoticed by the public at large, the school on the other hand is the place where all the half-solved problems and deblayed solutions come to a head. In general, schooling in a new language does not encounter resistance or raise major difficulties in the case of young children who are attending school for the first time. This is not true however of those who have

---

12. Cf. *Statistique sur la communauté portugaise (Quartier Saint-Louis),* n.d., p. 40.

already attended school in Portugal. These youngsters, because of the language problem, are at a disadvantage in terms of school credits and the difficulty is that much more keenly felt, the older the child and the higher the level of schooling. For the period of adjustment, there are primary schools designed exclusively for the children of immigrants.

In the case of immigrants, to all the normal problems of school is added the difficulty or even the impossibility of communication between teachers and parents, who are sometimes mutually unversed in each other's language and culture.

The problem of Portuguese immigrant schooling in Quebec cannot be attacked globally or resolved unless one studies and understands the limitations and conditions which have been placed on it in the country of origin. Not only has Portuguese legislation not encouraged more lengthy school attendance, but the families themselves have sometimes made this difficult because of a desire to see their children earn money beginning in their teens. Parents are often content to give their children the minimum schooling which is compulsory under law. Thus, many boys, instead of the compulsory four years of primary schooling, were taken out of school after the third year, not just for employment or financial reasons, but also for reasons of time and distance, because small schools only provided three years of schooling and the full four years were only taught in the central schools.

In Portugal, the level of schooling is even lower in the case of young girls. Even if, according to law, there is no discrimination as regards the compulsory minimum, there has in practice been less insistence on this obligation where girls are concerned.

The Portuguese immigrant milieu sometimes becomes an obstacle rather than an incentive, because parents whose children pursue higher learning may be considered pretentious.

The rate of illiteracy found in Portugal is necessarily reflected in the Portuguese immigrant. Thus, according to Adolfo Coelho, from 1897 to 1901, of the 105,392 immigrants who left Portugal during that period, 54.44% were illiterate. [13] The situation seems to have worsened during the next decade, so that in 1912, the percentage of illiterates among Portuguese immigrants reached 65.96% and was a whopping 91.52% among the immigrants from the area of Bragança. [14]

These highly representative ratios correspond to the present level of very limited schooling, even though rates of outright illiteracy among immigrants are much lower. Today, we are nowhere near these disgraceful numbers of illiterates, not because illiteracy has been eliminated in Portugal, but above all because of the selection procedures imposed by the manpower importing countries, which normally demand a certain level of schooling. Thus, in 1972, only 9.8% of all Portuguese immigrants aged seven or older were illiterate. [15] However, the overall statistics still reveal an alarming situation. [16]

Today, Portuguese parents are more and more inclined to judge the social advancement of their children by their level of schooling. In the choice of studies, one still finds a tendency towards vocational courses as opposed to an academic option which would normally lead to a university career. For immigrants,

13. Coelho, 1911.

14. Serrão, 1965, p. 25-26.

15. Portugal. Secretariado Nacional da Emigração, 1972, p. 67.

16. From an analysis of statistical data provided by the Quebec Ministry of Immigration on the number of immigrants with zero years of schooling admitted in 1973 by country of birth we find that Portugal contribued 39 such persons, or 70.9% of the total landed immigrants from Europe who were illiterate. This percentage is higher than that of all the countries of Africa, the Americas, Asia and Oceania taken together. (Cf. Québec. Ministère de l'Immigration. Direction de la Recherche, *L'Immigration au Québec: Bulletin statistique annuel,* Vol. 1, (1973), p. 53-58.

children's schooling continues to be regarded as a means of acquiring social prestige and guaranteeing the future rather than as a factor in integration. However, as we have already pointed out, many immigrant parents are still content to have their children receive a minimum of schooling and enter the labour market as soon as possible. Since in Quebec, compulsory schooling is longer than in Portugal, parents are readily inclined to compare the years of schooling they have themselves with the schooling which children receive today. By this criterion, they consider the compulsory minimum already adequate and even excessive.

In the choice of a school for their children, Portuguese parents are generally concerned both with the guarantees offered and with the level of education. Confessional schools are chosen or excluded depending on the religious beliefs of the parents. Some even go so far as to make sacrifices to pay their children's tuition at private schools to ensure that they get the very best education.

University attendance is proportionally low among the Portuguese of Quebec. [17] This may be attributed to the particular situation of first generation immigrants and to the fact that among the second generation very few have reached the age where they would be attending courses at this level.

Civic education

To judge the education of the Portuguese on the sole basis of their level of schooling would be highly unjust. The school is not the only means by which a people acquires a culture. The family, the

17. In the area of higher education, the situation of Portuguese immigrants is quite serious in the event of a return to the country of origin. There is no cultural agreement between Portugal and Canada. The provisions of Decree-Law No. 555-77, passed in Lisbon on December 21, 1977, and regulating academic equivalence, incline us to side with those who accuse the university authorities in Portugal of having closed minds. Thus, to the brain drain which has long afflicted Portugal is now added a barrier to the entry of brains into that country.

church, volunteer organisations and the milieu may also transmit standards and educational values, sometimes more effectively than the school itself. This appears irrefutable in the Portuguese case and it is sufficient to consider the high degree of civic responsibility which is generally evident within Portuguese communities. Listen to the following: ". . . the Portuguese community of Montreal shows a low rate of unemployment and delinquency and very few social problems".[18] If this statement is true of the Portuguese of Montreal, we can certainly apply it and more justifiably to the other Portuguese communities in Quebec, given their less complex nature.

We must underline the efforts made by the Portuguese group to maintain their culture of origin and to share in the cultural values of the new milieu. This is particularly evident in their concern with education and the social advancement of their children. Many Portuguese children are subjected to a very intensive curriculum, usually chosen by the parents, who find their fulfilment in the achievements of their children and who frequently tend to enroll them both in official schools and in the Portuguese school, sometimes adding private lessons in ballet, drama, piano, etc. While it is true that this involves a sacrifice for the parents, we must not forget the effort required of the children, who must handle a large number of subjects and assignments involving sacrifices no less significant than those made by their parents.

In spite of the relatively early age of school leaving, young Portuguese Quebecers generally achieve an educational level much higher than that of their parents, though the average is still below that of Quebec in general.

---

18. "Les Portugais à Montréal", in *Forum* (Montreal), January 18, 1974, p. 4.

Artistic values

Art is a mirror which reflects the culture of a people. Because of the conditions which surround human migrations, the transmission and affirmation of artistic values are particularly difficult initially. The social context in no way favours art, because the problems inherent in the search for employment and the psychological context of the new Portuguese immigrants in Quebec force them to satisfy their immediate vital needs, so that their higher values tend to take a back seat. We must however recognise that there is among the Portuguese of Quebec a more or less latent and sometimes manifest interest in artistic activities related to the culture of origin, such as folklore and folk music.

The Portuguese song, which has a very rich folk favour, is very varied. The fado is one of these variations, but not the only one. [19] Portuguese music and folklore are enjoyed and sometimes practiced by other ethnic groups who live in contact with the Portuguese.

It seems premature to speak of Portuguese handicrafts in Quebec. So far as we know, the Portuguese handicrafts found in commercial centres are strictly imported.

While we recognise the importance of the cultural values which may be transmitted by art, it is inevitable that art may appear as a luxury in a society which treats the immigrant as a work machine. In the pragmatism which is characteristic of immigration policies, the artist has no guarantee of employment and the labour market is not oriented towards the development of artistic talent. With the stability that comes from having resided for some time in the new milieu, we can expect new generations to do a better job of making Portuguese art known in Quebec through folklore, theatre and handicrafts.

---

19. Because of propaganda, the fado has become a Portuguese symbol for foreigners, and it is as a symbol that it is presented in Quebec, sometimes too exclusively.

168

Portuguese cuisine

Cooking is one of the characteristic aspects of a people's culture. Portuguese cuisine, which is still not widely known in Quebec, is maintained faithfully in the majority of Portuguese families. For those wishing to prepare a typical Portuguese meal, the main centres already have commercial suppliers of suitable products, generally imported from Portugal. There are also some typical Portuguese restaurants of repute with a clientele of the most diverse origins. Portuguese food is generally abundant and very healthful. It seems unfair to say that the Portuguese are slaves to their jobs and think only of hoarding savings. It would be more correct to say that Portuguese immigrants work well and eat well. Their meals, prepared at home "à la Portugaise", are characterised by good quality and an abundance of food.

A very significant percentage of the population continues to cook Portuguese style. Generally, there are traditional products on the table, in particular, green vegetables, olive oil, fresh fish and dried cod. At the Portuguese immigrant table, bread continues to be appreciated and home-made wine is indispensable, not just as part of the meal, but also as an expression of the culture itself.

In effect, oenology is a typical element of Portuguese culture. In Quebec as in Portugal, wine is a daily food and an essential part of the Portuguese table. Wine making as well as its consumption are accompanied by traditions and rituals which are retained even after the immigrants' arrival in Quebec. Given the impossibility, due to climate conditions, of cultivating vineyards on a large scale, some families purchase imported grapes and must and make their wine at home. The making and the tasting of wine become a social act which bespeaks mutual aid and sharing. We might even say that the social aspect is primordial in both its making and its drinking. Pathological alcoholism is rare among the Portuguese and they do not drink alone. Wine is served within the family circle, at meals, in friendly gatherings or at other social events.

Commemorations and feasts

The important events and festivities of both lay manifestations and religious feasts celebrated in the country of origin are generally transplanted to the new communities, and become a way of reliving and preserving the culture. Nowhere is the Portuguese soul manifested in its spontaneity and purity as in the gaiety of festivities. We might say that festivities express the vitality of a people and that in the case of immigrants, they are also a clear definition of identity. "The Portuguese love get-togethers where they can share the colour, the music and the gaiety of a festival or a special celebration." [20]

At the community level, the most important celebrations are those linked to the traditions of the ethnic group itself. Patriotic commemorations are generally observed in the new country. Religious feasts have a particular splendour in the large Portuguese-speaking areas, where they can be organised in the traditional manner. [21]

Sports activities

For individuals and groups, sport is an expression of unity, courage and fraternity. The taste for and the practice of certain types of sport typify and affirm different cultures. It is normal therefore that the Portuguese immigrant should be more interested in European football (soccer) or in the corrida than in American football or baseball. [22] Particularly among first generation Por-

---

20. Canada. Secrétariat d'État. Direction de la Citoyenneté Canadienne. *Les rameaux de la famille canadienne,* 1967, p. 298.

21. Although the style of the popular celebration is transplanted to Quebec with a certain regularity, there is however an introduction of new elements as well as a loss of certain traditional aspects. For example, rockets (*foguetes*) are no longer part of Portuguese festivities transferred to a new milieu.

22. In 1973, a Portuguese type corrida was organised in Montreal. It aroused general interest and also much polemic on the part of groups concerned with the protection of animals.

tuguese immigrants, European football continues to be regarded as *the* sport. Even if they do not play, football is the favourite sport of those numerous persons who follow direct broadcasts, which are listened to assiduously. Amateur football teams are formed and organised in the main Portuguese communities, usually as a leisure activity. However, since the winter is very long in Quebec and most of the year football cannot be played, the more avid fans generally limit themselves to following the championships in the mother country through the press or by radio.

* * *

While the preservation and transmission of a culture, and the support given it, pose problems at all times and in all places, these problems become more serious when the culture is suddenly forced to undergo a wholesale transfer and readaptation as occurs in migrations. These problems necessarily affect individuals, families and society in general.

At the individual level, the need to adapt to a new milieu is in itself a problem because of the contrasts and the conflict of values experienced. In the case of families, usually an attempt is made to keep the children within the confines of their own culture, which gives them a feeling of security. The problem arises when these same children go to school and experience the shock of a different culture which in practice is perceived by them as superior, at least in terms of survival.

Socially, the predominance of one culture over another may result in feelings of superiority which are readily reflected in attitudes and behaviours. Because of their lack of preparation, the educators themselves may aggravate a situation where the cultures, instead of being complementary, appear to be competing. This explains why the second generation in particular hesitates between one culture and the other, in a state of uncertainty, especially about the values of their origin, which are in practice considered marginal.

171

In Quebec, as already has happened in other older places of immigration, we can expect that future Portuguese generations, freed of the unjust opprobrium which is the lot of immigrants, will come to an awareness of the cultural values of their ancestors and will wish at some future date to return to these values, either to rediscover them or to reinstate them. Here and there, above all in the case of more evolved and involved persons and groups, we encounter initiatives which reveal a sensitisation to Portuguese values and an affirmation of their own ethnic group within the Quebec community.

As a yardstick of the interest of the local society in the culture of minority groups, we may take either its immigration policy or the welcome which it accords the immigrant population. The acquisition of new cultural values may be the most positive result of a good immigration policy for the manpower importing country.

A multiculturalism policy in which immigrants were regarded as work machines or their culture merely tolerated would indeed be an aberration. Within an honest policy, recognition of a culture brings with it a promotion of this culture based on the fulfilment of individuals. Vocational training, retraining and social promotion are the right of every immigrant, which means that there are corresponding obligations on the part of the country which accepts them, in the form of language courses, and job training and retraining. On the other hand, in an immigration system where all factors are essentially conditioned by the labour market, it is to be feared that the cultural values of a group may be sacrificed to expediency.

IX

WORK AND LEISURE

Work is a human right regardless of the status which is attributed to it. As early as 1919, the C.G.T. (Confédération générale du travail), meeting in Lyon (France) declared that "every worker, whatever his nationality, has the right to work wherever he can find employment". [1] The right to work implies an ethical code of duties which go to make up the offer and demand for manpower. Generally, the immigrant is motivated to work and throws himself completely into the tasks given him. Unfortunately, the job found by the immigrant on the labour market is often not the one he is competent to do, because he is assigned on the basis of a replacement policy which aims to fill the jobs considered most distateful in the receiving country. Thus, immigrants who occupied posts of some prestige in their country of origin are sometimes forced to accept jobs by far inferior to what their experience and their aptitudes qualify them to do. This is the case of numerous Portuguese immigrants who, upon arriving in Quebec, have to make a double effort to adapt to the new milieu and to a new type of work.

---

1. Gani, 1972, p. 9.

Occupations

A statistical table published by the Ministry of Immigration of Quebec showing the breakdown of immigrant workers admitted into this province in 1973 by country of origin and expected area of employment has given us the following data on the Portuguese: [2]

TABLE 9-1

Portuguese admitted to Quebec by sector of employment, 1973

Area of employment	Number
Specialised workers (manufacturing, assembly and repair)	241
Specialised service workers	166
Construction workers	163
Farmers, horticulturists and breeders	126
Workers in processing industries	65
Factory workers and similar	46
Workers not otherwise classified	32
Administrative personnel and similar	27
Sales personnel	20
Transport workers	17
Maintenance workers and similar	7
Directors, administrators and similar	6
Natural science workers	6
Other qualified workers and machine operators	4
Medical personnel, health technicians	4
Artists and writers	2
Teachers and equivalent	1

Source: Quebec, Ministère de l'Immigration. *Bulletin statistique annuel.* Vol. 1, 1973, pp. 45-46. Data compiled by the authors.

---

2. These data only refer to persons arriving as immigrants. Those who came as tourists and later obtained landed immigrant status are not considered. Prior to November 30, 1973, Canadian law permitted visitors to become landed immigrants.

Based on this table, we can identify four sectors: specialised workers, service workers, construction workers and agricultural workers, who together comprise 75% of the total. However, it is important to note that the areas of employment declared at the time of admission do not always correspond in practice to real competence or real possibilities of employment in these areas. The lack of specialisation and the limited job opportunities available open the way for exploitation of immigrants insofar as they are forced to accept work as "cheap labour". The low pay, immediate needs or the desire to save lead the immigrant to work overtime, which in turn can have repercussions on the worker and his family. [3] It may happen therefore that the jobs held in Quebec do not correspond to the real interests or qualifications of Portuguese immigrants. Even though these latter are, for the most part, natives of rural areas, the number of Portuguese working in the agricultural sector is very low in Quebec. This means that circumstances have forced a large number of them to suddenly do work about which they knew nothing beforehand. In a statistical survey, we found that out of 272 Portuguese workers in Montreal, 70.2% held a job different from that which they had held in Portugal, while only 29.5% were in the same area of employment. [4]

In all of Quebec, we found Portuguese employed in the most varied sectors, in particular the construction, service and industrial sectors. The men work mainly on building construction, in workshops, in the hotel industry and in trade. According to a

---

3. Based on types of occupations and their social status in Canada, we are entitled to conclude that the occupations which predominate among Portuguese immigrants are, for the most part, very low on the socio-economic ladder (cf. Porter and Pineo, 1967).

4. *Statistique sur la communauté portugaise (Quartier Saint-Louis),* n.d., p. 30.

survey conducted in the St-Louis District of Montreal, 53% of Portuguese heads of families worked in the maintenance sector and 27% were specialised workers. [5]

Portuguese women are for the most part employed in the maintenance sector in either offices or private homes (cleaning women). There are however a large number in the hospital sector. A high percentage work in textile industries or in clothing manufacturing. [6]

Even though their percentage is low, we do see some Portuguese in the liberal professions (doctors, veterinarians, architects, engineers, professors, etc.), especially in the last few years.

The following table, based on the sample of 272 Portuguese of Montreal, shows a breakdown of occupations:

TABLE 9-2
Portuguese of Montreal: breakdown by occupation

Employment sector	Portuguese group	Canadian average
Administrators	2.2	10.0
Liberal professions and technicians	9.4	13.6
Office workers	0.4	14.8
Sales sector	11.5	7.1
Services and recreation	2.6	12.3
Transportation and communication	2.2	5.3
Primary sector	1.1	8.1
Industrial workers	54.7	24.8
Undetermined	15.9	4.0

Source: *Statistique sur la communauté portugaise (Quartier Saint-Louis)*, undated, p. 32.

5.   *A Survey and an Action Plan for "Projet communautaire Pilote A"*, 1976, p. 95.

6.   Work as a cleaning woman does not in this case have the negative connotations sometimes attributed to it. As is pointed out by Anderson and Higgs (1976), cleaning women of Portuguese origin often own property worth more than that of their employers.

The Portuguese Worker

Accustomed to contact with nature and to the struggle for survival, the Portuguese have brought with them the physical robustness of their youth and their love of work.[7] We know the regard and the preference which employers show for Portuguese workers. This is because of their dedication to their work and the discipline with which they perform it.[8]

Either due to the influence of propaganda, or because of the impressions of foreigners who visit the coastal region of Portugal, the Portuguese worker is frequently thought of as a fisherman. Although fishermen represent only a small percentage of Portuguese workers, they have indeed always played an important role. Since the age of the maritime discoveries, they have maintained their contact with the Quebec coast; this is particularly evident in codfishing, where they show all the courage of men issued from a people of the sea. All this has reinforced the esteem earned by the Portuguese of Quebec, an esteem which is fully deserved in most cases.

Goals

It is fashionable to claim that it is not the love of work which motives immigrants but rather the love of money. It is true that money is both a goal and a stimulus for them, but this does not stop them from enjoying and taking a keen interest in their work. Generally, the Portuguese love work and show that they enjoy it. The privations and the insecurity earlier experienced by a number of them have become a stimulus to their advancement. It is certain

7. We found that among the Portuguese community living in the Saint-Louis district of Montreal, the age of 92% of the heads of families was between 25 and 54 years *(Logement du quartier Saint-Louis — Communauté portugaise,* xeroxed document, 1975, p. 84).

8. "In general, Portuguese immigrant workers are held in esteem by their employers and by the local people" *(Migration News,* 1968, No. 4, p. 3).

that money offers security and sometimes, for the sake of money, they sacrifice other values, taking several jobs or doing overtime.[9] However, this over-investment in work is usually in answer to a real need and cannot be regarded exclusively as an obsessive worship of the almighty dollar.

Thus, there seems to be a marked difference between the motivations of foreign workers and those of the Canadian population in general: "The immigrant tries to earn as much money as he can, since he is in a precarious situation and he agrees to work under very hard conditions [...]; the native worker, who is above all concerned with achieving a certain level of comfort, does not have the same motivation and does not submit to all the imperatives of production".[10] The primary goal of the immigrant is to improve his living standard, and work is the normal means of achieving it. Both from a social and an individual standpoint, integration into the labour market is the condition *sine qua non* which justifies the presence of immigrants and their continued stay.

---

9. "... because they are governed by an outmoded mentality and perhaps because of an uncontrollable greediness for the almighty dollar, they prefer to accept the first job which is offered them. Thus, they lose out on the possibility of learning the language of the country and remain outside the mainstream of social progress [...]. Very numerous are the immigrants engaged in building maintenance, who do unskilled jobs on building construction, or who, during the summer, collect earthworms to serve as bait in sport fishing. This last activity, in addition to making the workers look a bit silly, is also somewhat degrading, especially when the parents oblige their children to participate. Financially speaking, the fruits of this work may however be very enticing, because earnings are as high as 30 to 40 dollars an evening depending on the number of worms collected (Martins, 1971, p. 229).

10. Ageneau, *cit. in* Costa, 1970, p. 24.

Adaptation

We have already compared the milieu of origin with the receiving milieu. [11] As regards work, it is important to emphasise that many immigrants have moved from a rural area with a very primitive organisation to a highly structured urban milieu. This particularly affects immigrants coming from peripheral regions, which is the case of the majority of the Portuguese presently living in Quebec.

Rather than adaptation to work, we should speak of the problem of adaptation to the machine and to a whole system of technology. Often, the immigrant, who is accustomed to working the land using rudimentary tools and physical force, enters an industrial world where the machine replaces him, sometimes without his having to put forth any physical effort. This puts a distance between man and matter and forces the former to perform routine tasks in which there is no place for either creativity or personal initiative. Working hours are another factor making it difficult for many immigrants to adapt. Unlike the farm, where the seasons, the months and the days follow a natural rhythm, the factory imposes a rigid schedule and intense monotonous work which is prolonged in time without the slightest variation.

Working conditions

Either because they lack special skills, or because they have not mastered the language, Portuguese immigrants almost always find themselves on the lowest rungs of the occupational ladder.

On his arrival, the immigrant easily falls victim to certain kinds of exploitation. [12] The fact of not knowing the language leads

---

11.   See the chapter "Milieu of origin and the receiving milieu".

12.   On Isabel Romão's sample of Portuguese living in Montreal, two thirds of immigrant workers stated that at some time or other during their stay in Montreal, they had been victims of exploitation (cf. Romão, 1972, p. 119).

him to prefer a milieu where his employers, or at least his co-workers, speak Portuguese. Sad to say, it is sometimes conationals who abuse the new arrivals and exploit them in shameful fashion. We should like to believe that these cases are exceptions, since Portuguese immigrants are known for their spirit of mutual aid.

As we already said in the chapter on the family, it is not rare to see parents trying to place their children on the labour market, sometimes while they are still minors. Single children, even when they have reached their majority, customarily give their salaries to their parents. This does not mean that the children are exploited; they are compensated later, generally at the time of their marriage. Nevertheless, this procedure seems questionable both in terms of the lesson it teaches and in terms of fair remuneration.

Women working in clothing manufacturing are particularly vulnerable to exploitation by employers. Employers often limit salaries to the minimum permitted by law and almost always organise production so as to pay workers by the piece, which is considered a veritable attack on the dignity and health of the workers. [13] To say that immigrants accept these working conditions (long hours, piece work, unhealthy surroundings, low wages, etc.) out of a spirit of cupidity is both unjust and illogical. The fact that immigrants cannot defend themselves because of their ignorance of labour laws and workers' rights or lack of sufficiently strong representation in union organisations largely explains the sacrifices made by those who try to survive honestly.

---

13.   "According to the data of the Employment and Immigration Commission, immigrant women make up approximately half the workers in the textile sector and almost all the workers in the clothing sector, of which the most important centres are in Montreal, Toronto and Winnipeg. There are approximately 200,000 workers in these sectors throughout the country. More than any other group of workers in Canada, immigrant women hold jobs in the sectors paying the lowest wages: maid, chamber maid, cleaning woman, dishwasher, waitress, sewing machine operator, plastic manufacturing worker (Françoise Côté in *Le Devoir*, December 8, 1978, p. 2). See also Arnopoulos, 1979, p. 5 and Bernier, 1979).

During his initial period in Quebec, the Portuguese worker is inclined to compare what he earns with the wages he had in Portugal. There is here a danger of an anachronistic comparison and a false interpretation of the real standard of living, where immigrants come to consider remuneration advantageous when actually it is not. A certain "wealth" in escudos may in fact become relative poverty when converted into dollars.

Employment and unemployment

New immigrants arriving in Quebec look mainly to friends and relatives for help in finding lodging or employment, as Anderson found in her study on the Portuguese of Toronto. [14] In Hull, on a sample of Portuguese immigrants, Kemp and Morisset found that 80% of jobs were obtained through relatives and friends, 10% were found by the interested parties themselves and the remaining 10% through government manpower centres. [15] Though there is a danger that immigrants may centre their activities around their own ethnic group, we cannot deny that this procedure facilitates job-hunting. A large portion of Portuguese workers, from the very moment of their arrival, are forced to take jobs which are different from the ones they held in Portugal. With time, some have found work in their own specialties. Numerous immigrants having had experience in only one field in Portugal who come to hold a different type of job in Quebec gain an experience which can be more or less positive in terms of self-actualisation.

There seems to be great job stability among Portuguese immigrants. This is readily understood if we consider the family responsibilities which most immigrants must assume. What is known as horizontal mobility, that is to say, changing from one job to another with equivalent status, seems to be very low among the

---

14. See Anderson, 1974.
15. Kemp and Morisset, n.d., p. 2.

Portuguese workers of Quebec, as is demonstrated by the study of Romão conducted in Montreal. [16] This study shows that it is often on his own personal initiative that a worker changes jobs.

We already had occasion to point out that unemployment among Portuguese immigrants is low. [17] Though the unemployed are guaranteed subsistence thanks to unemployment insurance, it is rare to see the Portuguese of Quebec taking advantage of it to remain idle. [18]

For whom do the Portuguese work? It is a common assumption that their employers are Anglophones. It seems however that the Portuguese make their choice, not on the basis of language criteria, but rather according to the conditions and guarantees which are offered them. In the study on 272 Portuguese in the St-Louis district of Montreal, the ethnic background of employers was broken down as follows: English 28.2%, Jewish 21.6%, French 18.3%, Portuguese 11.3%, others 20.5%. [19]

Union membership

Quebec laws grant the immigrant the right to active and passive participation in union activities. In the struggle to protect workers' rights, the strike is a weapon often employed by unions. Even if the Portuguese worker feels a solidarity with his social class, his immigrant status and the problems of adapting to the new environment help foster feelings of insecurity, which cause him to

---

16. Cf. Romão, 1972, p. 128.

17. In Hull, Kemp and Morisset (n.d., p. 2) calculated that 94.2% of Portuguese men were employed, which corresponds to a real unemployment rate of almost 0%.

18. The Romão study on the Portuguese of Montreal indicates their almost total integration into the labour market and their low representation in the number of unemployed.

19. *Statistique sur la communauté portugaise (Quartier Saint-Louis),* n.d., p. 30.

hesitate because of the risks inherent in union struggles. In the study cited above, questions on attitudes towards unions gave the following results: 59.9% favoured union membership, 27.1% had no opinion, 12.7% were opposed or undecided. Lack of unionisation is particularly noteworthy in the case of women. [20]

The isolation and passiveness sometimes noted may reflect the feelings of insecurity common during the period of adaptation. Also, the failure of the Portuguese worker to participate actively in strikes, an attitude which sometimes earns him the epithet of "scab", may also be explained by the conditioning of his past experience. [21]

The majority of Portuguese immigrants living in Quebec were born and grew up in Portugal under a fascist regime, where freedom of association was very controlled and where the possibility of joining a free union was non-existent. This has prevented the development of class awareness among workers, and the old attitudes remain even after they arrive in Quebec. Thus, the choice of the area of employment is made quite independently of unionisation and union membership is rarely associated in the minds of Portuguese workers with union militancy. It is clear that the non-unionisation of a certain percentage of immigrant workers favours management insofar as it may pose an obstacle to the solidarity of

20. The Romão sample (cf. 1972, p. 184) indicates that only one sixth of the Portuguese of Montreal take an active part in union activities. The sample of Kemp and Morisset (n.d., p. 3) taken on the Portuguese of Hull, confirms the contrasts between the number of men and of women belonging to unions (57.7% and 35.8% respectively).

21. It is important to note that the majority of Portuguese immigrants have been conditioned by the dictatorial political regime described by Granotier as a regime where "the police state, the absence of democratic freedoms (absence of the right to strike), which are even more marked than in Spain, contribute to producing apolitical immigrants, docile workers esteemed by management and feared by militant workers, who know that they will be used at the first opportunity as 'scabs' and as strike breakers." (1970, p. 162).

the working class. [22] It is important however to note that this non-unionisation is typical of all immigrant workers in general and not just of Portuguese immigrants. [23]

Exploding a Myth

A simplistic and badly intentioned view of things might lead one to attribute the increase in unemployment to the presence of immigrants. In actuality, it is not difficult to see that the immigrant takes jobs which the local population does not want and that, through his work, he creates new jobs for this population. It should be added that with the filling of jobs which are going begging and the creation of new jobs, the immigrant, so to speak, helps to better the lot of the already established population which, of course, reserves the choice posts for itself. The epithet "job snatchers" proferred at immigrants is a misnomer which reflects either bad faith or a deplorable ignorance. The Parliamentary Committee on Immigration said in this regard that "the new arrivals are able to obtain jobs without contributing to the dismissal of Canadian workers." [24] The immigrant worker, by accepting wages which are lower than those of Canadian workers and also less favourable working conditions, reduces competition on the labour market and helps the local population to rise to the management level.

We find that the immigration policy of manpower importing countries is based on these countries' own interests, in that it is not simply a function of the immediate needs of the labour market, but is also a means of insuring that the offer exceeds the demand, thus making it possible to confront wage demands.

---

22. Cf. Bonacich, 1972.

23. Cf. Cappon, 1974, p. 38. See also *La Presse* (Montreal), April 2, 1979, p. C-2.

24. Canada. Special Joint Committee on Immigration Policy. *Report to Parliament,* 1975, p. 11.

Recourse to foreign manpower may have negative repercussions insofar as the immigrants' period of adaptation may cause a drop in productivity. Nevertheless, this factor is largely offset by the added value resulting from the play of forces which are unfavourable to the worker. The entry of the immigrant onto the job market does not automatically translate into a situation of justice. The immigrant, more than any other worker, is defenseless against the laws which govern supply and demand on the labour market. Going by Lenormand, most Quebec employers who try to engage workers through Canada manpower centres are exploiters who wish to offer lower wages. [25]

If the economy is the lever of the migratory phenomenon, employment is its fulcrum. However, to link work exclusively with economic goals would mean restricting its dimensions and condemning the worker to the status of a slave. While recognising that immigration is a function of the labour market which is itself a function of the economy, we must keep in mind that work is the key factor in the integration of immigrants across all human dimensions.

Leisure

To the proverb "man does not live by bread alone", we could add "bread does not come from work alone". The word bread thus takes on a broader meaning: it is not just food for the body, it is everything that contributes to the vitality and the development of the human person. In this sense, leisure may have the same value as does work if it, too, bears fruit. Rest is one of the conditions for work. Leisure is also a sort of release from built-up tensions. Closeness within the family circle permits a sharing of experiences and helps to promote culture. Leisure is not synonymous with a lack or absence of work but rather is a condition imposed by work. Insofar as this free time is used well, it fosters creativity and

---

25.   Cf. Luong and Luong, 1972, p. 73.

culture, and affords the opportunity for rest, recreation and hobbies and also socio-cultural contacts (reading, lectures, visits, etc.).

The time devoted to occupations of a cultural and recreational nature varies with the individual and is difficult to measure in terms of quantity or variety. It is logical that work, culture and tradition should be influencing factors. The person who works from ten to twelve hours a day has neither the time nor the energy to engage in leisure activities. The fact of not knowing the local languages poses limitations. In addition, acquired habits tend to create also a particular scale of priorities in the utilisation of leisure time.

Since the Portuguese devote a large part of their time to work, we must conclude that the percentage devoted to leisure activities is lower than the general average. Furthermore, it is logical that, given its customs and traditions, the group should use leisure time differently than the general population.

It appears that the Portuguese use a good part of their free time for social contacts with family and friends. A quite considerable percentage seem not to realise the advantages offered by, and the cultural needs inherent in, the new milieu. One often sees adults regularly whiling away their time in futile activities like playing cards. Although such occupations are, on the face of it, innocent, they may reflect a lack of higher interests.

We believe that the Portuguese of Quebec reduce their entertainment, in the strict sense of the word, to its simplest expression. Generally speaking, they rarely go to movies, theatres, cabarets or other like places. Diversions are often limited to weekend outings, visits to friends and Sunday church attendance, if one can, in this last case, actually speak of diversion.

In the regions with the highest ethnic concentration, dances are frequently held and here there is a certain form of socialising, but all cultural ambitions are absent. The gatherings, excursions and study tours organised, both to fill leisure time and to offer cultural enrichment, deserve a better fate.

The presence of community organisations and the availability of meeting places are essential to providing leisure activities. We note however that the Portuguese of Quebec tend more to receive friends or go to visit these friends than to plan outings or meetings in public places.

Reading and study are not generally a priority for the use of spare time and this is because a large percentage of immigrants come from rural areas. In their milieu of origin, a good part of this leisure time was spent outdoors. The climate conditions of the new country obviously make this option somewhat more problematic.

The Portuguese immigrant saves and accumulates not only money but also holidays, since long vacations are for him the preferred form of leisure. These vacations are ordinarily used for a trip to Portugal, to renew contacts with the people, the sun, the soil and the sea of the homeland.

In a society which has more and more leisure time on its hands, knowing how to occupy it is becoming increasingly important. Loafing about may not be the best way to live. Learning how to make good use of leisure time may be as basic as learning how to work.

Their new environment demands a spirit of creativity of the Portuguese immigrants living in Quebec, in order that they may strike a balance in the amount of time devoted to work, rest, social contacts and the promotion of their culture.

187

X

HEALTH AND WELFARE

Adaptation to a new country is a very complex process. The immigrant uprooted from his milieu of origin is forced into a psycho-social adjustment which generally results in a crisis situation. As is demonstrated in the works of Ruesch, Jacobson and Loeb, a change in cultural milieu is an event which engages the total personality.[1] Emigration forces individuals into sudden change, which is generally aggravated by distance, cultural differences and the conditions of adaptation imposed by the new milieu. According to Dodge, problems of adaptation are those which most seriously affect health.[2] Buzzanga emphasises the problems associated with moving from a society of the static type to a modern urban society of the dynamic type. In effect, experiencing a radically different social situation "arouses a deep feeling of insecurity and precariousness in the immigrant; he has difficulty seeing himself as an individual stable in time, and in identifying with himself; in extreme cases, this may even give rise to experiences of depersonalisation".[3]

---

1. Cf. Santos, 1975, p. 25.

2. *Idem,* p. 30.

3. Buzzanga, 1974, p. 169.

The Portuguese immigrant is generally very attached to his family and to his homeland, which he recalls with melancholy. The longing for the past and for what is far away is intensified by the solitude of the initial period and by the marginalisation often imposed by circumstances. The new immigrant only rarely causes social problems himself. Inwardly, however, he almost always suffers emotional conflicts which, on the short or long term, may be the cause of a large number of physical or emotional disorders.

Generally, adjustment to a new society fosters a situation of insecurity which seeks a resolution in memories of the milieu of origin and translates into a feeling of homesickness. Iida-Miranda, in her study on the Portuguese immigrants of Quebec, mentions certain symptoms of this homesickness, which include: lowered effectiveness on the job; concern for the security of family members who have stayed behind; decreased capacity for empathy; guilt feelings; a lowering of physical resistance; increased sensitivity and irritability; feelings of hostility; lowered frustration tolerance; a marked tendency to disease and accidents. [4]

The lack of direct contacts with the milieu of origin, the impact of a strange milieu, a different culture or a new value system, communication in a different language and adaptation to a new climate, are all factors which weigh heavily on the immigrant and which are sometimes beyond the strength and willpower of those who have embarked on the emigration adventure.

Work and the schedule that goes with it demand new types of relations within the family. The fact that parents, and in particular mothers, are too busy with their work to be able to follow their children's education and their adaptation to the new milieu, readily gives rise to feelings of insecurity and guilt.

---

4. Cf. Iida-Miranda, 1975, pp. 69-70.

We might compare the new immigrant to a transplanted tree which must undergo a process of adaptation to the new soil. However, in the case of immigrants, it is human beings and not plants who must undergo this trial. When changes are radical and sudden, health is affected. As Iida-Miranda points out, citing Holmes and Rahe, the number and intensity of changes are factors predisposing the individual to stress and disease. [5]

The initial period of adaptation to the new milieu puts a great strain on the immigrant's health. It must however be pointed out that the demands of adaptation are long term ones. Sometimes, the energies accumulated beforehand enable the immigrant to pass the initial test, but not the long term one. The newspaper "Forum" has this to say about the Portuguese of Montreal: "it appears that this group is particularly vulnerable to physical illness and that this vulnerability is linked to the stress caused by the brutal changes of immigration." [6] According to psychologist Ethel Roskies, cited in this same newspaper, the susceptibility of Portuguese immigrants to disease increases in proportion to the length of time they have been away from their country. We might say that these immigrants, upon entering Quebec, have a reserve of psychosomatic energy which is then gradually depleted.

First generation immigrants being those who most deeply experience this shock of adaptation to the new milieu, it is natural that it should be they who are most affected by the inherent health problems. Since, in addition, it is the man who takes the initiative to emigrate and who therefore has the longest contact with the foreign country, the woman who must depend on her husband's initiative suffers in a special way. Iida-Miranda's study on 303 Portuguese immigrants shows that women are more affected by change

---

5.   *Idem,* pp. 54-56.

6.   "Les Portugais à Montréal", in *Forum* (Montreal), January 18, 1974, p. 4.

than are men, and so are also more susceptible to disease. The author points out that, among women, increase in disease is in proportion to the changes experienced, while among men it seems to be the opposite. [7]

Health problems

Several factors need to be considered in any study of the health problems of a population. In the specific case of the Portuguese immigrants of Quebec, we believe it is important to consider not just the conditions of the receiving milieu but also those of the milieu of origin. Most Portuguese immigrants come from less developed areas where the educational level and economic conditions sometimes left very much to be desired. There appears to be a close correlation between health and social status, for we find that "the poorest groups from a socio-economic standpoint have a markedly higher rate of illness." [8]

Whether in the receiving milieu or in the milieu of origin, many Portuguese not only are not accustomed to using preventive medicine, they also have a habit of using family remedies to treat their ailments. Medical services are only consulted in more serious cases. The following table, prepared from the data provided by the survey connected with "Projet Communautaire Pilote A", is quite revealing.

7. Iida-Miranda, 1975, pp. 146 and 161.

8. Santos, 1975, pp. 30-31.

TABLE 10-1

Recourse to friends or family members in case of illness

Type of problem	Total sample	Portuguese
Minor illnesses or accidents	20%	71%
More serious illnesses or accidents	13%	41%
Nervous or emotional problems	27%	47%
Health problems of an intimate type	28%	71%
Dental care	16%	53%

Source: *A Survey and an Action Plan for "Projet communautaire Pilote A",* 1976,
p. 30.

As may be seen, the Portuguese group preferably consults family members or friends to resolve their various health problems. When the Portuguese consult a doctor, they are often more interested in getting rid of unpleasant symptoms than in following a treatment. [9]

We believe, like David Mechanic, that health and disease are directly correlated with social class, educational level, financial security, emotional stability of the family, housing and environmental conditions, cultural attitudes, an understanding of health and disease and the ability to make use of available health services. [10] It is logical that recourse to health services should be directly correlated with factors of a socio-cultural nature, both in the milieu of origin and in the receiving milieu. [11] These factors, as

9. According to the above survey on the Portuguese immigrants of the districts of Saint-Louis and Mile-End, "the tendency of the majority was to seek the help of a doctor to relieve symptoms such as abdominal pains, instead of trying to determine the cause of the trouble *(A Survey and an Action Plan for "Projet communautaire pilote A",* 1976, p. 25).

10. Cf. Santos, 1975, p. 33.

11. *Idem,* p. 136.

well as recourse to medical services, are influenced not only by the notions which immigrants have about them, but also by the conditions and constraints which surround them.

In the case of the Portuguese communities of Quebec, the lack of doctors, medical and paramedical personnel and social workers having the necessary language and cultural qualifications is well known.

The Parliamentary Committee on Canadian Immigration Policy concluded that immigrants' utilisation of social and health services is lower than the national average. [12] This finding is encouraging at first blush. However, our knowledge of the realities of the situation leads us to ask ourselves whether this low utilisation of health services by immigrants means that they are in good health or rather that there are factors making access to those services difficult.

The statement contained in the Green Paper on Canadian Immigration seems logical: "Since immigrants must meet certain health requirements in order to be admitted, it is very probable that on the average, they have a lesser need than natives for health services". [13] In effect, given the selection criteria for immigrants and the health requirements, we may conclude that immigrants admitted to Quebec are necessarily in good health. This being the case, the primary and most important requirements relate not to health but to social services. We might go further and hypothesise that the gaps in the area of social assistance are at least indirectly responsible for a large number of health problems.

Health services can be effective only to the extent that they consider immigrants in their specific situation and are organised as a function of the clientele which they are meant to serve. Though

12. Bonavia, 1978, p. 12.

13. Parai, 1974, p. 23.

we must admit that the competent authorities do make an effort to solve the particular problems and meet the particular needs of immigrants, by setting up services designed for these latter, it is also necessary to take initiatives designed to deal with hypothetical situations. As we seek to diagnose the reasons for the failures, we must remember that up to now these services have usually been planned without consulting the immigrants or seeking their co-operation.

Often the Portuguese immigrant has trouble filling in forms when he has to reply to surveys, make declarations or submit applications. Also, preconceived notions and suspiciousness about bureaucratic aims and requirements are not uncommon. This attitude may reflect the unfortunate experiences of a past in which bureaucracy was often synonymous with obscurantism.

Disease is not the only ill which threatens and besieges immigrants. Exploitation, the lack of education and moral and material poverty are other evils which afflict them. These are areas where social services can have an important influence.

The fact that Canada, including Quebec, is a preferred country for immigrants does not justify a certain type of propaganda which portrays this country to foreigners as a sort of Eldorado. If we are to be realistic and honest, we must also recognise certain negative aspects which may run contrary to the immigrants' expectations. [14]

More than material poverty, which is rare in Canada, there are instances of moral poverty which take the form of physical abuse,

---

14. Lenormand (cf. 1971) seems a bit extreme when he says that: nearly half the urban population of Quebec lives in a state of poverty which gets worse and worse; infant mortality is higher than that of the majority of European countries; longevity does not reach the average of the European countries; in certain places, one third of the children suffer from malnutrition. However, "statistics indicate that at least one Quebecer out of five lives on the threshold of poverty" (Bernard Descôteaux, in *Le Devoir*, March 8, 1979, pp. 1 and 6).

marital separation, desertion, alcoholism, drugs, etc. Though we freely admit that the Portuguese community is in a privileged position in this regard, we must however recognise that there are undesirable situations and make the community aware of their existence. Within the Portuguese community and in the receiving milieu in general, there are voluntary organisations whose aim is to combat both moral and material poverty. Even in the most developed countries, people may find it normal for charitable organisations to fill the gaps in and offset the deficiencies of official social services. But it is intolerable that charity should have to remedy situations of social injustice.

We sometimes hear of cases of discrimination and injustice in providing assistance to immigrants in Quebec. For instance, we find with regret that non-independent immigrants are not entitled to social welfare during their first five years of residence in Quebec and are not entitled to the old age pension until they have ten years of residence.

A survey conducted in the Saint-Louis District of Montreal yielded the following data on the Portuguese who live there and those who are dependent on welfare.

TABLE 10-2

Portuguese residents of the Saint-Louis District in relation to welfare

Have never received welfare	77.9%
Have sometimes received welfare	3.3%
Do not know what welfare is	17.7%
Are not interested in knowing about welfare	1.1%

Source: *Statistique sur la Communauté portugaise (Quartier Saint-Louis)*, undated, p. 48.

If this sample is representative, we must agree that these data are highly significant and require no further comment.

THE PORTUGUESE OF QUEBEC

Social assistance

To regard social assistance as a one-sided obligation on the part of the receiving country would be both unjust and undesirable. Immigrants, too, have obligations, both in terms of co-operation and in terms of individual or collective initiatives. Among the Portuguese of Quebec, the interest and initiative shown in providing assistance to conationals, especially family members, are well known. This aid takes the form of preparation of immigration documents, assistance in case of illness and in finding work or lodgings, etc.

Even though on the face of it, the services offered within the ethnic groups might appear to delay the process of integration, in actuality they may be an essential tool in normal integration. Individuals who are already established and accultured to the new milieu are in a better position to bring about a rapid, effective adjustment of the new arrivals. Thus, no one can object to the immigrants' tendency to use the services offered within their communities, provided that these services do not serve to "ghettoize" their clientele and the persons offering these services are sufficiently competent in the area in question.

The individuals and volunteer groups who work for the betterment of the Portuguese of Quebec have the support of some official agencies. We must however carefully consider the modalities of this support and the underlying motives. The amount of the grants seems in most cases to be insignificant, which forces some agencies to vegetate in a state of dependence and insecurity instead of going on to better things. In addition, the people who work in these agencies seem to be condemned eternally to do volunteer work, or at most to artificially reduce official unemployment figures by accepting starvation wages.

*   *   *

Everyone seems to agree that "immigration brings about stressful changes of a essentially psychosocial nature, which require considerable effort to adapt". [15] It is up to the health and social service sectors to play a primary role in assisting landed immigrants, at the time of their arrival and throughout the entire process of integration. The receiving milieu, by importing manpower, takes on a responsibility to create adequate living conditions which will make cultural shock more bearable. By doing this, the receiving milieu not only profits but also comes to realise that other human beings are important and that they are entitled to be treated with regard.

When they have recourse to health and social services, immigrants, whether individually or collectively, may adopt a negative attitude, believing themselves victims and accusing the receiving society of exploiting their labour and their health. In effect, in studying the health problems which affect immigrants and in diagnosing the diseases detected, we may confuse direct causes with circumstantial causes. Even admitting that immigration is in itself a source of numerous mental and physical disorders, it is necessary to take into account the case history of each individual, which may reveal factors that are completely alien to the fact of having immigrated. Frustrations and bad experiences in the country of origin and the presence of certain diseases in the latent state are examples of such factors.

It is generally those who have suffered the most in their country of origin, where they were victims of the prevailing system, who are condemned to leave their milieu and to suffer all the disadvantages of a new insecurity in the country of destination.

If the emigration adventure is a drama, it is particularly so for the pioneer immigrants on each territory, that is to say for heads of families. While today's immigrants can tell their children of the sacrifices they had to make, the immigrants of past eras endured

---

15.   Santos, 1975, p. 1.

even greater sacrifices beginning with the voyage, which in times past was a very great ordeal. [16]

Migrations are both an epopee and a tragedy. This tragedy is often to be found in the lives of those who have left their country to settle in a strange land. The comment of Miguel Torga seems to us verey apropos: "Those who have never felt like an extra wheel in their own country, to the point of being forced to leave it and to seek elsewhere the warmth that it refused them, cannot fathom the depths of this blow to the conscience, of this flogging of self-esteem, of the sorrow felt by the son who must leave his parents' home." [17]

How often, in actual fact, are health problems the result of a process of segregation which began in the country of origin? The health and social services must compensate for this segregation at the outset by offering a real welcome.

---

16. It is sufficient to consider that in 1847, 16% of the 109,690 immigrants who left Europe died during the voyage (Canada. Ministère de la Main-d'oeuvre et de l'immigration, 1974, p. 1).

17. *Cit. in* Serrão, 1974, p. 29.

XI

ECONOMIC FACTORS

Today more than ever, the terms migration and economy represent the two inseparable constants of a binomial. In effect, modern migrations are essentially the result of an imbalance between different levels of the socio-economic systems. They are not normally a direct response to a need to people territories as was the case in times past and they are not linked exclusively to industrialisation but rather to a process of accumulation of capital.

It is this process which has determined the destinations of Portuguese emigrants in recent decades. In other words, it is the countries with a greater accumulation of capital which have attracted Portuguese emigrants. "Portuguese workers head mainly for countries where the process of capital accumulation and industrialisation are already well advanced: France, the United States, Canada, Federal German Republic, Republic of South Africa, Venezuela and, increasingly, Belgium, Holland and Switzerland". [1]

Migrations and development

Migrations in general have ceased to be a process of land settlement to become what Seguí González calls "migrations towards

---

1. Almeida and Barreto, 1974, p. 239.

development''. It would be very simplistic to think that the use of immigrant manpower has as its immediate goal to establish a balance between the socio-economic systems involved. It is this imbalance which is the root cause of migrations, which in turn will serve to aggravate it. This explains why immigrants arrive mainly during periods of national prosperity when the demand for manpower is high.

Since the vast majority of immigrants come in answer to a demand for manpower, it is normal that immigrant populations should include a high percentage of individuals of working age. We find that in countries with a large number of immigrants, the percentage of wage-earners is higher among immigrants than among the local population.

Even if we agree that immigration is first of all a solution for the manpower importing countries, we must admit that the presence of immigrants brings with it other problems, while also being a source of controversy. Both the proponents and the opponents of immigration use mainly arguments of an economic type. The former feel that immigrants are essential in that they favour economic development; the latter accuse immigrants of increasing the cost of social services and taking jobs away from nationals.

It is certain that recourse to immigration occasions expenses both for the private sector and for the public sector. The recruitment of immigrants, transportation, preparation of infrastructures to receive and settle them, integration into the new milieu, social security and manpower training may represent burdens which compromise the economic equilibrium of the receiving country.

The objection of those who see the recourse to immigration and the increase in manpower as a means of postponing modernisation of industry, since the companies can thus avoid the expenditures which advanced technology implies, is certainly valid. However, the systematic utilisation of foreign workers is in itself a

200

proof of the advantages they offer. Immigrants may be used to fill manpower needs. In addition, with recourse to immigration, it is possible to increase production and more readily combat the threats of inflation. It is important to distinguish between real jobs and potential jobs when we talk about immigrants competing for jobs.

The arguments of those who feel that immigrants contribute to the economy of the receiving country include the following: most immigrants arrive in the country at their most productive age; the education and skills acquired in their country of origin represent clear profits for the receiving country; the selection criteria guarantee not only that the desired manpower is admitted but also that individuals in poor health are eliminated, which reduces the cost of social services. [2]

To this is added the fact that since their presence contributes to industrial expansion, immigrants bring about the creation of new jobs, so that the general population finds employment and social advancement. The admission of businessmen who bring with them more or less sizeable capital is also an advantage in that it favours the creation of new companies in which Canadians can find work. Even illegal immigrants may be very "profitable" because their work is productive and social security contributions are nil.

It should also be pointed out that by paying taxes, immigrants help to increase public revenue, which reduces the taxes of the population in general. Likewise, they favour the expansion of

---

2. It is interesting to cite the report of the French government which, in preparing the VIth Plan, estimated savings of three hundred and fifty million francs in welfare payments (not made) to one hundred and fifty thousand families who were not permanent residents of France; the heads of family had a certain amount deducted from their salaries for French social assistance. They received an average of a thousand francs in family allowances while the French average in 1967 was three thousand, six hundred francs (Loizu, 1975, p. 50).

public services and expand the domestic market by helping to increase consumption.

Another economic advantage is the possibility of opposing wage demands, to thus attenuate inflationary spirals. The complicity of government and management in this respect, reflecting their opportunistic policy of securing and exploiting a reserve army of workers, is well known. To these advantages of an economic type must be added others of a demographic nature. In the case of Canada, it should be emphasised that immigrants account for one third of the annual increase in the working population. [3]

The following table, which shows the percentage of active members of the immigrant population, is quite revealing:

TABLE 11-1
Percentage of workers among immigrants, 1968-1972

Year of admission	Quebec		Canada	
1968	$\dfrac{19{,}142}{35{,}481}$	: 54.0%	$\dfrac{95{,}466}{183{,}974}$	: 51.9%
1969	$\dfrac{15{,}821}{28{,}230}$	: 56.0%	$\dfrac{84{,}349}{161{,}531}$	: 52.2%
1970	$\dfrac{13{,}409}{23{,}261}$	: 57.6%	$\dfrac{77{,}723}{147{,}713}$	: 52.6%
1971	$\dfrac{10{,}709}{19{,}222}$	: 55.7%	$\dfrac{61{,}282}{121{,}900}$	: 50.3%
1972	$\dfrac{10{,}062}{18{,}592}$	: 54.1%	$\dfrac{59{,}432}{122{,}006}$	: 48.7%

Source: Quebec. Ministère de l'Immigration. *Une problématique des ressources humaines au Québec.* Montreal, 1974, p. 75.

---

3.   Québec. Ministère de l'Immigration. *Une problématique des ressources humaines au Québec.* Montreal, 1974, p. 37.

One could obviously speak at length about the ways in which immigrants contribute directly or indirectly to the prosperity of the countries which receive them. The yearly contribution of immigrants in Canada amounts to several hundred million dollars.[4] In the case of Quebec, immigration contributed 20% of the GNP (Gross National Product) between 1951 and 1974.[5]

Since our study is concerned with the Portuguese ethnic group in Quebec, it is proper to look specifically at the economic situation of the Portuguese established in that province. First of all, we should mention that the vast majority of the Portuguese communities in Quebec are made up of people from the lowest strata of the Portuguese economic pyramid. Once settled in the new milieu, they view their economic level in comparative terms. An economic improvement over the country of origin may not be an improvement in the context of Quebec society. In general, we do however find a rise in living standards within the Portuguese ethnic group at the level of the individual or the family.

The financial status of the immigrant rises not only in comparison with the wages paid in the country of origin, but also in terms of the buying power achieved in the new country. We find that the purchasing power of the Portuguese immigrants in Quebec is by far superior to that of their compatriots in Portugal. However, it would be ridiculous to say that the Portuguese community is rich. Thanks to their hard work and their thriftiness, the Portuguese generally achieve a satisfactory standard of living, which is almost always proportional to the length of time in the

---

4. Based on the statements given to the daily newspaper *Le Soleil* (June 19, 1972) by Minister Bryce MacKasey, immigrants contributed the sum of 385 million dollars to the Canadian economy in 1971. "In 1974-75, immigrants contributed more than 876 million dollars to the Canadian economy" (Cf. *Kaléidoscope ethnique du Canada,* publication of the Federal Department of Employment and Immigration, May 1977, p. 29. *Cit. in* Dejean, 1978, p. 75).

5. Françoise Côté, in *Le Devoir* (Montreal), December 8, 1978, p. 2.

province and also depends on the type of activity in which they are engaged.

Whether the Portuguese of Quebec are classified as a rich or a poor community will depend on how these terms are defined. When the Portuguese ethnic group is considered within the socio-economic context of that province, they must be regarded as belonging to the lower middle class.[6] Compared to Portugal and other less developed countries, the Portuguese of Quebec have a higher standard of living. However, we must take into account cases of real poverty caused by illness and unemployment not covered by welfare or unemployment insurance.

Every emigrant hopes to improve his financial situation. Although this goal is a valid one, the emigrant who pursues it to the exclusion of others is sometimes accused to making money his god. In a society overconcerned with economic security, the immigrant, who is no longer in his milieu of origin, risks sacrificing a whole set of values to money; this poses a threat to his own socio-cultural identity. As was pointed out by Jorge Dias: "For the Portuguese, the heart was the measure of all things; for the German, it was culture; and for the Frenchman, it was reason which gave a logical order to life and which made man capable of tasting its many fruits. Today, for the Portuguese, the German and the Frenchman, money threatens to replace sentiment, culture and reason".[7]

Subjects and objects

The economic factor acts as a double-edged sword in both the public and the private sectors. Neoclassical economists consider migratory movements as occurring in answer to the law of supply

---

6. According to the study of Maria Teresa Silva Santos, based on a comparative sample of the population of the Saint-Louis District, the work output of the Portuguese is superior to that of the Québécois (Santos, 1975, p. x).

7. Dias, 1971, p. 46.

and demand, which, on the international migration market, threatens to make commercial objects of human beings. The procedures and official decisions of the countries which export or which import manpower risk turning immigrants into simple production machines designed to promote the economy of these manpower importing countries. Seen in this optic, even the attention given to immigrants is perhaps motivated more by the desire to have them produce than by any altruistic concern. When this is the case both in the country of origin and in the receiving country, the immigrant becomes an object of capitalist manipulation, which threatens his identity and his socio-cultural integration.

The Portuguese immigrant is, by nature, attached to his country of origin and tries to invest his savings there. For more than a century, money sent home by emigrants has meant a substantial contribution to the Portuguese balance of payments. These remittances have been estimated "by Herculano (1873) at close to three million escudos per year [...]; at the time of Oliveira Martins (1891) at more than twelve million escudos; and during this century by Bento Carqueja at twelve million escudos and by Fernando Emídio da Silva (1917) at a sum ranging from twenty to twenty-four million escudos." [8] In the course of recent years, the following figures were recorded:

TABLE 11-2
Money sent by Portuguese emigrants, 1968-1979

Year	Amount in escudos	Year	Amount in escudos
1968	7,902,000,000	1974	22,913,000,000
1969	11,812,000,000	1975	20,975,000,000
1970	14,343,000,000	1976	26,566,000,000
1971	18,848,000,000	1977	43,232,000,000
1972	22,188,000,000	1978	74,226,000,000
1973	26,452,000,000	1979	119,758,000,000

Sources: *Estatísticas Financeiras,* Instituto Nacional de Estatística (Lisbon) and *Relatórios,* Banco de Portugal (Lisbon).

8.   Serrão, 1974, p. 175.

These remittances, which are destined essentially to aid family members, represent considerable revenue for the Portuguese economy. The presence of Portuguese banks in the Portuguese communities abroad only confirms Portuguese government policy, which is to profit from the money sent home by emigrants.

This raises a question: what basic reasons lead a country to open or to close its doors to immigration? It would be naive to think that these decisions are made chiefly for altruistic reasons. In principle, the country of immigration has the means of production but lacks cheap manpower. Its products are more competitive because they are cheaper to manufacture and are more numerous, which permits it to increase its margin of profit and its export capacity. We are thus forced to conclude that one can doubly exploit the country of origin of the immigrants by importing its cheap manpower on the one hand and exporting high-priced manufactured goods to it on the other.

We might also ask: just how high are the economic profits realised by the province of Quebec through the presence of Portuguese immigrants? Though we know of no other studies which could clarify this, suffice it to say that, between 1951 and 1974, "the national revenue of Quebec would have dropped by 11% without international immigration." [9] For reference purposes, we might also cite the VIth French Plan according to which: "France realises net profits of five billion francs per group of one hundred thousand immigrant workers." [10]

A policy which aimed at manipulating the labour force based on purely economic interests would be as reprehensible as the attitudes of those who, like the wolf in the fable of the wolf and the lamb, blame the immigrant for things which could not possibly be his fault. The goal of improving one's financial status, which the

---

9. Françoise Côté, in *Le Devoir* (Montreal), December 8, 1978, p. 2.

10. Loizu, 1975, p. 50.

Portuguese immigrant considers essential, has nothing in common with the Machiavellian manipulations of the world capitalist system of which he is a victim. For him, earning his daily bread honestly is a sacred principle. "Making good" is both a goal and a stimulus which brings him to put forward an extra effort and which often translates into numerous hours of work carried out in a spirit of true abnegation.

There is nothing more humiliating for the immigrant worker than to see himself viewed positively or negatively according to his profitability for the exploiting organisation. "We import immigrants to offset our deficiencies and, when an economic crisis comes, we accuse them of being their cause". [11]

The cultural differences between the majority and minority groups are sometimes enaggerated in times of conflict between these two groups, when in reality, economic factors are at the source of these antagonisms. In effect, the capitalist system fosters divisions within the working class by its recourse to immigration. This recourse guarantees the availability of cheap labour and also makes it possible to meet the demands of the elite of the organised working class. [12] Since the majority of immigrants are in the cheap labour category, certain conflicts which seem to have an ethnic character are in fact basically class conflicts.

One of the essential factors in immigrant socio-cultural integration is financial security, both collective and individual. We can recognise the importance of the economic factor without considering it to the exclusion of all others or accepting its arbitrary aspects. Economic development must be subjected to a political code regulating the process of migrations and their short or long term evolution. The Parliamentary Committee on Immigration Policy points out the danger of linking immigration to economic

---

11.   Baghdjian, 1976, p. 5.

12.   Cf. Bonacich, 1972.

development on the short term: "immigration is a long term invest-ment in human resources". [13]

Human resources

Quebec's economic situation is directly dependant on the presence of the ethnic groups which determine it. "For Quebec, im-migration may represent a contribution in terms of men, man-power, and know-how, and may possibly be a source of economically profitable investments." [14]

The ethnic groups of Quebec, for their part, are at the mercy of government, which must be able to make optimum use of the human resources it imports. "Quebec's difficulties will increase in the coming years because of its inability to industrialise effectively. In order for a country to become industrialised, it must be able to readily find the human resources needed by modern business, and to use them rationally and effectively." [15]

Immigrant workers, acting both as producers and as con-sumers, benefit the receiving country. As producers, they con-tribute to the development of natural resources by increasing pro-duction potential. On the other hand, they may improve the local economy by introducing new production methods. According to the Minister of Manpower and Immigration: "immigrants are a source of wealth insofar as they contribute their talents and their education and become consumers of Canadian products. Their im-pact on the economy has been considerable. Among the principal economic advantages of immigration, we should mention: growth

---

13. Cf. Canada. Special Joint Committee of the Senate and the House of Com-mons on Immigration Policy. *Report to Parliament*. Ottawa, 1975, p. 6.

14. Québec. Ministère de l'Immigration. *Une problématique des ressources hu-maines au Québec*. Montreal, 1974, p. 168.

15. Lenormand, 1971, p. 16.

of the domestic market, contribution to Canadian industrial expansion, enrichment of the country by new know-how and new art forms.'' [16]

The greatest wealth of a people is its human capital. For this reason, it would seem that manpower importing countries are poor compared to manpower exporting countries. Unfortunately, economic potential is becoming more and more the mark of distinction between rich and poor nations, thus creating an inhumane order in the scale of values. On this scale, man takes second place to the goods which he processes. In fact, the rich countries' potential in natural wealth has been realised because the recourse to imported human labour has made possible the transformation of this wealth.

We must conclude that the Quebec economy is strongly dependant on immigrant labour. We must not forget that human capital is the primary resource in a nation's economy. However, in immigration policy, whatever the interests of the parties concerned, it is essential that immigrants be regarded first and foremost as human beings and not as simple machines in the service of economic interests.

---

16. Canada. Ministère de la Main-d'Oeuvre et de l'Immigration. Service d'information. *Fiche d'information de l'immigration canadienne,* 1974, pp. 1-2.

XII

LEGISLATION AND POLICY

Since the period of French and English colonisation, immigration to Quebec has been linked to political and economic factors which have determined its nature and its course.

Present-day immigration is a vital factor in the survival policy of capitalist societies, which include Canada and with it the province of Quebec. The Special Senate and House of Commons Committee, in its report to Parliament dated November 6, 1975, expressed the opinion that "Canada must continue to be a country of immigration." [1] Canada's immigration laws and policy, at both the federal and provincial levels, have evolved considerably over time.

Legislation

Up to the First World War, immigration was generally recognised as a natural right. As proof of this, as early as 1889, the International Conference on Emigration made the following declaration: "We proclaim the right of each individual to the basic freedom, granted him by all civilised nations, to come and go and to dispose of his person and his destiny as he sees fit". [2] This same right is recognised in the Universal Declaration of Human Rights.

---

1. Bonavia, 1976, p. 11.
2. Thomas, 1962, p. 9.

The first Canadian immigration law dates back to 1869. This law limited the number of passengers which each ship could bring to Canadian territory.[3] In February 1919, Canada and fifteen European countries adopted an international protocol in Bern, article 9 of which established the following: "Prohibitions on emigration shall be abolished; prohibitions on immigration shall also be abolished as a general rule."[4] In 1966, the then Minister of Manpower and Immigration submitted to Parliament the first Canadian white paper on immigration which set standards for admission linked to the country's manpower needs, establishing a principle of non-discrimination and facilitating family reunions through less stringent requirements for the admission of close relatives.

Immigration to Canada in general and to each of the provinces in particular has been governed since very recently by law C-52, in force since April 10, 1978. This legislation was first submitted for public debate, while still in the embryo stage, through the famous "Green Paper", which gave rise to some differences of opinion and a lot of fears. The new law was greeted with reservations and many consider it a step backwards from Canada's traditional policy on immigration. After having studied this bill, several agencies expressed opposition to the new measures, calling these proposals deceptive, restrictive, repressive, discriminating and unworthy of the Canadian people.[5] Despite the valid arguments put forward and the strength of public opinion, the present law retains many

---

3. During the second part of the 19th century, Canada passed a restrictive law explicitly prohibiting the entry of *indigents, members of vicious classes* and *Chinese.* In the case of the Chinese, the prohibition was abolished for immigrants bringing with them a certain amount of money (cf. Canada. Department of Manpower and Immigration, 1974, pp. 4-5).

4. Gani, 1972, p. 10.

5. Cf. *Le Devoir* (Montreal), January 20, 1977, p. 14; *Idem,* January 11, 1979, p. 2. "It is striking to note the degree to which the new Canadian immigration law voted by the Parliament in Ottawa in July 1977 attempts to heap up precautions and barriers as if the country were threatened by a formidable and perfidious enemy, the immigrant!" (Dejean, 1978, p. 72).

restrictive clauses. It is sufficient to consider the different controll-
ing and discriminating measures which are evident in the selection
process.

Selective immigration is characteristic of the main countries of
immigration. Canada, in spite of the relatively positive attitude
which has always distinguished it, frequently shows certain prejudices in this area. In the House of Commons, it was explicitly
stated that: "We must choose as immigrants those who will have to
modify their habits as little as possible to adapt to the Canadian
way of life and contribute to the progress of the Canadian nation
[...]. This is why we clearly prefer immigrants from countries where
political and social institutions are similar to ours". [6]

Quebec's provincial policy on immigration has been particularly attacked because of its selective nature. The frankly stated
goal of ensuring the domination and development of the Francophone group in Quebec carries with it specific objectives as
regards ethnic and linguistic ratios. [7] Such a policy is overtly selective in attempting to limit "immigration to Francophones or prospective French speakers in order to strengthen the majority group,
which feels particularly threatened". In addition, it is recognised
that "the realisation of this goal demands highly selective immigration and strong measures to ensure adaptation". [8]

Unfortunately, this discriminatory policy in the selection of
immigrants to Canada seems on the way to becoming an institution. Such discrimination appears to be particularly directed at the
peoples of Mediterranean Europe and what is called the Third
World. Such was the orientation of former Immigration Minister J.
W. Pickersgill: "We try to select immigrants who are the least affected by changes in customs, so that they can adapt to Canadian

6. *Débats de la Chambre des Communes,* 1965, p. 13.

7. Cf. Québec. Ministère de l'Immigration. *Une problématique des ressources
    humaines au Québec.* Montreal, 1974, p. 81.

8. *Idem,* p. 166.

life and contribute to her development. This is why entry to Canada is, for all practical purposes, free to citizens of the United Kingdom, the United States and France, provided they are in good health and of good conduct. This is the reason for the preference which is deliberately shown to immigrants from countries having political and social institutions similar to our own."[9] Léger advocates a frankly selective immigration policy for Quebec, proposing the recruitment of immigrants likely to adapt more readily to the province of Quebec, because of their culture, their traditions, their occupation, and their religious beliefs.[10] He proposes as possible candidates French, Walloons, French-speaking Swiss, all the Latin peoples and the Slavs of Eastern Europe.

The point system presently in force has discriminatory connotations which pose an obstacle to the entry of many Portuguese. The large numbers of Portuguese entering Canada in the last twenty years represent in the main immigrants sponsored by relatives already established in the country. Furthermore, an immigration policy operating like a tap which one turns on or off depending on immediate manpower needs is too simplistic. As for the factors considered in the admission of immigrants, it must be taken into account that placement in a given employment sector is not final, because immigrants are always free to change jobs.

When considering Canada's immigration legislation, we must sometimes read between the lines to discover the hidden implications of certain provisions, above all when these have protectionist aims. The statement of the Canadian Council of Bishops is suggestive: "We must tell the members of parliament that we deplore the restrictive and protectionist policies on immigration and population matters."[11]

---

9. Cf. Hawkins, 1972.

10. Léger, 1956, p. 28.

11. Commission épiscopale canadienne des affaires sociales, in *La Documentation catholique* (Paris), 1975, p. 747.

In the working world, for example, we can easily fall into the discriminatory trap of assigning certain posts of responsibility according to the worker's status and not according to his professional competence. Frequently, natonals in a position of authority, when dealing with immigrants, display attitudes which reflect a ridiculous superiority complex. These attitudes may be reinforced by a corresponding submissive behaviour on the part of the immigrant, reflecting the latter's feelings of psychosocial insecurity.

Given the reactions aroused by the presence of immigrants, we may well ask ourselves to what degree they are wanted or unwanted in Quebec. Both at the level of political decision-making and at the level of public opinion, two extreme positions are normally taken: there are those who advocate the admission of unlimited numbers of immigrants and those who oppose almost any form of immigration. A Gallup poll conducted in 1971 and which asked whether or not there was a need for immigrants, gave a clear-cut picture of public opinion: in Quebec, 29% of respondents favoured immigration while 66% opposed it and 5% were undecided. [12] Based on 1,629 submissions made by the population in general to the Parliamentary Committee on Immigration Policy, the following conclusions were reached: 48.6% advocated a halt to all immigration or at least all non-white immigration, 22% advocated tight controls on immigration and 6% wanted immigration to be geared to economic conditions and manpower needs. [13] In 1975, the Canadian Parliamentary Committee on Immigration Policy took the following stand: "The Committee rejected the view contained in some submissions that Canada should close its doors to immigrants." [14]

---

12. Cf. Mvilongo *et al.,* 1972, p. 15.

13. Cf. Canada. Special Joint Committee of the Senate and the House of Commons on Immigration Policy, *Report to Parliament.* Ottawa, 1975, p. 65.

14. *Idem,* p. 5.

In spite of our criticisms of the conditions surrounding emigration to Canada in general and to Quebec in particular, we must commend the efforts and the good will of many authorities who are trying to eliminate discriminatory decisions and attitudes in legislation and in practice. Let us cite the example of the former Minister Fairclough. When this latter headed the former Department of Citizenship and Immigration, she attempted to establish immigrants' schooling and practical knowledge as the main conditions for admission to Canada, without distinction of country of origin. In recent years, the multiculturalism policy has also attempted to reflect the desire of the Canadian government to support the advancement of the different groups making up the national community and bring about a harmony and complementarity of these groups. While the principle of multiculturalism seems to have appeal for several ethnic groups, French culture cannot seem to accommodate this process, which is seen as a disguised attempt at domination by English culture and it is perhaps for this reason that separatist policy holds more attraction than multiculturalism.

Quebec, in spite of the xenophobia of which she is often accused, is still a preferred region, where the immigrant finds conditions more favourable than those afforded him by France or the Federal German Republic, for example. Thus, if we disregard certain key sectors to which access is in practice denied him, the immigrant can compete with the native on the labour market on a basis of legal equality.

Ends and means

It is universally recognised that immigration policy is designed to fill population deficits: overall deficits (demographic) and above all sectorial deficits (employment). Canada is no exception to this rule: "Owing to the spectacular decline in the Canadian fertility rate since 1960, immigration is becoming an increasingly important component of population growth." [15]

---

15. *Idem,* p. 4.

In the case of Quebec, as we already said, the particular goal of immigration seems to be to offset the drop in natality among the Francophone group, thus helping to guarantee the survival of the French language. [16] Based on the evidence, one is justified in questioning the pertinence and the effectiveness of Quebec immigration policy. Discussing this province, Lenormand speaks of false and contradictory interpretations, of tragic results and a gradual drop in European immigration, combined with the methodical, organised departure of specialised immigrants for other provinces. This author adds by way of conclusion: "As long as the federal government continues to find the Quebec immigration problem insoluble, it is logical to suppose that it will gradually have to give the Quebec government control over its own immigration." [17] This same author notes elsewhere: "The fact that in 1967, the province of Quebec adopted an immigration policy opposed to that of the federal government is consistent with the traditional ambivalence between Ottawa and Quebec, but this policy is catastrophic for the province of Quebec. The immigrant who has no traditional ties with Quebec will not tolerate being used as a pawn in a political game, either in domestic or in foreign policy". [18]

But there is a ray of hope. The following testimony shows that people can learn from past mistakes: "In Quebec [...], we have neither established an immigration policy nor taken a positive attitude towards the immigrant. Our hostility to the immigrant and our opposition to immigration must give way to an open policy based on ethnic balance." [19]

---

16. Québec. Ministère de l'Immigration. *Une problématique des ressources humaines au Québec.* Montreal, 1974, p. 160.

17. Lenormand, 1971, p. 76.

18. *Idem,* p. 13.

19. Morin, 1966, p. 124.

Rights and duties

In the beginning, the immigrant sometimes feels like a pariah, both in his country of origin where he has lost many of his rights, and in his adopted country where he has not yet acquired any. [20]

Even though we do not have enough information to support the opinions of the authors already cited, we have ourselves noted that today the ethnic minorities in Quebec are far more aware of their rights and their duties. If laws are to be respected, these laws must take into account the persons for whom they are intended. If we wish to prevent their alienation, immigrants must be made simultaneously aware of both their rights and their duties.

In the capitalist system of Quebec, immigrants cannot be expected to look solely to governments to protect their rights and less still, to the capitalist system which they serve. This leaves the unions, which cannot either guarantee the rights of immigrants if these immigrants are not adequately represented within their ranks. Thus, it is essential that within unions, immigrants be equal to other workers in terms of the right to vote and to be elected to posts of responsibility in their professional and union organisations.

If Quebec, and the rest of Canada, are to be truly democratic, we must make it possible for the immigrant to defend his rights and we can then expect that he will demand conditions which can better serve common goals. In a true democracy, the immigrant worker should be treated as an adult under law. It is also necessary that this same immigrant be able to actually avail himself in practice of this status which is granted him.

It may seem unrealistic to expect third parties to defend immigrant rights. Unfortunately, the Portuguese community of

---

20. To deal with this situation, there has been insistence on the need to give the immigrant worker international status so that he will not have just duties but also rights which can be guaranteed by legislation.

Quebec has not always been sufficiently cohesive or shown enough political awareness to be able to take up the promotion and defense of its own rights. This is because the community ties essential at all levels to protect common values and defend the rights of this community are still too tenuous.

Political awareness

The relationship among economic, political and legislative factors is evident. The immigrant generally and the new immigrant especially feels incapable of interrelating all these factors in his mind. It thus happens, and this is particularly frequent among the Portuguese, that immigrants show a certain political backwardness and even a certain aversion for things political. This may be attributed to a lack of previous experience and education. Political militancy is still confused with political formation. And it must be recognised that the best government policy can only be effective if the population is politically aware.

The majority of Portuguese immigrants now living in Quebec have suffered in their country of origin from the effects of certain political taboos existing under the dictatorship which lasted from 1926 to 1974. We should not therefore be astonished to see this past come back to haunt the Portuguese of Quebec. [21] A vast majority seem to be marked by prejudices about politics and by a stifled political awareness. With the sudden disappearance of these taboos, due either to the change in regime, or to their departure for a country which does not have them, some individuals, who are more motivated and more superficially politicised than others,

---

21. During the Portuguese elections, out of the immigrants in Montreal eligible to vote, only 3% took part in the election of the Constituent Assembly (in 1975), while 7% voted in the election of the Legislative Assembly (1976). In the first instance, all the voters were natives of continental Portugal and in the second, there were two voters from the Azores. (Data provided directly by the Consulate General of Portugal in Montreal on January 31, 1978).

218

voice their enthusiasm and preach their ideologies with messianic fervour or take the pretentious attitude characteristic of a still burgeoning political formation.

Political choices

In the battle of the dominant cultures, it becomes well-nigh impossible to resist the temptation of enlisting the minorities. It is clear that any form of conflict requiring a taking of sides creates distasteful situations, and it is understandable that ethnic minorities should feel uncomfortable when it comes to stating their convictions or when they must suffer the unpleasant effects of 'non-alignment'.

The present political situation in Quebec means constant pressure on ethnic groups to support one or the other of the dominant groups. Although the attitude of most Portuguese seems to be one of non-alignment, we must nevertheless conclude that these pressures do affect them. "When the immigrants feel that we accept them for what they are, that we love them as they are, they will feel more drawn to us. So long as we give them the impression that we want to use them as hostages of sorts in conflicts for which there is not even agreement among ourselves, we shall drive them psychologically further away from the Francophone community instead of bringing them closer". [22]

In Canada, the existing regime recognises freedom of political association, which facilitates free membership and participation in political parties for both immigrants and nationals. Once immigrants are naturalised, they become equal to nationals under law and this includes the right to vote. The attention shown by the different parties to immigrant minorities at election time in an attempt

22.   Ryan, *Cit. in* Mvilongo *et al.*, 1972, p. 16.

to win their votes is well known.[23] The Portuguese ethnic group, though aware that it is not well represented on the Quebec political scene, seems attentive to the main political forces at work, while remaining sensitive to all the manipulations that would use it as a pawn on the political chess board.

Given the secrecy of the ballot, it becomes practically impossible to determine the political leanings of the Portuguese. In regions with the highest concentration, it is impossible to advance hypotheses on their electoral behaviour based on the ballot results.[24] But on the other hand, it seems there is not a single agglomeration in Quebec where the Portuguese entitled to vote are numerous enough to permit us to draw sufficiently reliable conclusions.

Considering the large number of Portuguese immigrants, many of whom are naturalised Canadians, we should expect a certain political representation at the administrative level, but this is not the case.[25] Many factors can explain this absence. On the one hand, the Portuguese ethnic group is still first generation and thus is a population still in the process of adapting. On the other hand, as we already said, the majority of immigrants living in Quebec have been victims of the obscurantism of a dictatorial political regime which never encouraged them to participate in the social and political life of the community. We can thus better understand why

---

23. According to Cappon (1974, p. 75), "Immigrants' neutrality often goes to the extreme of refusing to express an opinion on intercommunity relations in Montreal, because they fear the consequences of aligning themselves on one or the other side".

24. As regards federal politics, in a survey conducted by the Centre portugais de référence et de promotion sociale (1975, p. 94) among a group of young Portuguese in Montreal, 45% of the respondents indicated a preference for the Liberal Party, 22.5% for the New Democratic Party and 3.2% for the Conservative Party or the Union Nationale and 29.2% had no opinion.

25. We estimate the percentage of Portuguese in Quebec who have taken out Canadian citizenship at 25%.

there is not yet a single Portuguese deputy in Quebec or a single political leader issuing from the Portuguese community. In spite of all these limitations, the lack of political education sometimes attributed to the Portuguese ethnic group of Quebec, even if real, should not be a reason for washing one's hands of the problem or justify a process of marginalisation. [26]

---

26. The politicising of the worker should in principle be one of the functions or aims of unions. These latter however seem to have had other concerns and to have forgotten immigrant workers. So we ought not to be surprised if immigrants regard unions rather like a company which controls them or an employer to whom they are subservient, instead of seeing them as a forum where they might participate actively, stating their convictions and defending their rights.

XIII

THE RELIGIOUS DIMENSION

The religious heritage is a integral part of the cultural values which define a people. In the case of Portugal, religion, and more specifically Catholicism, is intimately bound up with its history. In fact, the Catholic religion has been and continues to be the religion of most Portuguese. [1] Being Portuguese and being Catholic are two traditionally inseparable conditions. Both in collective decisions and in individual beliefs, religion has left a deep imprint on the Portuguese way of life.

The socio-historical context

Portuguese expansion has always been closely linked with religious concerns. "The discovered territories were placed under the temporal authority of the Holy See, which sometimes granted the right of ownership to the discovering king. The right to expand the faith took precedence over the right of conquest, not as a political factor but as a supranational reason. Popes Nicholas V (1554) and later Calixte II confirmed the granting of territories to the king of Portugal in papal bulls". [2]

---

1. In 1975, according to the bulletin *Pro Mundi Vita,* 98.1% of the Portuguese population was Catholic (July-August, 1978, No. 73, p. 9).

2. Bettencourt, 1961, pp. 37-38.

At the time of the planning of the Portuguese commercial and maritime empire, there was also concern with establishing a religious empire. Thus, in the 16th century, Afonso de Albuquerque founded a large Christian metropolis in Goa which up to our day has remained the Rome of the Orient.

Adding to what was said in Chapter V "The milieu of origin and the receiving milieu", we shall describe some facets of the religious life of the Portuguese living in Quebec.

Every people has its own image of God, at least in the way it identifies Him and in the traits which it attributes to Him. How can we describe the God of the Portuguese? We cannot go wrong if we say that He is the God of the Bible, personified in the Old Testament and known under the titles of Father, Judge and Lord. These attributes are reflected in the traditional Portuguese culture, which is of the patriarchal, authoritarian, paternalistic type.

Popular religious belief is often laced with superstition, just as worship is often associated with magic. This confusion manifests itself not only at the conceptual level but also in overt behaviour. For the Portuguese, in Portugal as in Quebec, both devotions and receipt of the sacraments often reflect a certain magical approach or a more or less determinant socio-cultural conditioning.

Traditionally, the Portuguese Catholic Church has been almost exclusively guided by the clergy, with which it identifies. Even today, the Church is equated with its pastors in the minds of many Portuguese. It is credited with connivence in the maintenance of the status quo and the stability of the reigning social order.

In their conception of God, the Portuguese, as we just said, emphasise the attributes of Father, Judge and Lord. These same attributes are projected onto priests as representatives of God. Paternalism, moralism and authoritarianism are the marks of the traditional Portuguese clergy. Both because of what he does and because of his social status, the parish priest is generally a dominant figure, especially in rural areas. However, the respect which is shown him seems to be more a situational automatism than the result of any real conviction. The remarks of Cutileiro concerning the people's relations with the clergy may perhaps be applied generally: "Although he is given the respectful treatment reserved for the upper class in face-to-face contact, behind his back he is never referred to as *o senhor padre* or *o senhor prior* but simply as *o padre* or *o prior* and derogatory terms are often used in conversations about him".[3]

Even if material wealth is the ideal of the majority of immigrants, including the Portuguese, the priest who acts like a rich man is looked at askance. The immigrant readily agrees to contribute to the priest's upkeep but objects if the priest becomes a "capitalist". One might call it a mixture of jealousy and zeal.

The reasons for the anticlericalism of the Portuguese people, which is reflected in their literature and in their popular expressions, are quite complex. "The anticlericalism of our people is an attitude which we all deplore but it is only rarely that it leads us to Christian reflection on its causes and its effects. The root source of this anonymous undercurrent of contention, criticism and defensiveness, in my opinion, lies in the clericalism of the attitudes, language, standards and demands of the world to which the priests belong. The authoritarian, moralistic and omniscient sermons, pronounced in a singsong tone, are almost always prepared (when they are prepared) without the participation of lay people and are often directed against them [...]. There are some who make the sermon a rendering of accounts or a *chapter* in the manner of the medieval monks".[4]

---

3. Cutileiro, 1971, pp. 265-266.
4. Azevedo, 1973, p. 81.

Anticlericalism is an obstacle to the religious education of immigrants. Nevertheless it can be an incentive for certain priests responsible for this education to bring their lives more in line with doctrine. "It is easy to become propagandists of the things of heaven, traders or even black marketeers of things which we *pass off* as being of God. Excessive religiosity almost always degenerates to the point where we see priests, their book under their arm, receiving the remuneration considered due for each sacrament administered. These attitudes run counter to the prophetic mission which is essential in the life of the priest". [5]

Unfortunately, in the immigrant milieu, one still finds examples of a type of clericalism engendering forms of interference and authoritarianism which are particularly distasteful. Some see a parallel between certain expressions of clerical arrogance and the public service, where arrogance towards the public is a way of making the individual feel helpless in the hands of the all-powerful bureaucrat.

Typology of religious practice

Though it is possible to consider the Portuguese as a whole, it is important to note that there are differences in their religious beliefs, among the various regions of the continent and also between the continent and the adjacent islands of which the majority of Portuguese immigrants to Quebec are natives.

As regards religious expression, the distinction usually made between the North and South of Portugal, though well-founded, is nevertheless somewhat simplistic. Abrunhosa e Sousa, proposing a more elaborate typology, divided the continent into five geographic regions:

---

5. *Idem*, p. 78.

1. *Northern inland region*: characterised by strong religious practice, traditionalist. Very closed communities which exercise strict control over their members.
2. *Northern coastal region*: very religious with stable family values, very extended family, great propensity for religious feasts and celebrations. Church attendance high.
3. *Central region*: region of transition particularly along the coast; other values oppose Christianity. Church attendance varies from subregion to subregion. Less expansive Christianity.
4. *Southern region*: The South of Portugal is markedly de-christianised. Loss of religious and family standards, poorly defined values. Absence of priests: this region is not adequately served.
5. *Estremadura*: undergoing industrialisation and urbanisation, its Christianity is of the type found in developed countries. [6]

We are of the opinion that the religious characteristics described for the coastal and inland regions of the North also apply to the adjacent islands. This typology is reflected in the immigrant milieu, where the characteristics of the milieu of origin tend to be reproduced.

Over and above the regional differences, there are also differences among social strata. As happens elsewhere, the more sophisticated milieux are much more progressive and agnostic. More isolated persons and groups generally show an attachment to traditional beliefs and standards.

Religious confessions

Catholicism is so linked to the history of Portugal that for many Portuguese, religion and Catholicism are synonymous. However, it would be wrong to think that all Portuguese believers are

---

6. *Cit. in* Silva, 1976, p. 121.

Catholic or even Christian. The Portuguese in both Quebec and Portugal count members of other religious confessions, and of certain Protestant churches in particular, although their overall number is very small.[7] The Portuguese Jews have been part of the Portuguese community of Quebec for a long time. Even today on rue St-Kevin, in Montreal, there is a synagogue called the "Spanish and Portuguese Synagogue". Founded in 1768, it is the oldest in Canada. Despite its name, which certainly attests to the presence of Portuguese Jews in Quebec, the Portuguese believers attending this synagogue are presently limited to two families.

Rites of passage and religious practice

The rites of passage are a constant of all traditional cultures. They are observed by the majority of the Portuguese population including the so-called non-practising Catholics. For example, children continue to be baptised both in the receiving milieu and in the milieu of origin.[8] The Catholic marriage is still the usual way of tying the knot.[9] Religious funerals are almost an absolute norm, even among those who have dropped their religious practice.[10] Although there is agreement that religious beliefs must translate into a way of life which is consistent with faith, it has become common to judge the degree of religious fervour by the more or less

---

7.   In Montreal, there are about a hundred Portuguese who attend Portuguese Protestant churches.

8.   In 1976-77, 430 Portuguese babies were baptised at the "Santa Cruz" Mission in Montreal. In 1975, the Portuguese mission in Hull registered 52 baptisms.

9.   In 1975, 80.01% of marriages in Portugal were celebrated in the Catholic Church. There are however very marked differences among the various geographical regions. Non-Catholic marriages totalled 58.27% at Setubal and barely 1.47% at Braga in 1975 (Cf. Portugal. Instituto Nacional de Estatística, 1975, p. xxiii).

10.   In spite of the belief professed by many Portuguese in eternal life and the beatitude of that life, both death and the religious rites which accompany it are times of great mourning which may touch on the melodramatic.

regular attendance at religious rites, so much so that such attendance becomes a way of distinguishing practising and non-practising Catholics. It is however practically impossible to determine the extent of religious practice among the Portuguese of Quebec, since some attend church in non-ethnic parishes which cannot provide the necessary statistical data.

Church attendance is found to be high among Portuguese from the Azores. Not only do they form a majority among the ethnic group, but they also boast a higher percentage of church-goers. There are many possible explanations for this phenomenon, among which the socio-cultural influences of the milieu of origin hold a prominent place.

In Montreal, Laval and Hull, where there are religious services specifically for the Portuguese, church attendance seems to have risen in terms of absolute numbers, coinciding with the increase in the size of the Portuguese ethnic group. If we were to find a drop in attendance at ethnic religious services, we might conclude either that religious practice is neglected or that immigrants have been absorbed by the respective local parishes. Romão, in a study on the Portuguese of Montreal, found that only one third of this sample attended church in the Portuguese language parish. [11] An approximate calculation based on personal observations leads us to estimate the percentage of immigrants who attend church regularly at 15%, those who attend church irregularly at 15% and the percentage who practice their religion occasionally at 45%. Those who have abandoned their religious practice make up the remaining 25%. [12]

---

11.   Cf. Romão, 1973, p. 170.

12.   "A survey conducted at the request of the Portuguese Bishops' Conference shows that 32.5% of Portuguese Catholics attend Mass regularly every Sunday. This figure comprises 61% women and 39% men" (*La documentation catholique,* April 16, 1978, No. 1780, p. 392).

The drop in religious practice does not however mean that the faith is about to disappear. Also, participation in religious rites is not necessarily a reflection of enlightened religious belief. Among the Portuguese, it seems safe to say that social considerations motivate attendance at religious rites much more than does personal conviction.

Along with those whom we consider practising Catholics, we must not forget the high percentage of those who are indifferent. The majority of these latter do however show a religious undercurrent insofar as religion often interests them, even if only in a socio-cultural optic.

Expressions of religious belief

The Portuguese milieux of both Quebec and Portugal abound in religious symbols. The wearing of crosses and medals, either out of devotion or for decorative purposes, is very widespread. In homes, we frequently find religious pictures or statues which are used for personal devotions or simply out of tradition.

Quite aside from the beliefs and preferences of each individual, collective devotions can in part serve to define the culture of a people. And certain devotions are characteristic of each region within a nation. The Portuguese in Quebec are easily distinguished by devotions typical of their milieu of origin. The immigrants from the Azores have special devotions to the Holy Ghost and to the "Senhor Santo Cristo dos Milagres" (Lord Christ of Miracles). Among natives of the continent, the feasts of popular saints (St. Anthony, St. John and St. Peter) are special occasions. Devotions to the Virgin under her different names, in particular Our Lady of Fatima, are vested with special significance within both groups.

The religious convictions of the Portuguese people find particular expression in the celebrations organised in honour of the patron saints of the different towns and cities. Numerous feasts have their roots in ancient traditions, which are characterised by special rituals and formalities. In Quebec, Portuguese immigrants tend to continue the devotions and rituals of their milieu of origin. In the large Portuguese communities of Montreal, Hull, Laval and Ste-Thérèse, some religious processions take on the character of popular demonstrations. These manifestations are strongly imprinted with folklore and we see traditional figures from the milieu of origin merging with figures and symbols which are typically Québécois.

Popular religious belief frequently translates into vows and the keeping of vows made to God, either directly or through the intercession of the saints. Pilgrimages to holy places, to fulfill a promise or out of devotion, are a typical mode of popular Portuguese religious expression. They are veritable acts of penance, above all along the routes which lead to the large sanctuaries.

Once established in Quebec, the Portuguese immigrants keep up their traditional devotions rather than replacing them with local devotions. This applies to both the saints which they invoke and the places to which they make their pilgrimages. It is thus more probable that a Portuguese from Montreal, in keeping a vow, will make a pilgrimage to Fatima, in Portugal, rather than to St. Joseph's Oratory in the city where he lives.

Two dimensions, the future and life beyond the grave, are the essence of Portuguese religious belief. Praying for favours from heaven, taking care to ensure the salvation of one's soul and praying for the dead are reflections of these dimensions. For the immigrant, as his attachment to tradition brings the past to life, the insecurity of his new situation and his hope of a better future imbue religious manifestations with new meaning. Thus the religious feast takes on particular significance as past and future meet, which explains the zeal shown in the organisation and celebration of these feasts.

230

The pastorate

Immigrants like religious leaders who work and struggle side by side with them in their daily lives. Conversely, they are less and less tolerant of the pastor who remains distant, content to pass on the directives received from above and to welcome those who practice their religious duties as his faithful, while considering the others as infidels and lost sheep. In view of the persistence of the rectory pastorate, it would almost seem that the order given to the missionaries to "go and teach" has been changed to a bureaucratic decree to "come and learn". There is another accusation levelled at the religious hierarchy; in the form of criticism of the nonchalant manner in which missionaries to the immigrant communities are appointed.

It seems logical that the religious guidance of immigrants ought to be entrusted to specialised people who know the new milieu. [13] It is also important that directives from higher authorities be adapted to the particular circumstances of each group and that the immigrants' immediate spiritual advisors be given the leeway and the support which they need to show initiative and creativity. If the religious advisor is not sufficiently knowledgeable, he will have difficulty in understanding the people, who will then suffer the consequences of his mistakes. On the other hand, if this advisor is merely a yes-man of the higher authority or if he is content to be nothing more than an intermediary between this latter and the people, he runs the risk of being viewed as a bureaucrat, unable to devote time to the religious community that he was sent to educate.

---

13. "Pastoral work among immigrants must, insofar as possible, be entrusted to a priest with sufficient preparation and whose virtues, doctrine, knowledge of languages and other moral qualities ideally equip him to take on such a demanding mission" (Paul VI, "Instruction", *De pastorali migratorum cura,* Chap. V, No. 36-4, in *Acta Apostolicae Sedis,* 1969, Vol. 61, No. 10, p. 633).

Active participation and education

The abandoning of religious practice, which is quite widespread, seems to reflect a casting off of the force of authority and of the weight of tradition. This decision becomes easier in the new context created by immigration. The passive participation in religious activities to which many believers are accustomed seems unable to arouse the interest of the young in religious practice. Leaving the Church is thus more common among young people and sometimes we might ask ourselves whether certain religious services are not conducted solely with the older representatives of the community in mind. Religion is only very rarely abondoned because of atheism. At the very most, this "loss of faith" may represent a transition to unbelief or agnosticism.

In spite of their zeal, certain priests sometimes have difficulty in obtaining the cooperation of lay people or else have occasion to bemoan their lack of preparation. Even admitting that immigrant workers are very busy, their cooperation in religious works may serve as a measure of the religious fervour of a people. [14]

Systematic religious teaching continues to be given only to young children. Catechism classes in the Portuguese language are offered by religious missions in Montreal and Hull. They are taught by native Portuguese in these two places, while in centres with a lower concentration of Portuguese, children are enrolled in the local parishes. By constitutional right, religious instruction is offered in Catholic schools, which are those attended by the majority of Portuguese children.

---

14. Entering religion or making a career of the priesthood can be an indicator of the interest shown in religion. It seems to be extremely rare for a Portuguese Quebecer to either become a priest or enter a religious congregation.

The attitude of local churches

Is the Church in Quebec fully aware of the large number of immigrants in her midst and is she concerned with their fate? It says something that in the eight volumes published recently by the *Commission d'Études sur les Laïcs et l'Église* of Quebec, there is no explicit mention of pastoral work among immigrants. This attitude runs contrary to the guidelines given in this same document: ''The Church has the duty ot assist creatively at the emergence of new cultures, at the resurgence of particular heritages, at the new chapters written in the book of human adventure''. [15]

Prejudices and even indifference are contrary to Christian principles, and all the more so in the case of the local churches in Quebec established long ago by immigrant peoples. [16] The warning of the Holy Scriptures seems apropos: ''Do not mistreat the stranger and do not oppress him, because you too, were once strangers [...]. If you afflict him, he will cry to me and I shall hear his cry''. [17]

The Church in Quebec has been accused of aloofness and of being content with merely accepting the presence of immigrants, almost always passively. The appeal of Pope Paul VI to local communities concerning the welcome to be given immigrants is very pointed. ''We again invite the receiving churches to humbly and loyally meet the different pastoral needs of immigrants [...]. The initial welcome and the initial experience are very significant in the temporary or permanent integration of the ethnic groups. It is very difficult for the inhabitants of countries that consider themselves

---

15. Commission d'études sur les laïcs et l'Église, 1971, p. 148.

16. It was a French Canadian who made the following comment: ''Unfortunately, up to now, at the parish level, and at other levels as well, our very mixed societies have paradoxically almost always ignored the immigrant and his problems'' (Léger, 1956, p. 25).

17. Exodus, 22, 20-23.

developed to become poor with the poor, to learn to see them, to hear them and to receive their gifts. However, this fundamental attitude will make it possible for emigrant people and communities to be themselves, to express themselves, to understand their problems of integration, and to gain confidence in their ability to gradually resolve them". [18]

Social impact

The religious expression of the Portuguese group has always been highly personal, rarely emphasising the social dimension. Although religious devotions have a collective character, the underlying motivations are still personal in nature. Religion is a sort of eternal-life insurance and religious devotions are regarded mainly as individual obligations and are the premium to be paid for the divine insurance policy guaranteeing personal salvation.

The Portuguese immigrant generally moves from a uniformly religious (and almost always Catholic) world to a world of multiple religions which is sometimes indifferent to religion. Especially in the large urban centres, the immigrant who encounters many and varied beliefs comes to adopt either an attitude of scepticism or an eclectic position. The receiving milieu, especially in the cities, makes possible his psychological liberation from the religious practices he observed in the milieu of origin because of tradition, due to social pressure or out of human respect.

For those who attend church, Sunday Mass is the socio-religious act par excellence. It is not just the fact of gathering in church which is significant. The possibility of meeting friends and renewing social contacts, before and after the religious service, plays an important role. As institutions, the different churches still have moral ascendancy over a large percentage of the population.

18. Paul VI, Discourse pronounced on October 17, 1973, at the 1st European Congress on the Ministry to Migrants.

Churches do not limit themselves to spiritual matters and extend their action to problems of a material order, offering aid to persons in need. Frequently, immigrants appeal first to the church to resolve both their spiritual problems and their material difficulties.

The religion of the Portuguese of Quebec is one of their cultural traits. This does not of course mean that all the members of the Portuguese community consider themselves religious and even less that they attend Mass. However, as a general phenomenon, religious behaviour still prevails.

Like the traditional Quebec culture, Portuguese culture is imbued with Christian values and customs. The Catholic religion has always been dominant in both societies. However, for the Portuguese, it is not simply a question of transplanting the religious culture of their milieu of origin. The same religion does not necessarily take the same form in the new milieux. The meeting of different cultures is reflected in religious behaviour. [19]

Religion may be regarded as an important force within the Portuguese group insofar as an adequate socio-religious culture may result as may a process of alienation. A church which limited itself to preaching resignation to those who suffer, to demanding the performance of "religious duties", to imposing religion as a moral code and threatening believers with Hell, would indubitably be an alienated and alienating church. A church which, having taken refuge in its ivory tower, did nothing but teach, would condemn itself to indifference and isolation. A pastorate based exclusively on traditional religious practices unrelated to day-to-day

---

19. Unlike the Québécois, the Portuguese are not in the habit of "swearing" (Cf. Chapter "Milieu of origin and receiving milieu"). Nevertheless, expressions of religious origin like: "vai com Deus" (God keep you); "até amanhã se Deus quizer" (God willing, I'll see you tomorrow); "meu Deus!" (my God!); "ai Jesus!" (oh, Jesus!); "Santíssimo Sacramento!" (Holy Sacrament!); "Nossa Senhora!" (Virgin Mary!), etc. are very popular. However, these words are used in a suitable context and are not expressions of disrespect.

life can indeed be regarded as an alienating factor or as an opium of the people. The traditional religious practice of the Portuguese of Montreal has already been described as both "a consequence of and a new factor in [...] alienation and resignation bordering on fatalism." [20]

The interest shown in offering religious guidance to the ethnic groups is certainly praiseworthy but also implies certain risks, not the least of which is that of encouraging parochialism, and thus favouring cultural marginalisation. The acquisition of a religious culture must not be synonymous with colonialist assimilation or with the perpetuation and systematic stagnation of atavistic values. "It is not enough to transplant a pastorate, a religious expression, regional devotions or even to tie people to the past through a nostalgia for what they have left behind in the village." [21]

The religious guidance offered to immigrants should neither isolate them on an island nor lose them on a continent. A pastorate conducted solely by members of the same ethnic group may be limited to transferring of cadres from the milieu or origin without adapting them to the new context. Conversely, a service improvised in local churches will not readily give way to new values.

Providing immigrants with religious guidance appears to us indispensable. However, in the process of acquiring a culture, the religious mission must serve as a bridge and not as a dam. When rites are conducted solely by the Portuguese clergy, in the Portuguese language, these rites gradually come to lose interest, especially for the second generation. In order for the religious mission to be a bridge, its piles must be built on both banks of the river. When religious services are conducted by a clergy from both

---

20. Centre portugais de référence et de promotion sociale. *Le groupe portugais à Montréal: la situation sociologique, La problématique et les lignes d'intervention,* (xeroxed document), Montreal, 1976, p. 7.

21. Azevedo, 1973, p. 82.

the milieu of origin and the receiving milieu, it will be possible to retain the immigrants' heritage and to guarantee continuity at the same time. It will then no longer be a question of transplanting the church from the milieu of origin or imposing the local church. Religious culture will be acquired in a spirit of harmony and not one of conquest.

The presence of immigrants is both an established fact and a test of the Catholicism which is regarded as a common trait of the Portuguese and Quebec peoples. As Pope Paul VI said, "immigrants facilitate mutual understanding and universal cooperation, thus contributing to the unity of the human family. They very clearly confirm the fraternal bonds between peoples insofar as both parties give and receive at the same time." [22] Pluralism and the coexistence of different cultures offer a challenge for religious doctrines. Respect for the uniqueness of cultures and fraternal communication between these cultures are consistent with the Christian principles shared by the majority of the Quebec people.

---

22.   Paul VI, *Pastoralis Migratorum Cura,* 1969, No. 2.

XIV

COMMUNITY ORGANISATIONS

The use of the expression "community" to designate the main Portuguese agglomerations in Quebec may be a source of controversy or even judged premature by some. Under certain aspects, the use of this expression nevertheless seems legitimate. The anthropologist Jorge Dias, whose thinking is very close to that of Robert Redfield, defines the community as "a local group made up of individuals living on a well-defined territory, who enjoy interpersonal relations and who share a common cultural heritage." [1] Ferdinand Tönnies, in *Gemeinschaft und Gesellschaft,* distinguishes between "community" and "society", emphasising that the primary characteristic of a community is a veritable life in common which is of a permanent nature, while the basic characteristic of a society is an apparent life in common which is of a temporary nature. While the community represents a living, spontaneous organism, society, on the other hand, is nothing more than a mechanical grouping of individuals living in an artificial situation which has been imposed on them. [2]

---

1.   Dias, 1961, pp. 39-40.

2.   Cf. Tönnies, in Jürgen Moltmann, *L'homme.* Paris: Le Cerf-Mame, 1974, p. 75.

For the purposes of this work, we shall define communities as groupings which have their own organisations, insofar as these latter are active and represent the collectivity. The adjective "community" is used to designate these organisations, because it is felt that their goals and in fact their very existence are indications of the community spirit which moves them forward.

Based on this definition of community, we would identify as such the Portuguese groups in Montreal, Hull, Ste-Thérèse, Laval and Quebec City. Here below, we shall offer a brief description of the community organisations and mass media, present or past, in each of these communities.

EXISTING COMMUNITY ORGANISATIONS

Below is a summary of the history and objectives of existing community organisations, listed in order of length of existence and size of the communities served.

MONTRÉAL

Official institutions

— *Consulate General of Portugal.* This Consulate first came into being on October 1, 1947. First located on rue Bishop, it later moved to rue l'Esplanade, in the area with the largest Portuguese population, then to rue Sherbrooke and finally, it moved from centretown and set up on Avenue de Maisonneuve (Westmount), following the events which marked the Portuguese political life of the early 1960s.

Coming under the jurisdiction of the Consulate General of Montreal, there is presently an honorary consulate in Quebec and other consulates in St. John's (Nfld), in Halifax (N.S.) and on the

French islands of St-Pierre and Miquelon. [3] The jurisdiction of the Montreal consulate extends to all of Quebec (with the exception of the Hull region), as well as to Newfoundland and Prince Edward Island. [4]

The functions of the consulate include consular protection, registration of births, marriages and deaths, notarising of documents, issuing of visas and authentication of documents relating to trade and navigation. [5] The consulate is also required to report to the Ministry of Foreign Affairs and to the Embassy in Ottawa. There are representatives of the Secretary of State for Emigration and of the Export Development Fund at the Consulate General in Montreal. [6]

— *Portuguese Tourist Bureau* — *Montreal Office.* This is a state agency attached to the Portuguese Ministry of Trade and Tourism. The Montreal office has been open since 1975 and it serves all of Quebec. This government agency has the specific aim

3. These data were provided by the Consultate General of Portugal in Montreal, following consultation with the Ministry of Foreign Affairs in Lisbon. This Ministry also mentions more or less regular consular activities in several parts of the Province of Quebec since the end of the 19th century: Chicoutimi (1893-1905); Gaspé (1896-1927); Montreal (1888-1947); Paspébiac (1888-1927); Quebec City (1888-1927); St-Étienne du Saguenay (1893-1905).

4. Since 1970-71, the Hull region has come under the Consular Section of the Portuguese Embassy in Ottawa. Up until very recently, the consular office in Port-au-Prince (Haiti) also came under the Consulate of Montreal.

5. "Red tape" seems to be one of the factors in the aversion and dislike shown by many Portuguese immigrants towards their consulate, whether it be the Montreal one or another. Former Consul Luís Augusto Martins (1971, p. 229) recommended that "the bureaucratic formalities of consular services be made as simple as possible so that emigrants will be more favourably inclined toward us".

6. The purpose of the Delegation of the Secretary of State for Emigration is to provide social assistance to Portuguese nationals, along with interpretation services and aid in dealing with Portuguese authorities.

of promoting Portuguese tourism among the local populations, and thus encourages closer ties between the Portuguese and Quebec peoples.

Associations

— *Portuguese Association of Canada.* Founded on January 7, 1956, it was one of the first Portuguese associations in Canada.[7] Though it began with only about twenty members, by 1978, this number had grown to 316. This association was originally set up to give immigrants the chance to meet one another. Its chief aim is to bring Portuguese nationals together by organising cultural, artistic, recreational and sports activities. The achievements of this association include the formation of a philharmonic orchestra, along with sports, folklore and theatre groups.[8]

— *"Santa Cruz" Portuguese Mission.* Officially opened in 1965, following a canonic decree of 1964, this is an extra-territorial ethnic parish, though coming under the jurisdiction of the Montreal diocese and the *Obra Católica Portuguesa de Migrações*. It was founded by a group of members of the Portuguese Catholic Union of Canada, an organisation dating back to 1956-57. At that time, the Portuguese Catholics gathered in Notre Dame Church, where religious services were conducted by a Quebec priest of the "Congrégation de St-Sulpice" aided by a Brazilian priest. In 1960, the Portuguese bishops, at the request of the Catholic Union, sent a

---

7. This organisation was brought into being by a Portuguese group initially formed to promote the study of French and English. In 1955, there was already thought of setting up an association, which materialised the next year. It had its first headquarters in a building situated at the corner of Sherbrooke and St-Laurent, and later moved to St-Laurent, between Prince Arthur and Avenue des Pins. The Association presently has its headquarters at rue St-Urbain, in a former synagogue.

8. The newspaper *O Luso-Canadiano,* which is no longer published, was founded by this association.

Portuguese priest (of the Franciscan order) to minister to the Portuguese of Montreal. At that time, Sunday Mass for the Portuguese was held in Notre-Dame Church and in the chapel of the Hôtel-Dieu. [9] In 1962, it was a Canadian priest of the Dominican order who ministered to the Portuguese. That year, Sunday Mass in Portuguese was also celebrated in the chapel of the "Soeurs du Bon Pasteur" (Sisters of the Good Shepherd), on rue Sherbrooke. By 1965, the mission was already set up and it was a Portuguese lay priest from Toronto who conducted religious services.

In December of 1964, a building situated on rue Clark was made available to the Portuguese by the Montreal Diocese. On February 16, 1977, the Catholic Mission of "Santa Cruz" purchased this building from the same diocese. Today, religious services are held both in the building on rue Clark and in Enfant-Jésus Church.

Besides religious services, the mission organises recreational and cultural activities, which include the operation of a Portuguese language school. [10]

— *Portuguese Democratic Movement of Montreal.* Founded in 1964 by about thirty people, it had 300 members in 1978, including several women, something which distinguishes it from other Portuguese organisations. [11] The now defunct "Casa dos Portugueses" was the precursor of this organisation. While in the

---

9. According to one of the persons we interviewed at the time, a statue of Our Lady of Fatima was brought to Notre Dame Church on October 13, 1958, on the initiative of the *Union catholique portugaise du Canada.* Today this statue still stands in the Santa Cruz Church (Clark St.). This was apparently the first religious celebration organised by the Portuguese immigrants of Montreal.

10. Affiliated with the "Santa Cruz" mission, there is a St-Vincent de Paul Society, which provides aid to the poor and the ailing needy within the Portuguese community.

11. Up to April 1974, the *Portuguese Democratic Movement of Montreal* was called *Portuguese Democratic Movement.*

beginning, the headquarters of the Portuguese Democratic Movement of Montreal was on rue St-Denis, it has now moved to rue St-Laurent. The aims of this association are essentially socio-political and cultural. It has to its credit the organisation of French courses, Portuguese classes for natives and literacy campaigns. [12] Since its foundation, this association has played a very active role within the community, following a political line which has become its imprint, especially in its stance vis-à-vis the political regime existing in Portugal up to April 25, 1974.

— *Portugal Club of Montreal.* It was founded in April 1965, on the initiative of some members of a sports group, who were also former members of the Portuguese Association of Canada. Today, it has close to two hundred members, most of whom belong to the working class. Its main activities are in the areas of recreation and sports and involve in particular the holding of parties and dances. [13] The Club has been located at rue Ste-Catherine, rue St-Laurent, rue Prince-Arthur and finally, rue St-Laurent, in that chronological order. [14]

— *Portuguese Folklore Group of Montreal.* Founded in 1966, this group is today made up of a few dozen young men and girls. The primary aim of this group is to encourage youth and help them to preserve Portuguese folklore, at the same time giving public performances.

— *Portuguese Pentecostal Church.* This was the name adopted in 1966 by a small group that met in the Italian Pentecostal Church. Since 1968, Sunday services have been conducted in the Ukranian Pentecostal Church, on rue St-Urbain.

---

12. For a few years, this group sponsored a Suzuki violin school for children.

13. A soccer group was connected with this association which, in the beginning, offered support for initiatives of a cultural type.

14. Efforts aimed at the merger of the *Portugal Club of Montreal* and the *Portuguese Association of Canada* have not yet borne fruit, given the difficulty of agreement on common interests and goals (Cf. *Jornal O Emigrante,* April 15, 1978, p. 9).

— *Portuguese Businessmen's Association of Quebec.* Founded in 1967 by a small group of Portuguese businessmen, the aim of this association is to help its members to invest their money profitably.

— *Portuguese Savings Cooperative of Montreal.* Its foundation, which dates back to 1969, is attributed to a group of Portuguese interested in the co-operative movement. This institution, which in 1979 had 2,000 members, has assets of about six million dollars, and is affiliated with the "Fédération des Caisses d'Économie du Québec". [15]

— *Montreal Luso-Stars.* This is a soccer team reorganised in 1971 by some former members of the Sporting Club Azores, later renamed the Montreal Luso Sporting. [16]

— *Portuguese Reference Centre.* Established in 1972, this centre's main purpose is to welcome and integrate new Portuguese immigrants, and it also organises cultural and recreational activities. It has offered French courses and literacy training and has an ongoing service to assist the Portuguese population.

— *Federation of Portuguese Organisations of Quebec.* This federation founded in 1974 includes a limited number of Portuguese organisations. It claims to represent the different organisations of the Portuguese ethnic group. [17]

---

15. "This bank was founded by a small group of Portuguese residing in Montreal who first met for the purpose of setting up a housing cooperative. However, after a few meetings, it was instead suggested that a savings bank be set up". (*Ma Caisse d'Économie* (Montréal), Vol. 3, No. 1, Spring 1979, p. 20).

16. This team, which is affiliated with the *Montreal Soccer Club,* is part of the *Quebec Major Soccer League Federation.* Although legally, it comes under the *Portuguese Association of Canada,* it nevertheless enjoys a certain autonomy.

17. It is to this federation that we owe the founding of the newspaper *A Voz do Imigrante* first published in 1975.

— *Portuguese Evangelical Church of the Pentecostal.* This church, which was founded in 1976, serves a small number of Portuguese Christians affiliated with the Pentecostal Church of Canada. Its religious activities consist essentially of religious services and Sunday school, which are held in a church situated on rue St-Dominique.

— *Portuguese-Quebec Cultural Centre.* Founded towards the end of 1976, and boasting autonomy vis-à-vis the different Portuguese organisations, its immediate aim is research on the Portuguese of Quebec.

— *Portuguese Theatrical Group of Montreal.* The activities of this group began in 1976 and its chief activity is the interpretation of Portuguese authors in the literary and artistic fields.

— *Portuguese Soccer League of Montreal.* Founded in August 1977, this league is made up of several amateur soccer teams representing Portuguese businesses.

— *Azores Club of Quebec.* This is an association established in 1978 for the purpose of making Azorean culture known to Canadians, and more particularly those of Quebec and Montreal. It also provides information on the Azores in general and helps Azorean immigrants to integrate into the new milieu.

— *Portuguese Oriental Club of Montreal.* It was recently founded in 1979. Purposes: sports and cultural activities.

Schools

— *School of the "Santa Cruz" Portuguese Mission.* Since 1965, this school, which comes under the Portuguese parish, offers Portuguese courses for children on Saturday during the school year. More than 600 pupils were enrolled during the academic year

245

1977-1978. Portuguese language and culture are taught outside the regular school curricula. [18]

— *"Português do Atlântico" Primary School.* Affiliated with the "Banco Português do Atlântico", it has been offering Portuguese courses to school-age children since 1972. During the academic year 1977-1978, 355 pupils were enrolled. [19]

— *Lusitanian Secondary School.* This school began operating in 1975-76 under the designation "Ensino secundário unificado". Some 60 pupils were enrolled during the academic year 1977-1978. While encouraging the study of the language and culture of origin, this school organises its programme so as to meet the requirements of the Portuguese Ministry of Education, something which facilitates schooling at the secondary level, both for students arriving in Quebec and for students returning to Portugal.

HULL

— *"Amigos Unidos" Portuguese Centre.* The Portuguese community of Hull has been gradually organising since the 1950s. From 1961 to 1965, the only Portuguese language religious services were provided by a priest residing in Kingston. In 1965, it got its own priest. In 1974, the Portuguese Catholic Mission of Hull aided in the establishment of the *"Amigos Unidos" Portuguese Centre,* which has as its aim to encourage unity among the Portuguese, offer them religious guidance, promote Portuguese culture and

---

18. This school receives financial support from the Ministry of Immigration of Quebec, the federal Secretary of State and the Portuguese Government.

19. This school not only is sponsored by the "Português do Atlântico" Bank, but also receives subsidies from the federal and provincial governments. In the beginning, it was linked with the *Portuguese Association of Canada.*

favour integration into the receiving milieu. [20] Some of the activities sponsored by this centre are:

Religious services — The religious services formerly held in St. Bernadette Church are now held in the community centre. It was in the basement of this church that the Portuguese first held meetings to organise celebrations for the feast of Our Lady of Fatima. As soon as the community centre was built, space was set aside for worship. In addition to Sunday Mass, catechism classes and other parish activities, two large annual feasts are also organised: the Feast of the Holy Ghost in summer and, on the first Sunday in September, the Feast of the Blessed Sacrament. The Christian community also publishes a weekly bulletin providing information on socio-cultural activities and religious matters.

Our Lady of Fatima Philharmonic Ensemble — Even though it is now part of the Centre, this music group preceded it. Ousted from several places because of too noisy rehearsals, the ensemble set up in a garage. Since the construction of the centre, it has had its own premises there.

Portuguese School of the Outaouais — The activities of this school, which comes under the "Amigos Unidos Portuguese Centre", began in 1976-1977. In 1978 the number of pupils taking courses in Portuguese language and culture totalled sixty. [21]

20. Construction of the headquarters on rue Front began in May 1974 and it was officially opened on December 15, 1974. The Portuguese community provided all the necessary manpower. We cannot but praise the spirit of mutual aid demonstrated and the danger incurred by workers who carried main beams weighing 1,200 kg to the top of the building, using only sweat and tears.

21. This school receives financial support from the Ministry of Immigration of Quebec and from the federal Secretary of State.

Unidos Soccer Team — Also forming part of the Community Centre, this sports group was founded on May 27, 1974. It comprised two teams: the senior team and the junior team, which are part of the Quebec League.

Among other socio-cultural activities of the "Amigos Unidos Portuguese Centre", we might mention the establishment, in 1975, of a theatre group and a folklore group made up of children and adults.

STE-THÉRÈSE

— *Ste-Thérèse Portuguese Association.* The idea of establishing an association, which took root within the community towards the end of 1973, only materialised in 1974. The aims of this association are social and cultural and sports-related and take into account both the culture of origin and that of the receiving milieu, with a view to effective integration and good co-operation with local institutions and groups. Within this association, there is a cultural committee responsible, among other things, for teaching activities. There is also a festivities committee responsible mainly for the annual celebrations in honour of St. Peter. We should also emphasise that there is a women's committee which works to promote women's participation in the life of the association. It is this committee which organises sports activities (volley-ball), fashion shows and manual craft competitions.

— *Bravos Sporting of Ste-Thérèse.* This sports group, which dates back to 1966, is now part of the "Ste-Thérèse Portuguese Association". It is in fact within this sports group that the idea of founding an association comprising several juvenile teams was born. Since 1971, the team *Bravos Sporting of Ste-Thérèse* has been part of the Metropolitan Soccer League.

— *School of the Ste-Thérèse Portuguese Association.* This is a new school, which began operating at the beginning of the

248

academic year 1977-1978, with 40 children attending. French and Portuguese courses designed for adults have been offered with the support of the Deux-Montagnes School Board and the Ministry of Immigration of Quebec.

LAVAL

— *Our Lady of Fatima Parish Association of Chomedey-Laval.* Founded in 1974, this association is the first Portuguese association in Laval. Its chief goals are to overcome the isolation of the Portuguese and to offer reasons and opportunities for encounters, while promoting the Portuguese culture. Among its other accomplishments, it has set up a Catholic mission for the Portuguese of Laval and organised annual festivities in honour of Our Lady of Fatima, the Blessed Sacrament and the Holy Ghost.

— *Saint-Esprit Laval Philharmonic Group.* Recently set up by the Portuguese community in Laval, this orchestra already boasts more than 30 musicians. The group is also known under the name of the "Portuguese Philharmonic Orchestra of Chomedey".

QUEBEC CITY

— *Portuguese Association of Quebec.* Founded in 1972 by a group of Portuguese, with special support from the Ministry of Immigration of Quebec, its immediate goals are to preserve the Portuguese culture and to facilitate integration into the Quebec milieu. This association does not have its own offices and limits itself mainly to recreational activities, given the low interest shown by most of the Portuguese population in the culture of their ethnic group.

DEFUNCT COMMUNITY ORGANISATIONS

From the beginning, in regions having large Portuguese communities, there was a poliferation of initiatives aimed at the creation of associations, often on an experimental and precarious basis. Some of these associations never did get beyond the stage of good intentions. Some people claim that, in certain cases, such associations served as a stage on which upstarts posing as leaders could strut about. We must however recognise that most of these initiatives did to a large extent reflect the real aspirations of the community. They were frequently a first step in the creation of other, more sophisticated organisations.

Here below, in alphabetical order, is an almost exhaustive list of community organisations which are now defunct and some historical notes concerning them:

TABLE 14-1

Quebec: Defunct Portuguese community organisations

Organisation	Historical information
Casa de Portugal	The *Casa de Portugal* had a very precarious existence.
Casa dos Portugueses	Organisation of a political type, it had its headquarters at rue St-Denis and later gave way to the *Portuguese Democratic Movement.*
Centro Cultural Português do Canadá	This centre owed its existence to persons connected with the magazine *Portinhola,* now also defunct.
Club Soccer de Montréal	Sports group which gave rise to the *Portugal Club of Montreal,* founded by dissidents of the *Portuguese Association of Canada.*
Luso Sporting de Montréal	This was a soccer group founded in 1969, which was so to speak a successor to the *Montreal-Stars* and the *Sporting Club Azores.*

Montreal-Stars	This soccer club, set up informally at Jeanne Mance Park, existed from 1965 to 1968. It formed part of the Quebec Junior League, where it became recognised as a champion, participating in several tournaments.
Movimento da Juventude Portuguesa de Montreal	Established in 1965 through the merger of a group of young girls called *The Optimists* and a group of young men called *Young Men's Club* both connected with the "Santa Cruz" Mission, this group remained more or less active up to 1975-76. It sought to meet the needs and aspirations of young people in socio-cultural, recreational and religious areas.
Grupo de Escuteiros Corte Real	This group was organised in 1959 and it was active up to 1970. Its main goal was to co-operate with parents in educating youth in the spirit of scoutism. It formed Scout Troop 163, affiliated with the Catholic Scouts of Montreal, and came under the Portuguese parish of "Santa Cruz".
Portuguese Canadian Community School	Linked to a former group known by the name of *União Católica Portuguesa do Canadá,* this was a small Portuguese school in Montreal. Founded in 1958, with a small number of pupils, it gave courses in the Jean-Jacques Olier School building.
Soccer Portugais du Québec	This was a semi-professional team set up in 1968 and financed by a group of Portuguese. The team only survived for one sports year.
Sporting Club Açores	Founded in 1966 by a group of Azoreans, its primary goal was the playing of soccer. It also worked to promote and preserve the culture of the Azores. Because its members became dispersed, this group ceased to exist in 1970.
União Caólica Portuguesa do Canadá	Established in the 1950s, it was concerned with solving the religious problems of the Portuguese community of Montreal. During the 1960s, the union had its headquarters in Notre Dame Church and published the bulletin *Ecclesia*. This organisation later gave birth to the Portuguese Mission of "Santa Cruz" and ceased to exist in 1962.

MASS MEDIA

As regards mass media, there have been several initiatives within the Portuguese community, some of them commercial in character, but most of them having aims of a socio-cultural nature. We shall first discuss the mass media in existence, to later deal with those which are now defunct.

EXISTING MEDIA

Newspapers

— *Voz de Portugal.* Founded as a successor to the bulletin *Ecclesia* of the Portuguese Catholic Union of Canada, it was published for the first time on April 25, 1961. [22] This newspaper was initially intended to reflect the views of the political regime then dominant in Portugal. The manifestations of discontent current at that time, such as the diversion of the Portuguese ship "Santa Maria", coincided with the appearance of this publication. Today, the priority aim of *Voz de Portugal* is to create bonds between the milieu of origin and the receiving milieu.

— *Voz do Imigrante.* Established in 1975 by the Federation of Portuguese Organisations of Quebec, its stated purpose was to "deal with the political confusion created by the Portuguese revolution of April 25, 1974".

— *Jornal O Emigrante.* Designed to serve Portuguese immigrants, this newspaper, which has appeared twice monthly since May 1977, is sponsored by the "Société de publications de Montréal".

---

22. This newspaper was printed first in Portugal, later in New York and finally in Montreal.

Radio and television

The Portuguese language radio and television programmes in Quebec are currently the following:

MONTREAL

— *Hora Portuguesa.* Sunday programme on radio station CFMB, of the commercial and community service type, it began in December 1962. In its broadcasts, emphasis is placed on matters of interest to the ethnic community and those relating to the culture of origin.

— *Portuguese Section of Radio Centre-Ville.* Daily programme of the community service type, which has been on the air since 1972. Its main purpose is that of assisting immigrants.

— *Radio Portugal de Montréal.* This programme, which started up in 1975, is broadcast by cable and is commercial in nature. At present, the programme time totals 40 hours per week, approximately 5 to 8 hours per day. It serves the Portuguese community, offering it news and football (soccer) direct from Portugal.

— *Télévision communautaire portugaise de Montréal.* A small group interested in communication media instituted this programme, which tries to help Portuguese immigrants to integrate into the receiving milieu. Programmes are televised by cable and are usually limited to fifteen minutes a week. [23]

HULL

— *Voz da Saudade.* This programme went on the air in 1973 and is broadcast on Sunday by radio station CIMP-FM. Commercial in nature, its aims is to promote Portuguese culture and provide information on the home country.

---

23. Other Portuguese programmes had been telecast earlier on this same channel under various names.

— *Portugal Presente.* This is a community service type programme telecast twice a week since 1973, on "Cablevision Laurentien".

DEFUNCT MEDIA

The proliferation of initiatives in this area is both the cause and the effect of the amateurism which characterised them and the absence of catalysing forces which might serve to prevent dissipation of effort. These factors, which make these initiatives no less praiseworthy, explain why very often, attempts have been made to impose quantity instead of quality, with the results which we all know.

Based on written documents and verbal information, we were able to compile the following list:

TABLE 14-2

Quebec: Portuguese media which have disappeared

Media	Historical information
Caravana	This was a cultural magazine with texts in Portuguese, French, English and Spanish.
Comunidade	This periodical, which was multilingual and informative, was published in Hull from 1973 to 1974.
Ecclesia	This bulletin, founded in 1960, was an organ of the Portuguese Catholic Union of Canada, and was the predecessor of the newspaper *Voz de Portugal.*
Ecos de Portugal	Radio programme broadcast by cable around the middle of the 1960's.
O Lusitano	Newspaper founded in 1964, on the initiative of dissident personnel of *Voz de Portugal.*

O Luso-Canadiano	Newspaper founded in 1958 and evolving out of the bulletin of the Portuguese Association of Canada, of which it was the press organ up to 1960. Once it broke its ties with the Association, it took on a clear political line vis-à-vis the regime in power in Portugal. It stopped publication in 1971.
Luso-Québécois	This was a cable T.V. programme started up in 1974 and was the successor of the programmes *Reflets du Portugal* and *Estamos no Quebec*.
Portinhola	Begun in 1970, this magazine was linked to the *Centro Cultural Português do Canadá* and published only three issues.
Reflets du Portugal	Begun in 1971 and telecast by National Cablevision, it was the first Portuguese T.V. programme in Quebec.
Tribuna Portuguesa	Newspaper founded in 1972 and which folded in 1974.

THE SITUATION AND THE PROBLEMS

The Portuguese are often accused of lacking community spirit and of being unable to get together on anything. Observing the emotional climate of some volunteer associations, one is inclined to share this view. It is important however to note that this accusation often ignores a deeper reality. As participant observers, we have in fact concluded that a large number of the Portuguese living in Quebec, belonging as they do to a social stratum with a low level of education, are in a state of "intransitive awareness" which, according to Paulo Freire, is particularly characterised by a polemic spirit. The emotional climate does not always favour common action. However, a proper understanding of this phenomenon should help those wishing to work disinterestedly for unity among and promotion of their fellow nationals.

255

Anderson and Higgs see the Portuguese communities of Canada as differentiated by class, politics and regionalism. [24] Iida-Miranda is of the opinion that "the main obstacles to veritable cohesion seem to lie in political differences and the diversity of regional origins." [25] According to the sociologist Breton, the Portuguese immigrant group shows a low capacity for social and institutional cohesion. [26] These factors are however more circumstantial than structural. The degree of participation and social cohesion seems to depend essentially on the level of awareness achieved by the Portuguese population, or any other population. According to a former Consul of Portugal in Toronto, "in spite of the efforts to set up an organisation of the federative type able to unite and represent the entire Portuguese community, the results up to now are frankly discouraging. The reasons for this failure perhaps lie in the individualistic temperament of the Portuguese, in the ambition of certain "leaders" who place their personal interests above those of the community, and in the diversity of regional origins of our emigrants". [27]

On the other hand, individualism and the absence of community spirit are not peculiar to the Portuguese ethnic group. Castelli has this to say about the Italians in Montreal: "We are distressed to find an almost total lack of interest in everything which concerns the community, other individuals, political, religious or social problems, entertainment, etc." Unfortunately, the most common remark is: 'mind your own business and let others mind theirs' ". [28]

---

24. Anderson and Higgs, 1976, p. 153.

25. Iida-Miranda, 1975, p. 84.

26. Cf. Breton, 1964.

27. Martins, 1971, pp. 227-228.

28. Cf. Giuseppe Castelli, *La fête patronale italienne,* Université de Montréal, Département de théologie, 1974, p. 5.

Based on the survey for the "Projet communautaire Pilote A", which covered several ethnic groups established in Montreal, we were able to compile the follow table:

TABLE 14-3

**Degree of yearly sharing of activities with
other individuals of the same nationality**

Type of activity	Yearly participation by families					
	Never		From 1 to 5 times		15 times or more	
	Total	Portuguese	Total	Portuguese	Total	Portuguese
Encounters with neighbours speaking the same language	52%	12%	36%	65%	12%	23%
Activities of own ethnic group or association within the community	86%	70%	13%	24%	1%	6%
Activities of own ethnic group or association outside the community	90%	82%	10%	12%	0%	6%

Source: *A Survey and an Action Plan for "Projet communautaire Pilote A"*, 1976, p. 72.

The table which precedes suggests that participation by the Portuguese group is quite encouraging. The claim that the Portuguese is an individualist may be only partly true. It is true that he is generally reticent when asked to enter into "gesellschaft" type relations, which place him in a impersonal, complex type of society. However, he is particularly altruistic in the "gemeinschaft" type relations which are closer to his daily life. This can perhaps help to explain the paradox which we find in the Portuguese communities of Quebec: while, on the one hand, the majority is little disposed to participate actively in the new society, on the other, mutual assistance within their own ethnic group is quite phenomenal.

The presence of conflicts within organisations is not necessarily a reflection on the population in general. These conflicts are often created by "pseudo-leaders" and are not everyday fare within the Portuguese community, which is generally peaceful, long-suffering and sometimes indifferent. One may be led to dramatise this situation because of fears and prejudices and not because of any desire to provide solutions. The conclusion of the Ministry of Immigration of Quebec is quite telling: "The ethnic communities, rent by internal strife and unable to act as serious, competent, representative spokesmen to government because they lack direction and cohesion, have the distinct impression of being left out of things and fear becoming the third solitude." [29]

It would be astonishing if there were no problems within any group of individuals. However, it is important to emphasise that the most serious misunderstandings result from conflicts of interest or of ideology among leaders who seek to obtain the support of both government and the masses. Therefore, a distinction should be made between what is rule and what is exception. [30]

---

29. Québec. Ministère de l'Immigration. Comité consultatif de l'immigration du Québec. *L'immigration québécoise et les communautés ethniques.* Minutes of the colloquium held on June 4 and 5, 1977, p. 31.

30. By way of example, we would cite the lack of preparation and the audacity of some pseudo-leaders of the Portuguese community who in no way represented the community but who, either through their actions or through written articles, were able to compromise their community, especially when outside observers took to be a rule what in reality was only an exception.

True leadership may be regarded as basic and essential to the affirmation and progress of any human group, and this is especially true in the case of immigrants. It must be recognised that lack of leadership is in effect one of the most serious problems of the Portuguese community and one of its weaknesses. Within the different associations and in contacts with individuals and groups outside the community, not only is it difficult to find leaders who are both competent and available, but it is also impossible to prevent certain leaders from neutralising one another in their internal rivalries.

According to the former Consul whose views on the Portuguese of Canada are cited above, the community life of Portuguese immigrants is undermined by the proliferation of small clubs and associations, by their lack of cohesion, and by the limited financial means made available to them to carry out large-scale projects. [31]

The aims of almost all the Portuguese organisations in Quebec seem to centre around transmission of the culture of origin and adaptation to the new milieu, among adults. The limited resources allotted to serve young people are a well known fact.

In the binomial made up of the mass media and the public, the low appeal of the communication media and the lack of interest and co-operation shown by a part of the Portuguese population seem to become a vicious circle. What is needed is an appeal to the true values of the community to promote effective leadership and real representation and a united effort which can bring this community to affirm itself both as a community and as part of the receiving milieu.

Looking at the aims and the accomplishments of the different Portuguese organisations in Quebec, we must admit that almost all of them reflect a humanitarian community spirit. Even if all their

---

31.   Martins, 1971, p. 227.

goals have not been achieved, this detracts nothing from their good intentions. The role of community organisations in the social integration of individuals and groups is well known. They help friendships to develop, vehicle ideologies and polarise interests. Ethnic associations are necessary and must be preserved and encouraged. It seems nevertheless advisable to promote exchanges and relations among different ethnic groups, because this is essential to mutual adaptation and is also a means of combatting ethnocentrism.

The government of Quebec is undecided as to the significance and the merits of the ethnic organisations established in this province: "We must say that it is difficult, without more in-depth study, to determine the exact importance of all the ethnic associations presently existing in Quebec. Certain persons judge them negatively because it is felt that they serve to delay the integration of immigrants into Quebec society. We believe on the contrary that a large number of them greatly assist immigrants over the difficult period of adaptation to our society, while helping them to retain a feeling of pride in their origins. In this sense, they play a very positive role among immigrants and within Quebec society." [32]

---

32. *Annuaire du Québec,* 1974, p. 284.

PART FOUR

REALITIES
AND
EXPECTATIONS

XV

AN ATTEMPT AT TYPOLOGY

While recognising the value of the different typologies of migrations, we must also be aware of their limitations. When confronted with a particular instance of migration, we may find that certain existing typologies are inadequate or that no applicable typology can be found.

Any typology must be designed *a posteriori*, and take its inspiration from the elements which it aims to characterise and distinguish. When a population is classified on the basis of an existing typology, one runs the risk of squeezing reality into too tight a framework. This is why we are offering some relatively new typologies with the risks inherent in "creativity". Based on the factors analysed, we arrived at a certain classification of types of immigration encountered and of types of Portuguese immigrants in Quebec.

Types of immigration

— *Admission of immigrants* — Based on the ways in which immigrants are admitted, we identified the following three types: *informal, formal,* and *selective.* The first type, which was common up to the end of the last century, equated with free access to Canada for all those who wished to settle here. [1] The formal type immigration that followed was regulated by fairly liberal legislation. Immigration of the selective type, which dates back to 1967, is characterised by a point system applied to prospective immigrants, and is more strictly regulated.

In the particular case of the Portuguese of Quebec, we might conclude that immigration of the informal type has been very limited, while that of the formal type has been quite common. However, most of the present Portuguese population of Quebec has in fact been admitted under the system of selective immigration. [2]

— *Number of admissions* — Based on the number of admissions, we may distinguish two types of immigration: *sporadic* and *massive*. While the former is characterised by occasional admissions, the latter involves a collective phenomenon of a certain magnitude.

From the age of the discoveries up to the middle of our century, Portuguese emigration to Quebec had been an occasional phenomenon. Beginning at that time, it became a mass movement.

— *Type of settlement* — As regards immigrant settlement, we consider two modalities: *concentrated* and *scattered*. Close to 90% of the Portuguese population in Quebec is concentrated in urban centres, and scattered settlement is therefore very limited. [3]

— *Social structures* — Based on the social structure of the milieu or origin and that of the receiving milieu, we may consider

---

1. There have however been exceptions to this rule, for instance the barriers raised to Chinese immigration (Cf. Chapter XII - "Legislation and Policy").

2. See Chapter III - "Historical Background".

3. See Chapter IV - "Places of Settlement".

them either *identical* or *different*. In our opinion, Portuguese immigration to Quebec involves adaptation to a different social structure.[4]

— *Length of stay* — According to the length of stay in the receiving milieu, we would distinguish *temporary* immigration and *permanent* immigration. The latter term may be applied to 95% of the Portuguese immigrants received by Quebec, insofar as they settle permanently in that province.

Based on the foregoing, we would offer the following summary.

TABLE 15-1

Typology of the Portugal-Quebec migratory movement

Area	*Type*
— Admissions of candidates	— Informal — Formal — Selective
— Number of admissions	— Sporadic — Massive
— Type of settlement	— Concentrated — Scattered
— Social structure	— Identical — Different
— Length of stay	— Temporary — Permanent

---

4. The typology of Heberle (1956) distinguishes between migrations which do not affect social relations and those which imply adaptation to a new social structure. The colonisation of Canada is considered an example of the first type of migration, while Portuguese immigration to Quebec involves a transition to a different social structure.

REALITIES AND EXPECTATIONS

Types of immigrants

— Time of settlement — Looking at the settlement of Portuguese throughout time, we are led to propose a distinction between *pioneers* and *contemporaries*. [5]

We regard as pioneers all those who settled in Quebec from the age of the discoveries up to the end of the 19th century. Among the pioneers, we may further distinguish between those who have been *identified* and those who remain *unknown*. We have identified some pioneers and more thorough research could uncover more. [6] The category of unknowns includes, among others, the various seamen, fishermen, mercenaries and adventurers who settled in Quebec in olden times, and whose identity and number remain a question mark.

We regard as contemporaries all those who arrived since the beginning of our century. Among the contemporaries, we may further distinguish the *dispersed*, the *founders*, and the *consolidators*.

Falling into the category of the dispersed are those who, because of their small numbers or their isolation, have had neither the opportunity to form or belong to an ethnic group nor any interest in doing so. Necessarily forming part of this category are the limited number of Portuguese who settled in Quebec during the first half of the 20th century.

All those who have had the initiative and the opportunity to establish community organisations in the receiving milieu merit the name of founders. Many of them belong to the waves of immigrants admitted to Quebec in the 1950s. [7]

---

5. See Chapter III - "Historical Background".

6. See "The genealogy of the founding peoples", in Chapter III.

7. The first contingents of that time were made up mainly of individuals with a low level of schooling, recruited in rural areas and destined for work in the fields. In a search for better working conditions, they moved little by little to the urban centres where, thanks to their spirit of initiative, they laid the foundations of the main Portuguese communities today existing in Quebec.

266

The immigrants who have arrived since the beginning of the 1960s may be regarded as consolidators. Welcomed by those whom we have called founders, they encountered Portuguese organisations already in the process of formation. Most of the Portuguese population of Quebec falls into this category.

— *Classification of applicants* — The Canadian government has established a classification of prospective immigrants based on the following categories: *independent, nominated* and *sponsored*.

The point system in force being very strict, only a small percentage of Portuguese immigrants belong to the independent category. Most of the Portuguese in Quebec have been admitted as nominated or sponsored immigrants.

— *Type of occupation* — We may distinguish four general sectors of employment into which the occupations of immigrants fall. These are *unskilled* workers, *specialised* workers, *entrepreneurs* and *professionals*.

Coming under the category of unskilled workers are all those who do lack a particular skill or trade, as well as those who work at jobs outside their speciality. They are characterised by high mobility, the holding of more than one job and low remuneration. A high percentage of the Portuguese of Quebec fall into this category of workers; they are particularly visible in the service sector, where there is a high predominance of female labour.

Classified as specialised workers are those individuals who are recognised as having a special skill, whether acquired in the place of origin or in the place of residence. Work in this sector is stable and well paid, which encourages a certain social mobility. The criteria used in this classification are often arbitrary; nevertheless, we can include a large segment of the male population in this category.

Considered to be entrepreneurs are those individuals who act as middlemen within their ethnic group. They have an unquestionable influence on the community and may either serve the interests of the population or exploit this same population. In the Portuguese case, this sector is made up of individuals whose level of schooling is generally above the average for the Portuguese population and who have a working knowledge of the official languages, all of which facilitates their task as go-betweens. We find them in several areas of endeavour, but mainly in business.

The professional group is normally comprised of persons practicing the liberal professions. By definition, the members of this group have a university degree and are a minority in all societies. Among the Portuguese of Quebec, this group is especially small, something which is readily understandable given the conditions in the milieu of origin. The second generation, which has had more advantages, may however increase Portuguese representation within the professional ranks.

— *Legal status* — To the extent that the admission of immigrants is covered by some type of legislation, we may conclude that there are two types of status under law, which implies a distinction between *legal* and *clandestine* immigrants.

Although clandestine immigration is difficult to calculate, it is nevertheless realistic to assume the presence of a certain number of illegal immigrants. [8] However, they are the exception and not the rule. Consequently, we must regard the vast majority of the Portuguese in Quebec as legal immigrants.

— *Level of awareness* — Paulo Freire uses the following terminology to describe level of awareness: intransitive, transitive

---

8. In 1973, the Canadian government took a look at the situation of illegal immigrants and encouraged them to legalise their status through the "My Country" campaign. For further in-depth study of illegal immigration, see Anderson 1971.

naive and transitive critical. Following closely on this nomenclature, we would propose the following typology: *alienated* awareness, *aroused* awareness, *informed* awareness.

The first type implies a state of alienation in terms of the dialectic relationship between man and his environment. This state is characterised by an imperviousness to problems which go beyond those of biological survival and by a magical and mediational interpretation of events. The low level of schooling and the obscurantism which have plagued the Portuguese population mean that the state of awareness of a certain percentage of these immigrants is still of the alienated type.

Aroused awareness goes hand in hand with a simplistic perception of problems and is characterised by vague, generalised reasoning, explanations which have something of the magical, a large dose of emotionalism, feeble arguments, a predominance of polemics over dialogue and premature solutions. This state of awareness is frequently associated with a certain inferiority complex and sometimes with a penchant for exhibitionism. We find tendencies towards assimilation into the "grey masses" and a spirit of "follow the leader". We have the impression that a large percentage of the Portuguese of Quebec have not progressed very far beyond this level.

Informed awareness lies at a higher level and these individuals have overcome the processes of alienation and achieved a sense of identity. The specific characteristics of this level of awareness are, among others: replacement of magical explanations by a knowledge of real causes, identification of the problems, predominance of dialogue over polemics and solid arguments. At this level of informed awareness, there is an openness to innovations and a recognition of the values of the past. This phase being the result of a slow process of evolution, it is not astonishing that a large majority of these immigrants have not yet achieved it.

— *Links with the ethnic group* — Based on immigrants' ties with their ethnic community, we have distinguished the following types: *merged, casual* and *isolated*. We would describe as merged those immigrants who have almost daily contact with their ethnic group. Given the type of concentrated settlement which predominates among the Portuguese of Quebec, we must include most of them in the merged category. [9]

We would classify as casual the ties of those who normally live outside the community but who remain linked to it, either because they serve it or because it serves them. We include under this designation a certain number of Portuguese who are interested in the life of the associations or who are entrepreneurs.

The term isolated applies to those far removed from their ethnic group, whether this distance be physical or psychological. Such isolation may be forced or voluntary. The Portuguese scattered throughout Quebec and geographically separated from their ethnic group belong to this category. Those who, while being physically close to their ethnic communities, do not maintain contacts with them, also belong to this same category. We have in mind a small number of individuals of bourgeois or pseudo-bourgeois origins, who have never felt motivated to join their ethnic group, and others who have placed a distance between it and them for other reasons.

— *Degree of integration* — Since the integration of immigrants into the new milieu is a gradual process, we feel it is important to establish a typology relating to it. [10]

Here we distinguish four categories: *assimilating, assimilated, integrating,* and *integrated*. Regarded as assimilating are those who are in a state of anomie in relation to the values of origin. The

9. See Chapter IV - "Places of Settlement".
10. See our Introduction and Chapter VI - "Factors in Adaptation".

assimilated are those in whom these values have been replaced by those of the adopted culture. When immigrants attempt to preserve their culture, while adapting to that of the new milieu, we may say that they are in the process of integrating. When they have succeeded in reconciling the culture of origin with that of the receiving milieu, they must be considered to have in fact become integrated.

— *Family roots* — In discussing the Portuguese of Quebec, it is normal to include not only the immigrants who have arrived recently, but also the Quebecers whose ancestors were offspring of the Portuguese immigrants of bygone days. The different processes and circumstances of acculturation lead us to distinguish *first generation, second generation* and *descendants*.

Those who originally came from abroad belong to the first generation. Their children comprise the second generation, while those of subsequent generations are considered simply to be Quebecers of Portuguese descent.

First generation Portuguese immigrants are today very numerous in Quebec, due to quite recent large-scale immigration. The second generation is increasing in numbers in the natural course of events. Among those classified as descendants, we must include all Quebecers who are descended from Portuguese pioneers and, in future, all those whose Portuguese origins extend beyond the second generation.

Following is a table prepared as an attempt to classify the Portuguese immigrants of Quebec.

TABLE 15-2

Typology of Portuguese immigrants in Quebec

Area	*Terminology*

— Time of settlement	— Pioneers
	   — Identified
	   — Unknown
	— Contemporaries
	   — Dispersed
	   — Founders
	   — Consolidators

— Classification of applicants	— Independent — Nominated — Sponsored
— Type of occupation	— Unskilled — Specialised — Entrepeneurs — Professionals
— Legal status	— Legal — Clandestine
— Level of awareness	— Alienated — Aroused — Informed
— Links with the ethnic group	— Merged — Casual — Isolated
— Degree of integration	— Assimilating — Assimilated — Integrating — Integrated
— Family roots	— First generation — Second generation — Descendants

*   *   *

We feel that the typologies just proposed could prove useful to persons wishing either to gain knowledge of the Portuguese ethnic community or to typify immigrants belonging to this group.

Before planning or starting up any activity whatsoever, these classifications should be taken into account, in order to have the best possible grasp of the Portuguese ethnic reality.

Given the dynamic nature of history and of society, it would be wrong to let these tentative typologies become an absolute or static model. They are intended simply as a term of reference and as a starting point.

XVI

HOPES AND PROSPECTS

For the immigrant, entry into Quebec is not a simple anticlimax to an adventure. Living in a new milieu calls for acculturation, which is a more or less lengthy and complex process. Having left a culture with which he identified, and finding himself immersed in a new one, the immigrant lives through a period of transition, when it is not easy for him to meet the imperative of adopting new values while still retaining those he brought with him. If settlement is to be permanent, the acculturation process becomes still more vital and draws on all the immigrant's resources.

In the case of the Portuguese of Quebec, immigration is almost always seen as a temporary experience and not as a final solution. However, concrete circumstances usually intervene to alter the initial plans. In fact, when plans are made to emigrate, there is ordinarily an implicit intention of returning. In practice, however, this intention of returning soon gives way to the hope of returning "some day", finally yielding to the imperative of remaining permanently.

The determinant factors which contribute to this decision almost always include: the guarantees offered in Quebec, the higher standard of living, the children's familiarity with the new milieu and the degree of socio-cultural integration achieved. The decision to settle permanently may be a more painful one for the immigrant than was the original decision to emigrate. This is part of the agony of living in one place while one's heart is in another.

Though he has moved to a country with a different culture, the immigrant continues to identify with his culture of origin, which he is called upon to transmit in a climate that does not always favour a complementarity of values.

Within the confines of his family, the immigrant generally is able to maintain an atmosphere which permits him to feel quite at home. But it is up to the receiving milieu to create a social climate which will also enable the immigrant to feel at home in his new country, recognising his right to his own identity based on the values of his origin, but without allowing this to become a source of discrimination in any form.

The immigrant established in Quebec is, generally speaking, far from meriting the derogatory epithets of mercenary and foreigner. Once he adapts to the society to which he has decided to entrust his children, he makes a double contribution in the work he performs and in the culture he transmits.

It would be utopian to idealise immigration and to view it as a social panacea that offers ideal solutions without creating any con- comitant problems. The presence of new immigrants gives rise to specific problems which test the ingenuity and the good will of those who arrive and of those who receive the new arrivals.

Most problems inherent in the immigrants' new situation fall within the hierarchy of basic needs described by Abraham Maslow (1970), namely: physiological drives and problems of survival, safety drives, belongingness and love drives, esteem drives and self-actualisation drives. [1]

Participant observation has afforded us close contacts with the Portuguese population of Quebec, and permits us to state that this population is generally well accepted, which speaks highly both for the Portuguese capacity to adapt, and for the humanitarian spirit of the receiving society.

Some Quebecers will point to the happy expression on Portuguese faces and to their friendly smile. [2] Others emphasise the characteristic "saudade" which seems to mirror a homesickness and a state of malaise. The immigrant's happiness depends both on the inner strengths he has brought with him and on accomodations provided him by the receiving milieu. One should not attribute his sometimes obvious discontent to feelings of frustration, but rather to the difficulties inherent in his ideal of improving his status and guaranteeing his future.

There are numerous testimonies of the Portuguese ethnic group's ability to integrate. However, this ability is not sufficient to guarantee acculturation and there are other factors to be considered. On the one hand, the concomitant presence of different ethnic groups may make a cultural pseudo-synthesis of the melting pot type seem desirable. On the other hand, the fact that a group

---

1. One of Grace Anderson's informants made a striking comment about the Portuguese community of Toronto: "The issues that are really important, essential and useful to the community are: how to get work; how to learn English; how to get more education; how to qualify as a skilled worker, how not to be exploited by travel agents; how to get correct information about immigration laws; and how to survive in a different and often hostile society" (Anderson, 1974, p. 183).

2. Human warmth is the first quality which the immigrant looks for. We might say metaphorically that the coldness of the climate causes less of a shock than the coldness and insensitivity of people. The pen of Rodrigues (1976, p. 219) expresses the immigrant's disappointment in a few poignant words: "But what are they made of, these people? Dollars, machines and ice!"

forms an absolute majority gives it certain advantages and makes it tempting for the dominant culture to become a dominating one.

Without advocating defensive attitudes, we must however encourage critical evaluation, to be able to distinguish between progressive integration and regressive integration. The former is evolutionary in nature and leads to social acculturation. The latter is an involutional process ending in cultural assimilation and implies a disappearance of the values of origin.

The Portuguese presence in Quebec cannot be dissociated from the specific values of the milieu of origin, which are destined to become an integral part of the cultural heritage of the receiving milieu. Insofar as acculturation does not consist in the winning over of one culture to another, but rather implies a goal common to all the cultures involved, the situation of the Portuguese ethnic group ceases to be a special case and can be situated within a more general framework.

This study has attempted to show the Portuguese of Quebec as they really are and to identify those factors which facilitate or hinder their participation in the common goal of socio-cultural integration.

Immediate goals

Without losing sight of the ultimate goal to be achieved through acculturation of the Portuguese in the different spheres of Quebec life, we shall now propose a number of immediate goals expressed either as plans or as hopes.

Family environment — As regards the family unit, we must point out that the traditional Portuguese family tends to be maintained in the receiving society. The desirability of reconciling traditional values with the requirements and the pace of life of the new milieu suggest the following immediate goals:

—To lessen the generation conflict, which tends to become more severe as the contrast between country of origin and country of residence reveals itself. The gaps between standards and values must be narrowed, through a rapprochement of the first and second generations in the socialisation process.

—To view traditional values in a dynamic and complementary framework, to prevent both disacculturation and isolation.

—To encourage the harmonious development of couples, attempting to reach a compromise in the rapid evolution of the immigrant woman's role and the persistence of the phenomenon known as "machismo".

—To devote particular attention to young people, who lack suitable activities and space to engage in them.

—To overcome the isolation and lack of social support experienced by the elderly.

Educational environment — The educational area is as vast as it is important. The majority of community initiatives revolve more or less directly around it. While applauding the efforts and the achievements in this sector, we must recognise the factors which tend to limit progress. Following are some aspirations which might translate into goals:

—To combat the tendency toward cultural assimilation, through a policy of true multiculturalism.

—To encourage activities of a multi-ethnic type and promote language teaching as a means of gaining access to other cultures.

—To favour cultural expression, especially as regards creativity and the arts.

—To help parents to follow their children's school progress, so that they will encourage these children to continue their schooling.

—To train cadres qualified to teach the Portuguese language, emphasising both the professional competence of the teachers and a high quality of instruction.

—To make teachers aware of the particular problems of immigrant students in their classes.

—To promote continuing education for adults.

Manpower sector — Here, we should say at the outset that the hard-working qualities of Portuguese immigrants are generally known. One might say that they make it a point of honour to earn their living honestly. Their presence on the labour market nevertheless brings with it various problems which range from vocational training to unions, and include such things as exploitation through low wages.

—As regards vocational training, it appears essential to provide training and upgrading courses to permit more immigrants to qualify as specialised workers.

—As regards remuneration, it appears urgent to deal with all forms of exploitation of human labour. [3]

—Also related to the working world is the union movement, which is sometimes as complex and arbitrary as the management sector. The immigrant worker must begin to participate fully and directly, if he does not wish to be manipulated by one or the other of these forces.

---

3. Just consider for a moment the working conditions of female labour, the early placement of children on the labour market and the excessively long working hours; all these are facets of the process which channels immigrant workers into the "cheap labour" sectors.

Use of leisure time — If we accept the principle that the immigrant is not just a production machine, it is by providing him with leisure time and helping him to fill it profitably that we can enable him to develop as a human being and to participate in community life. In this area, the Portuguese group appears to lack direction and encouragement, especially as regards the following:

—Organising leisure time activities of a cultural type.

—Finding suitable places for fraternising.

—Providing green spaces and premises designed for leisure, particularly in areas with a high population density.

—Planning and good use of vacations.

—Promoting physical culture and amateur sport, both indoor and outdoor.

Health and welfare — Once he has left the milieu of origin which was familiar to him, the immigrant must cope not only with the effort required by his work, but also with problems of adaptation to his new environment and with his working, family and social responsibilities, all of which combined frequently brings about a situation of stress. Knowing the importance of health to the immigrant's feeling of security and the hazards to which this health is exposed, it is essential that we make him aware of the problems and offer him support in this area. In particular, priority must be given to helping immigrants to:

—Make systematic use of preventive medicine.

—Know what they have a right to demand in terms of healthy working premises and accident prevention.

—Strike a balance between hours of work and well-earned rest.

—Find doctors, nursing personnel and social workers familiar with their language and with their specific problems.

The economic context — We have discussed the way in which migrations are regulated by essentially economic factors, thus making immigration a function of the labour market. At the same time as they attempt to use the immigrant as cheap labour, those who wield economic power also create consumer needs which lead him to extend his working hours to put aside savings, in the hope of improving his purchasing power. The immigrant thus risks sacrificing his being to a cult of material possessions. Given the dangers inherent in this situation, emphasis must be placed on the following goals:

—Encouraging the immigrant to define the meaning of money within a context of other values, including work.

—Counselling effective use of the savings put aside, preferably in community-type investments.

—Denouncing the system which tends to see the immigrant solely as a producer and a consumer.

The political context — The migratory process is directly linked to interests and decisions of a political nature, both national and international. Not only does the immigrant run the risk of becoming a pawn in a political game, he is also frequently incapable of recognising alienating processes and of defending himself against them. Because of this situation, certain goals become more immediate. These include:

—Providing basic political education, to enable immigrants to situate ideologies and events within their true context.

—Taking a stand for a less defensive and more humane immigration policy in Quebec and one that is truly multicultural in its aims. [4]

—Neutralising the improvised, immature militancy of certain individuals who, working at loggerheads with the community, manage to discredit political causes which may in themselves be valid.

—Providing effective Portuguese representation at different levels of government.

—Helping the Government of Portugal to improve its present emigration policy, which is more or less limited to a fascination with the foreign currency poured into the country's coffers by Portuguese living abroad. [5]

---

4. "Quebec immigration policy attempts to favour the harmonious integration of immigrants into the Francophone majority. But it appears difficult to discern this intention in practice. Too often, the immigrant asks himself whether the government wants to integrate him or assimilate him" (Québec. Ministère de l'Immigration. Comité consultatif de l'immigration au Québec, 1977, p. 4). See also Jacques Couture, "Voeux du ministre", in *Québec-Monde* (Dec. 1978), No. 34, p. 1.

5. So long as the facts seem to indicate that the Motherland cares only about the profits coming from her emigrants, and does nothing to show them her appreciation and her support, it is probable that it will continue to be called the "Stepmotherland" (See A. Barqueiro, in *Voz de Portugal* (Montreal), January 17, 1970, p. 1).
    Today, more than one quarter of the Portuguese population lives outside that country. If Portugal wants to develop channels able to capture and disseminate the voice of this throng, she must adopt guidelines and measures which take into account the reality lived by these immigrants as well as their expectations. Otherwise, they will lose any interest they have in their culture of origin and in the government which represents it.
    The Portuguese immigrants of Quebec would like their governments to take steps to establish agreements on, among other things, cultural exchange, recognition of school and university credits, promotion of workers, double nationality, investment of capital, support to community projects and old age pensions.

Religious expression — Religious expression is a trait which identifies Portuguese culture, both in the milieu of origin and in the receiving milieu. The claim that immigrants have traded their religious ideal for a worship of the almighty dollar seems exaggerated, at least in the case of the Portuguese. In a climate which favours its disappearance, religion is nevetheless maintained and, in some cases, is enhanced as a means of preserving cultural identity.

In religious matters, the greatest danger seems to lie in the lack of cohesion between religion and real life and in an attachment to expressions of the past which disregard the requirements of the present. In order that ethnic churches may free themselves of their present ritualism and isolation, the following pastoral approaches should be envisaged:

—Helping believers to go beyond religious individualism and systematic attachment to traditional rites and ceremonies.

—Giving priority to religious instruction for adults, to bring these latter to an informed, responsible and socially committed faith.

—Drawing the attention of local churches to the presence of immigrants and the need for a framework and programmes to permit their direct involvement, based on the principle that the future is as important as the past in the lives of these immigrants.

—Urging religious authorities to take into account the opinions and the needs of the ethnic communities when training and appointing priests, or establishing and replacing pastoral groups.

Community action — The intensity of community life and the forms it takes may serve as a gauge of the dynamism of a population. Using this criterion, the numerous initiatives coming from the

Portuguese group can be taken as a sign of its vitality. However, in making value judgments concerning these initiatives, we must also distinguish between quantity and quality. Most aspirations aim at an improvement in quality. Here are the principal ones:

—Urging the Portuguese population to take an interest in the life of the associations and in the socio-cultural level of these associations.

—Identifying the real leaders and neutralising the actions and the opportunism of pseudo-leaders.

—Encouraging professionalism in the Portuguese mass media and in community workers.

—Developing a financing policy which will enable organisations to cope with a scarcity of means, a climate of insecurity, a state of immobility and the ambiguities arising out of the use of volunteers and dependence on subsidies.

—Establishing an umbrella organisation which is truly representative of the interests of the Portuguese communities.

The paths of acculturation — As we already said, Portuguese emigration to Quebec tends to be characterised by permanent settlement. The long-term presence of immigrants in the adopted country is an incentive to combine efforts to bring about their integration. The acculturation process threatens to be retarded and discredited if we fail to take into account the values of the respective cultures and if we neglect the means available to promote these values. If we wish to have the Portuguese of Quebec become full citizens of Canada, the following deserve special attention:

—Persuading immigrants to avoid attitudes and behaviours of an ethnocentric type.

—Encouraging the established populations to receive their immigrants openly, making them aware of the pitfalls inherent in xenophobia.

—Helping immigrants to gain an awareness of and to affirm their own ethnic values, to prevent a state of anomie from developing in these immigrants.

—Developing a sense of complementarity of values in the different groups so that the acculturation process does not degenerate into assimilation or disacculturation.

The goals proposed reflect essentially what we were able to identify as the factors most likely to influence the acculturation of the Portuguese ethnic group. Without a doubt, responsible persons in each area will be able to make use of them to arrive at more specific objectives as they plan their activities.

Prospects for acculturation

To recognise and proclaim the typical values of a culture is not enough. It is also essential to adapt to concrete situations, if we are to implant these values. In any effort to achieve acculturation, the values of the milieu of origin deserve equal attention and there is no way in which they may be subordinated.

The permanence and stability of the cultural values which typify the new milieu are not easily threatened by the admission of minority groups. These latter groups, on the other hand, when represented by a deprived, dependent population, have difficulty in asserting their own values and in escaping cultural assimilation. True integration implies a socio-cultural symbiosis open to all values, and which eventually will become a common heritage.

Even the nomenclature used to describe the more recently settled populations makes distinctions which sometimes reflect prejudices and thus favour discrimination. In Quebec, the term immigrant is often equated with that of alien and may have emotional connotations which are unfavourable to integration. The former Quebec minister of immigration, Jean Bienvenue, suggested that immigrants should be called Québécois, adding an indication of their origin: Québécois of French, English, Italian, Greek or Portuguese origin, etc. [6] The present minister Jacques Couture calls them "Québécois de nouvelle souche". [7]

The recent statement by René Lévesque, the present Prime Minister of Quebec, is in the same vein. "All those who earn their living in Quebec, who pay their taxes in Quebec, who have or expect to have the right to vote, all citizens who have been legally recognised, or who are in the process of being recognised, all without exception are and must be regarded as Québécois". [8]

The use of the terms "Néo-Québécois" or "New Canadian" is a new step forward in the direction of rapprochement, but it also implies a certain distinction susceptible of continuing for several generations, because it is difficult to say when a "Néo-Québécois" or a "New Canadian" becomes simply a Québécois or a Canadian.

Sometimes, the process of acculturation gives rise to situations which are beyond anyone's ability to foresee or to control. In fact, acculturation is a complex phenomenon and cannot be restricted to the fields of sociology, psychology or politics. Rather, it straddles all of them, along with others areas of knowledge and know-how.

------

6. See *Le Devoir* (Montreal), March 14, 1974, p. 11.

7. See *Québec-Monde* (Dec. 1978), No. 34, p. 1.

8. Address delivered at the University of Montreal, on Saturday, June 4, 1977, during the colloquium "Quebec - Immigration - Ethnic communities", organised by the Immigration Advisory Committee of Quebec (Quebec Ministère de l'Immigration 1977, appendice I, p. 3).

In the case of ethnic groups, we must also remember that the values of origin are not necessarily totally and integrally represented in the populations or social strata that have emigrated. It may also be that the cultural values of the country or origin have been poorly assimilated or distorted by the persons who transmit them. The level of awareness achieved, both individually and collectively, in terms of cultural identity, conditions the goal of acculturation.

*   *   *

The elements of socio-cultural analysis which it was given us to compile in this study on the Portuguese of Quebec suggest optimistic conclusions and expectations as regards their integration. However, if we are to achieve the desired degree of acculturation, we shall require a joint effort to identify and neutralise the involutional forces which hinder or retard the normal course of this process. The goals of multiculturalism are incompatible with the cultural imperialism of an already established group and with the fanatical attachment of a new group to its traditional *modus vivendi*.

The democratic acceptance and encouragement of cultural values proclaimed by the multiculturalism policy call for the creation of suitable social structures. Such a policy is only true to its principles when, recognising the cultural identity of each group, it encourages an affirmation and integration of the values which characterise it. It is only in a climate of equality that all the cultural values can achieve their full dimension. The transmission of these values is inevitably conditioned by the status of the population which is called upon to transmit them. It would be contradictory to promote a culture while denigrating the people who represent it.

If the labour market continues to be the decisive factor in the treatment given to immigrants, it is logical to suppose that employer-employee relations affect other areas, too. So long as immigrants continue to be regarded chiefly as units of production, we have reason to fear that individuals and the cultural values of which they are vehicles will be sacrificed to the pragmatic interests of a manpower purchasing society.

The history of Quebec is essentially a history of migrations. For as long as there is a category defined under the name of immigrants, it is in identifying with them that the Quebec people will be able to welcome them. It is up to the immigrants of yesteryear to join with those of today to build the Quebec of tomorrow with the contribution of each.

The Portuguese touched Quebec territory even before the arrival of those who became the chief founding peoples. Though their numbers were initially small, they have lived there at least since the beginning of French colonisation. In modern times, Portuguese settlement in the Province of Quebec has been so considerable that this ethnic group is already regarded as one of the largest in that province.

Portuguese immigrants, in addition to their labour, have brought to Quebec certain cultural values destined to become an integral part of the Quebec heritage, which will be enriched by the marks of the Portuguese soul. The term *luso-québécois* must evoke a synthesis, never a confrontation. May the Portuguese culture in Quebec be both a guardian of the past and a beacon for the future.

BIBLIOGRAPHY

BOOKS

AGUIAR, Armando de, *O mundo que os portugueses criaram.* 2nd ed. Lisboa, Empresa Nacional de Publicidade, 1945.

ALACOQUE, Roger, *Les importés: essai-témoignage sur l'immigration au Québec.* Sherbrooke, Éditions Naaman, 1977.

ALMEIDA, Carlos and BARRETO, António, *Capitalismo e emigração em Portugal.* 2nd ed. Lisboa, Prelo, 1974.

ALPALHÃO, J.A., LEFEBVRE, J.-J. and DA ROSA, V.M.P., *La créativité et les milieux défavorisés.* Montréal, Conceptions 2001, 1976.

ANDERSON, Grace M., *Networks of Contact: The Portuguese and Toronto.* Waterloo, Ont., Wilfrid Laurier University Publications, 1974.

ANDERSON, Grace M. and HIGGS, David, *A Future to Inherit: The Portuguese Communities of Canada.* Toronto, McClelland and Stewart, 1976. (In French: *L'héritage du futur; Les communautés portugaises au Canada.* Montréal, Le Cercle du Livre de France, 1979).

ANIDO, Nayade and FREIRE, Rubens, *L'émigration portugaise: présent et avenir.* Paris, Presses Universitaires de France, 1978.

ANTUNES, A. M. Marinho, *A emigração portuguesa desde 1950; dados e comentários.* Lisboa, Gabinete de Investigações Sociais, 1973.

ATHERTON, William, *Montreal 1535-1914; Under British Rule 1770-1914.* Montréal, The S. J. Clarke Publishing Company, 1914.

ATKINSON, William C., *A History of Spain and Portugal.* Harmondsworth, Penguin Books, 1965.

ÁVILA, Fernando Bastos de, *Economic Impact of Immigration. The Brazilian Immigration Problem*. Westport, Conn., Greenwood Press Publishers, 1970.

AYDALOT, Philippe and GAUDEMAR, Jean-Paul de, *Les migrations*. Paris, Éd. Gauthier-Villars, 1972.

BALTAZAR, Diamantino, *A congregação geral das comunidades portuguesas: Os Portugueses na América*. Lisboa, Sociedade de Geografia de Lisboa, 1965.

BARATA, Oscar, *Migrações e povoamento*. Lisboa, Sociedade de Geografia de Lisboa, 1965.

BARBOSA, Jorge Morais, *A língua portuguesa no mundo*. Lisboa, Agência-Geral do Ultramar, 1969.

BEATTIE, John, *Introduction à l'anthropologie*. Paris, Payot, 1972.

BERTLEY, Leo W., *Canada and its People of African Descent*. Pierrefonds, Qué., Bilongo Publishers, 1977.

BETTENCOURT, José de Sousa, *O fenómeno da emigração portuguesa*. Luanda, Instituto de Investigação Científica de Angola, 1961.

BOISSEVAIN, Jeremy, *The Italians of Montreal; Social Adjustment in a Plural Society*. Ottawa, Queen's Printer, 1970.

BÖHNING, W. R. and MAILLAT, D., *The Effects of the Employment of Foreign Workers*. Paris, O.C.D.E., 1974.

BORRIE, W. D. *et al.*, *The Cultural Integration of Immigrants*. Paris, U.M.E.S.C.O., 1959.

BOXER, Carles R., *Four Centuries of Portuguese Expansion, 1415-1825*. Johannesburg, Witwatersrand University Press, 1961.

BOXER, Carles R., *The Portuguese Seaborne Empire, 1415-1825*. London, Hutchinson, 1969.

BRAZÃO, Eduardo, *La découverte de Terre-Neuve*. Montréal, Les Presses de l'Université de Montréal, 1964. (In Portuguese:*A descoberta da Terra Nova,* Lisboa 1964).

BRAZÃO, Eduardo, *The Corte-Real Family and the New World*. Lisboa, Agência-Geral do Ultramar, 1965. (In French: "Les Corte-Real et le Nouveau Monde", in *Revue d'Histoire d'Amérique Française* (1965), Vol. 19, Nos. 1, 2 et 3, pp. 3-52, 163-202 et 335-349).

BRAZÃO, Eduardo, *Os descobrimentos portugueses nas histórias do Canadá.* Lisboa, Agência-Geral do Ultramar, 1969.

BRETON, Raymond, ARMSTRONG, Jill and KENNEDY, Les, *Les répercussions sociales des changements survenus dans la taille et la structure de la population: réactions devant l'immigration.* Ottawa, Information Canada, 1974.

BRYANS, Robin, *The Azores*. London, Faber and Faber, 1963.

BUZZANGA, Mario, *L'intégration socio-culturelle et ses problèmes.* Sherbrooke, Éditions Paulines, 1974.

CAPPON, Paul, *Conflit entre les Néo-Canadiens et les francophones de Montréal.* Québec, Les Presses de l'Université Laval, 1974.

CARDOZO, Manoel da Silveira, *The Portuguese in America 590 B.C.-1974; A Chronology and Fact Book.* Dobbs Ferry, N.Y., Oceana Publications, 1976.

CARLOS, Serge, BÉLANGER, Diane and PETIT-TESSIER, Pierrette, *Monographie sur l'immigration au Québec.* Montréal, Centre de Sondage de l'Université de Montréal, 1974.

CASTLES, Stephen and KOSACK, Godula, *Immigrant Workers and Class Structure in Western Europe.* New York, Oxford University Press, 1973.

CASTRO, Armando, *Estudos de economia teórica e aplicada.* Lisboa, Seara Nova, 1968.

CASTRO, Augusto de, *O portuguesismo no mundo*. Lisboa, Sociedade de Geografia de Lisboa, 1964.

CEDETIM, *Les immigrés: contribution à l'histoire politique de l'immigration*. Paris, Lutter/Stock 2, 1975.

CERASE, Francesco, *L'emigrazione di ritorno: innovazione o reazione?* Roma, Instituto di Statistica e Ricerce Sociale, 1971.

CINANNI, Paolo, *Emigrazione e imperialismo*. Roma, Editori Riuniti, 1968. (In German: *Emigration und Imperialismus: zu Problematik der Arbeitsemigration*. München, Trikont Verlag, 1970).

COELHO, F. Adolpho, *Nouveau dictionnaire de pédagogie et d'instruction primaire*. Paris, Hachette et Cie., 1911.

COMMISSION D'ÉTUDES SUR LES LAÏCS ET L'ÉGLISE, *L'église du Québec: un héritage, un projet*. Montréal, Fides, 1971.

CORNELL, Paul *et al.*, *Canada: unité et diversité*. Montréal, Holt, Rinehart et Winston, 1968.

CORTESÃO, Jaime, *Os portugueses no descobrimento dos Estados Unidos*. Lisboa, Seara Nova, 1949.

CORTESÃO, Jaime, *Portugal, a Terra e o Homem*. Lisboa, Portugália, 1968.

COSTA, Afonso, *O problema da emigração*. Lisboa, Imprensa Nacional, 1911.

COSTA, Florencio, *Emigrantes obreros en Europa*. Algorta (Viscaya), Zero, 1970.

CUTILEIRO, José, *A Portuguese Rural Society*. Oxford, Clarendon Press, 1971.

DEJEAN, Paul, *Les Haïtiens au Québec*. Montréal, Les Presses de l'Université du Québec, 1978.

292

DELGADO, Jesus Manuel, *Die Gastarbeiter in der Presse: eine inhaltsanalytische Studium.* Opladen, Leske, 1972.

DESCAMPS, Paul, *Histoire sociale du Portugal.* Paris, Firmin-Didot et Cie., 1959.

DIAS, António Jorge, *Ensaios etnológicos.* (Estudos de Ciências Políticas e Sociais, No. 52). Lisboa, Junta de Investigações do Ultramar, 1961.

DIAS, António Jorge, *Portuguese Contribution to Cultural Anthropology.* Johannesburg, Witwatersrand University Press, 1964.

DIAS, António Jorge, *Estudos do carácter nacional português.* Lisboa, Junta de Investigações do Ultramar, 1971.

DIAS, Manuel Vaz, *Cri d'un immigré.* Paris, Éditions Ouvrières, 1974.

DIDIER, René and BORDELEAU, Yvan, *Le processus des choix linguistiques des immigrants au Québec.* (Commission d'enquête sur la situation de la langue française et sur les droits linguistiques au Québec). Québec, Éditeur officiel, 1973.

DOLLOT, Louis, *Les migrations humaines.* Paris, Presses Universitaires de France, 1965. (In English: *Race and Human Migrations.* New York, Walker, 1964).

EISENSTADT, S. N., *The Absorption of Immigrants.* Glencoe, Illinois, The Free Press, 1955.

ELKIN, Frederick, *La famille au Canada.* Ottawa, Institut Vanier, 1964.

ÉLOI-GÉRARD, Frère, *Recueil de généalogies des comtés de Charlevoix et Saguenay, depuis l'origine jusqu'à 1939.* La Malbaie, Société Historique du Saguenay, 1941.

ÉLOI-GÉRARD, Frère, *Recueil de généalogies des comtés de Beauce-Dorchester-Frontenac.* Beauceville, Collège du Sacré-Coeur, 1948.

ENGELS, Friedrich, *La situation de la classe laborieuse en Angleterre*. Paris, Éditions sociales, 1960.

EVANGELISTA, João, *Um século de população portuguesa (1864-1960)*. Lisboa, Centro de Estudos Demográficos, 1971.

FERGUSON, Edith, *Newcomers in Transition*. Toronto, International Institute of Metropolitan Toronto, 1964.

FERGUSON, Edith, *Newcomers and New Learning*. Toronto, International Institute of Metropolitan Toronto, 1966.

FERREIRA, Eduardo Sousa, *Origens e formas da emigração*. Lisboa, Iniciativas Editoriais, 1976.

FIGUEIREDO, Mário Manuel d'Oliveira, *Considerações sobre os valores socio-culturais dos núcleos portugueses na França e na América do Norte*. Lisboa, Sociedade de Geografia de Lisboa, 1965.

FLASCHE, Hans ed., *Aufsätze zur portugiesischen Kulturgeschichte*. Münster in Westfalen, Aschendorff, 1961.

FRANCO, António de Sousa, *A emigração para a Europa no conjunto da emigração portuguesa*. Lisboa, Edição da Obra Católica Portuguesa de Migrações, 1974.

FREIRE, Paulo, *Pédagogie des opprimés*. Paris, Maspero, 1974.

FREITAS, Joaquim Francisco, *Portuguese-Hawaiian Memories*. Honolulu, The Printshop Company, 1930.

FREIDMANN, Wolfgang G., *German Immigration into Canada*. Toronto, The Ryerson Press, 1952.

FRIEDLANDER, Stanley L., *Labor Migration and Economic Growth*. Cambridge, Mass., M.I.T. Press, 1965.

GAFFAREL, Paul and GARIOD, Charles, *Découvertes des Portugais en Amérique au temps de Christophe Colomb*. Paris, Ernest Leroux Éditeur, 1892.

GALLOP, Rodney Alexander, *Portugal, a Book of Folk-Ways*. Cambridge, The University Press, 1961.

GANI, Léon, *Syndicats et travailleurs immigrés*. Paris, Éditions Sociales, 1972.

GEORGE, Pierre, *Les migrations internationales*. Paris, Presses Universitaires de France, 1976.

GIRÃO, Aristides de Amorim, *Geografia de Portugal*. 3rd ed. Porto, Portucalense Editora, 1960.

GNEHM, Adrian H., *Ausländische Arbeitskräfte*. Bern und Stuttgart, Haupt, 1966.

GODINHO, Vitorino Magalhães, *Os descobrimentos portugueses na economia mundial*. Lisboa, Arcádia, 1963.

GODINHO, Vitorino Magalhães, *L'économie de l'empire portugais aux XVe et XVIe siècles*. Paris, S.E.V.P.E.N., 1969.

GOLDSCHMIDT, Walter ed., *Exploring the Ways of Mankind*. 3rd ed. New York, Holt, Rinehart and Winston, 1977.

GONÇALVES, José Júlio, *Portugal no Mundo*. Lisboa, Sociedade de Geografia de Lisboa, 1967.

GONÇALVES, José Júlio, *Portugueses dispersos pelo mundo*. Lisboa, Agência-Geral do Ultramar, 1971.

GORDON, Milton M., *Assimilation in American Life: The Role of Race, Religion and National Origins*. New York, Oxford University Press, 1974.

GORDON, Milton M., *Human Nature, Class, and Ethnicity*. New York, Oxford University Press, 1978.

GRANOTIER, Bernard, *Les travailleurs immigrés en France*. Paris, François Maspero, 1970.

GROULX, Lionel, *La découverte du Canada*. Montréal, Fides, 1966.

GROUPE DE RECHERCHES SOCIALES, *La situation des immigrants à Montréal.* Montréal, Conseil des Oeuvres de Montréal, 1959.

HAMILTON, Jon, *Portuguese in Transition.* Toronto, Board of Education for the City of Toronto, 1970.

HAWKINS, Freda, *Canada and Immigration: Public Policy and Public Concern.* Montréal, McGill-Queen's University Press, 1972.

HERSKOVITS, Melville J., *Cultural Relativism; Perspectives in Cultural Pluralism.* New York, Vintage Books, 1973.

HOUTE, Hans and MELGERT, Willy, *Foreigner in Our Community.* Amsterdam, Keesing, 1972.

HUNTER, L. C. and REID, G. L., *European Economic Integration and the Movement of Labour.* Kingston, Ontario, Queen's University, 1970.

ISAAC, Julius, *Economics of Migration.* New York, Oxford University Press, 1947.

ISHWARAN, K., *The Canadian Family; A Book of Readings.* Toronto/Montreal, Holt, Rinehart and Winston of Canada, 1971.

JACKSON, J. A., ed., *Migration.* Cambridge, Cambridge University Press, 1969.

JANSEN, Clifford J. ed., *Readings in the Sociology of Migration.* Oxford, Pergamon Press, 1970.

KAYSER, Bernard, *Les retours conjoncturels de travailleurs migrants et les effets de l'émigration.* Paris, O.C.D.E., 1972.

KAYSER, Bernard, *Rapport sur l'immigration.* Paris, O.C.D.E., 1973.

KINDLEBERGER, Charles P., *Europe's Postwar Growth; The Role of Labor Supply.* Cambridge, Mass., Harvard University Press, 1967.

296

KROHN, Roger, FLEMING, Berkeley and MANZER, Marilyn, *The Other Economy: The Internal Logic of Local Rental Housing.* Toronto, Peter Martin and Associates, 1976.

KRYCHOWSKI, T. W., *Polish Canadians; Profile and Image.* Toronto, Polish Alliance Press Limited, 1969.

LANCTÔT, Gustave, *Histoire du Canada; des origines au régime royal.* Montreal, Librairie Beauchemin, 1959.

LAROQUE, E., *Ventaja y inconvenientes de l'emigración.* Madrid, Instituto de l'Emigración, 1961.

LÉGER, Jean-Marc, *Le Canada français face à l'immigration.* Montréal, Éditions Bellarmin, 1956.

LENORMAND, Jean-Claude, *Québec-Immigration: Zéro.* Montreal, Les Éditions Parti Pris, 1971.

LIMA, Joaquim A. Pires de, *A emigração portuguesa em França.* Lisboa, Editorial Estampa, 1974.

LIVERMORE, Harold V., *A New History of Portugal.* Cambridge, The University Press, 1966.

LIVI BACCI, Massimo, *A Century of Portuguese Fertility.* Princeton, Princeton University Press, 1971.

LIVI BACCI, Massimo ed., *The Demographic and Social Pattern of Emigration from the Southern European Countries.* Firenze, Dipartimento statistico matematico dell'Università e Comitato italiano per lo studio dei problemi della popolazione, 1972.

LOIZU, Máximo, *Capitalismo europeo y emigración.* Barcelona, Avance, 1975.

LOPES, Francisco Fernandes, *Os irmãos Corte-Real.* Lisboa, Centro de Estudos Histórico-Ultramarinos, Agência-Geral do Ultramar, 1957.

LOPES, Norberto, *Emigrantes.* Lisboa, Sociedade de Geografia de Lisboa, 1964.

LUONG, T .M. and LUONG, C. M., *The Great Image Sellers; The Study of the Causes of Difficulties among Immigrants in Canada.* Brooklyn, N.Y., Pageant-Poseidon Ltd., 1972.

MAILLAT, A. D., *Effets économiques de l'emploi de travailleurs étrangers: le cas de la Suisse.* Paris, O.C.D.E., 1974.

MALSERVISI, Mauro, *La contribution des Québécois des groupes ethniques autres que français et britannique au développement du Québec.* Québec, Éditeur officiel du Québec, 1973.

MARQUES, A. H. de Oliveira, *History of Portugal.* New York, Columbia University Press, 1972.

MARQUES, Domingos and MEDEIROS, João, *Imigrantes portugueses: 25 anos no Canadá.* Toronto, Movimento Comunitário Português et Festival Português de Toronto, 1978.

MARTINS, Joaquim Pedro de Oliveira, *Fomento rural e emigração.* Lisboa, Guimarães & Co., 1956.

MARX, Karl, *Le Capital.* Paris, Éditions Sociales, 1948.

MASLOW, Abraham H., *Motivation and Personality.* 2nd ed., New York, Harper and Row, 1970.

MINCES, Juliette, *Les travailleurs étrangers en France.* Paris, Seuil, 1973.

MINGARELLI, Giosafat, *Gli Italiani di Montreal.* 2nd ed., Montréal, Centro Italiano Attività Commerciale-Artistiche, 1971.

MONTEIRO, Waldemar, *As histórias dramáticas da emigração.* Lisboa, Prelo, 1969.

MORIN, Rosaire, *L'immigration au Canada.* Montréal, Édition de l'Action Nationale, 1966.

MORISON, Samuel Eliot, *Portuguese Voyages to America in the Fifteenth Century*. Cambridge, Harvard University Press, 1940.

MURTEIRA, Mário, *Emigração e política do emprego em Portugal*. Lisboa, Fundo de Desenvolvimento de Mão-de-Obra, 1966.

MVILONGO, Anselme *et al.*, *Les minorités ethniques à Montréal*. Montréal, Bureau de la Consultation Jeunesse, Inc., 1972.

NAVARRO, Modesto, *Emigração e crise no Nordeste Transmontano*. Lisboa, Prelo, 1973.

NAZARETH, J. Manuel, *O envelhecimento da população portuguesa*. Lisboa, Editorial Presença / Gabinete de Investigações Sociais, 1979.

NIKOLINAKOS, Mario, *Politische Ökonomie der Gastarbeiterfrage*. Reinbeck bei Hamburg, Rowohlt-Verlag, 1973.

PAP, Leo, *Portuguese-American Speech: an Outline of Speech Conditions among Portuguese Immigrants in New England and elsewhere in the United States*. New York, King's Crown Press, 1949.

PARAI, Louis, *L'incidence économique de l'immigration*. Ottawa, Information Canada, 1974.

PERES, Damião, *Como nasceu Portugal*. Porto, Portucalense Editora, 1946.

PERES, Damião, *História dos descobrimentos portugueses*. 2nd ed., Coimbra, Edição do Autor, 1960.

PORTER, John, *The Vertical Mosaic*. Toronto, University of Toronto Press, 1965.

PORTER, John, *Canadian Social Structure: A Statistical Profile*. Toronto, McClelland and Stewart, 1967.

REYNOLD, Gonzague de, *Portugal*. Paris, Éditions Spes, 1936.

RIBEIRO, Aquilino, *Aldeia: Terra, Gente e Bichos*. Lisboa, Livraria Bertrand, 1964.

RIBEIRO, Orlando, *Portugal, o Mediterrâneo e o Atlântico*. 2nd ed., Lisboa, Sá da Costa, 1963.

RICHMOND, Anthony H., *Post-War Immigrants in Canada*. Toronto, University of Toronto Press, 1967.

RODRIGUES, L., *Bastardos das Pátrias*. Lisboa, Distribuidora "O Século", 1976.

ROGERS, Francis Millet, *Americans of Portuguese Descent: A Lesson in Differentiation*. Beverly Hills/London, Sage Publications, 1974.

ROGERS, Francis Millet, *Atlantic Islanders of the Azores and Madeiras*. North Quincy, Mass., The Christopher Publishing House, 1979.

ROSA, Eugénio, *Problemas actuais da economia portuguesa*. Lisboa, Seara Nova, 1974.

ROSE, Arnold M., *Migrants in Europe: Problems of Acceptance and Adjustment*. Minneapolis, University of Minnesota Press, 1969.

SAUVY, Alfred, *Théorie générale de la population*. Paris, Presses Universitaires de France, 1952. (In English: *General Theory of Population*, New York, Basic Books, 1970).

SAYERS, Raymond S. ed., *Portugal and Brazil in Transition*. Minneapolis, University of Minnesota Press, 1968.

SCHERMERHORN, R. A., *Comparative Ethnic Relations*. New York, John Wiley and Sons, Inc., 1967.

SCOTT, Franklin D. ed., *World Migration in Modern Times*. Englewood Cliffs, N.J., Prentice-Hall Inc., 1968.

SCOTT, Franklin D., *The Peopling of America: Perspectives on Immigration*. Washington, D.C., American Historial Association, 1972.

SEARY, E. R., *Place Names of the Avalon Peninsula of the Island of Newfoundland*. Toronto, University of Toronto Press, 1971.

SEGUÍ GONZÁLEZ, Luis, *La inmigración y su contribución al desarrollo*. Caracas, Monte Avila Editores, 1969.

SERRÃO, Joel, *A emigração portuguesa*. 2nd ed., Lisboa, Livros Horizonte, 1974.

SERRÃO, Joel et al., *Testemunhos sobre a emigração portuguesa: Antologia*. Lisboa, Livros Horizonte, 1976.

SILVA, António da, *Para uma pastoral em Portugal*. Lisboa, Sampedro, 1972.

SILVA, Fernando Emídio da, *Emigração portuguesa*. Lisboa, Tipografia Universal, 1917.

SIMÕES, Nuno, *Os portugueses no Mundo*. Lisboa, Edição do Autor, 1940.

SOARES, Celestino, *California and the Portuguese*. San Francisco, R & E Research Associates, 1970. (First edition 1939).

SOUSA, Francisco de, *Tratado das ilhas novas e dos descobrimentos dellas et outras . . . et dos Portugueses que forao de Vianna, et das ilhas dos Açores a povoar a Terra nova do Bacalhao vae en 70 anos, deque suceden o que adiante se trata. Anno de Senhor 1570.* 2nd ed., Ponta Delgada, Typ. do Archivo dos Açores, 1884.

STANISLAWSKI, Dan, *The Individuality of Portugal; A Study in Historical-Political Geography*. Austin, Texas, University of Texas Press, 1959.

STATHOPOULOS, Peter, *The Greek Community of Montreal.* Athens, National Centre of Social Research, 1971.

TAFT, Donald, *Two Portuguese Communities in New England.* New York, AMS Press, 1967. (First edition 1923).

TANGUAY, Cyprien, *Dictionnaire généalogique des familles cana-diennes depuis la fondation de la colonie jusqu'à nos jours.* Québec, Eusèbe Senécal, 1871-90.

TAPINOS, Georges Photios, *L'économie des migrations internatio-nales.* Paris, Armand Colin, 1974.

THOMAS, Brinley, *International Migration and Economic Develop-ment.* Paris, U.N.E.S.C.O., 1961.

THOMAS, Brinley, *Migration and Economic Growth.* 2nd ed., Cambridge, The University Press, 1973.

TRINDADE, Maria Beatriz Rocha, *Immigrés portugais: Observation psycho-sociologique d'un groupe de Portugais dans la ban-lieue parisienne (Orsay).* Lisboa, Instituto Superior de Ciências Sociais e Política Ultramarina, 1973.

TRUDEL, Marcel, *Histoire de la Nouvelle-France.* Montréal, Fides, 1963.

VANGILISTI, Guglielmo, *Gli Italiani in Canada.* 2nd ed., Montréal, Chiesa Italiana de N.S. della Difesa, 1958.

VASCONCELLOS, José Leite de, *Etnografia portuguesa.* Lisboa, Imprensa Nacional, 1933-1958.

VATTIER, Georges, *Essai sur la mentalité canadienne-française.* Paris, Librairie Ancienne Honoré Champion, 1928.

VAZ, August Mark, *The Portuguese in California.* Oakland, California, I.D.E.S. Supreme Council, 1965.

WILLIAMS, Robin, *Stranger Next Door.* Englewood Cliffs, N.J., Prentice-Hall, 1964.

WILSON, Charles *et al., Economic Issues in Immigration*. London, The Institute of Economic Affairs, 1970.

WOLFORTH, Sandra, *The Portuguese in America*. San Francisco, R & E Research Associates, 1978.

WOODSWORTH, James S., *Strangers Within our Gates*. Toronto, University of Toronto Press, 1972.

THESES

BOULTER, Alison Isobel, "Constituting Ethnic Difference: An Ethnography of the Portuguese Immigrant Experience in Vancouver". M.A. thesis in Anthropology, University of British Columbia, 1978.

FERNÁNDEZ, Ronald Louis, "A Logic of Ethnicity: A Study of the Significance and Classification of Ethnic Identity among Montreal Portuguese". Ph.D. dissertation in Anthropology, McGill University, 1977.

HENRY-NIEVES, Rohn, "Ethnicity: The Canadian Experience and the Portuguese in Toronto". B.A. thesis, Friends' World College, 1975.

IIDA-MIRANDA, Maria Lia, "La relation entre les changements récents et les maladies chez les immigrants portugais à Montréal". Ph.D. dissertation in Psychology, University of Montreal, 1975.

LEDER, Hans, "Cultural Persistance in a Portuguese American Community". Ph.D. dissertation in Anthropology, Stanford University, 1968.

ROMÃO, Isabel, "Le processus de migration, la mobilité professionnelle, la mobilité sociale et l'acculturation chez les ressortissants d'origine portugaise à Montréal". M.A. thesis in Sociology, University of Montreal, 1972.

SANTOS, Maria Teresa Silva, "Étude comparative de la situation de santé d'enfants immigrants portugais et d'enfants québécois d'âge scolaire". M.A. thesis in Nursing, University of Montreal, 1975.

MIMEOGRAPHED DOCUMENTS

ANDERSON, Grace M., "Illegal Immigration: A Sociologically Unexplored Field". Paper delivered at the American Sociological Association meeting in Denver, Colorado, in September 1971.

ARNOPOULOS, Sheila McLeod, *Problèmes des femmes immigrantes sur le marché du travail canadien*. Ottawa, Conseil consultatif canadien de la situation de la femme, 1979.

CENTRE PORTUGAIS DE RÉFÉRENCE ET DE PROMOTION SOCIALE, *Le passé, le présent, l'avenir — Résumé historique*. Montreal, 1974.

CENTRE PORTUGAIS DE RÉFÉRENCE ET DE PROMOTION SOCIALE, *Enquête concernant les abandons scolaires des jeunes portugais au niveau secondaire*. Montreal, 1975a.

CENTRE PORTUGAIS DE RÉFÉRENCE ET DE PROMOTION SOCIALE, *Statistiques sur la population portugaise*. Montreal, 1975b.

CENTRE PORTUGAIS DE RÉFÉRENCE ET DE PROMOTION SOCIALE, *Le groupe portugais à Montréal: la situation sociologique, la problématique et les lignes d'intervention*. Montreal, 1976.

GRUPO DE ASSISTÊNCIA SOCIAL A PESSOAS COM BAIXO RENDIMENTO, *Statistique sur la communauté portugaise (Quartier St-Louis)*. Montreal, n.d.

KEMP, Madeleine and MORISSET, Claude, *Rapport statistique de l'enquête sur la population portugaise de Hull*. Hull, Quebec, n.d.

MOTA, Avelino Teixeira da, "Portuguese Navigations in the North in the Fifteenth and Sixteenth Centuries". Paper delivered at Memorial University of Newfoundland, on September 28th, 1965.

PUBLISHED ARTICLES

AGENEAU, Charles, "Étrangers dans la ville" in *Esprit* (April 1966), Vol. 34, No. 348, pp. 770-798.

ALMEIDA, Carlos C., "Émigration, espace et sous-développement" in *Migrations Internationales* (1973), Vol. 11, No. 3, pp. 112-117.

ALMEIDA, Carlos, C., "Movimentos migratórios, espaços socio-culturais e processos de aculturação" in *Análise Social* (1975) segunda série, Vol. 11, Nos. 2-3, pp. 203-212.

ALMEIDA, J. C. Ferreira de, "Dados sobre a emigração portuguesa em 1963-1965: alguns comentários" in *Análise Social* (1966), Vol. 4, No. 13.

ALPALHÃO, J. A., DA ROSA, V. M. P. and LEFEBVRE, J.-J., "A educação para a criatividade nos meios subdesenvolvidos" in *Andragogia,* Rio de Janeiro (1977), Ano 2, Nos. 4-5, pp. 74-88.

ALPALHÃO, J. A. and DA ROSA, V. M. P., "Presença portuguesa no Quebec" in *Boletim da Sociedade de Geografia de Lisboa* (1978), Série 96, Nos. 1-6, pp. 69-82.

ALPALHÃO, J. A. and DA ROSA, V. M. P., "Aculturação religiosa dos imigrantes no quadro das comunidades portuguesas do Québec" in *Brotéria* (Jan. 1979), Vol. 108, No. 1, pp. 71-85.

ANDERSON, Grace M., "The Educational Ladder and Success" in *The Journal of the American Portuguese Cultural Society* (Fall 1971), pp. 13-18.

ANDERSON, Grace M., "Spanish—and Portuguese—Speaking Immigrants in Canada" in *Two Nations, Many Cultures; Ethnic Groups in Canada,* ed. Jean L. Elliott, pp. 206-219. Scarborough, Ont., Prentice-Hall of Canada, 1979.

ANGEL, Alfred, "Théologie de l'Église Particulière par rapport au fait migratoire" in *La Documentation Catholique* (1973), Vol. 55, No. 1642, pp. 962-972.

ANIDO, Nayade and FREIRE, Rubens, "A existência de ciclos emigratórios na emigração portuguesa" in *Análise Social* (1976) segunda série, Vol. 12, pp. 172-186.

ANTUNES, M. L. Marinho, "Twenty Years' Emigration from Portugal" in *Migration News* (1973), No. 1, pp. 11-14.

AUBIN, Henry, "A Little Bit of Portugal Brightens City Core" in *The Gazette* (Montreal), February 26, 1974, p. 3.

AZEVEDO, Alexandre, "A pastoral junto dos emigrantes" in *Migrações e Turismo* (Dec. 1973), Vol. 1, No. 3, pp. 76-84.

BAGHDJIAN, Kévork, "Pourquoi voudrait-on que les immigrants soient à jamais 'les autres' parmi nous?" in *Le Devoir* (Montreal), 8 juin 1976, p. 5.

BEAUPRÉ, Pierre, "Rénovations des Portugais au quartier Saint-Louis" in *Décormag* (March 1976), Vol. 4, No. 7, pp. 16-20.

BEIJER, Gunther, "Modern Patterns of International Migratory Movements" in *Migration,* ed. J. A. Jackson, pp. 11-59, London, Cambridge University Press, 1969.

BERNIER, Bernard, "Main-d'oeuvre féminine et ethnicité dans trois usines de vêtement de Montréal" in *Anthropologie et Sociétés* (1979), Vol. 3, No. 2, pp. 117-139.

BÖHNING, W. R., "Immigration Policies of Western European Countries" in *International Migration Review* (1974), Vol. 8, No. 2, pp. 155-164.

BÖHNING, W. R., "Some Thoughts on Emigration from the Mediterranean Basin" in *International Labour Review* (1975), Vol. 3, Nos. 1-3, pp. 6-25.

BONACICH, Edna, "A Theory of Ethnic Antagonism: The Split Labour Market" in *American Sociological Review* (1972), Vol. 37, pp. 547-559.

BONAVIA, George, "Coup d'oeil sur l'immigration" in *Ethnic Kaleidoscope/Canada .Ethnique* (Feb. 1976), Vol. 3, No. 4, pp. 11-18.

BOYD, Monica, "The Status of Immigrant Women in Canada" in *Canadian Review of Sociology and Anthropology* (1975), Vol. 12, No. 4, pp. 406-416.

BRETON, Raymond, "Institutional Completeness of Ethnic Communities and the Personal Relations of Immigrants" in *American Journal of Sociology* (1964), Vol. 70, No. 2, pp. 193-205.

BRETTELL, Caroline Bieler, "Ethnicity and Entrepreneurs: Portuguese Immigrants in a Canadian City" in *Ethnic Encounters; Identities and Contexts,* eds. George L. Hicks and Philip Leis, pp. 168-180. North Scituate, Mass., Duxbury Press, 1977.

BUCHANAN, M. A., "Notes on Portuguese Place-Names in North-Eastern America" in *Estudios Hispánicos: Homenaje a Archer M. Huntington,* Wellesley, Mass., 1952.

CALLIER, Colette, "Soajo: une communauté féminine rurale de l'Alto Minho" in *Bulletin des Études Portugaises* (1966), No. 27, pp. 237-278.

CALLIER-BOISVERT, Colette, "La vie rurale au Portugal; Panorama des travaux en langue portugaise" in *Études rurales* (Jul.-Sept. 1967), No. 27, pp. 95-134.

CALLIER-BOISVERT, Colette, "Remarques sur le système de parenté et sur la famille au Portugal" in *L'Homme* (Revue Française d'Anthropologie) (1968), Vol. 8, No. 2, pp. 87-103.

CERASE, Francesco, "Movimenti Migratori e Transformazioni Strutturali nella Società di Arrivo e di Partenza: Considerazioni Introductive" in *Revue Internationale de Sociologie* (1971), Vol. 7, No. 2, pp. 233-238.

CINANNI, Paolo, "Consequenze Economico-Sociali dell' Emigrazione" in *Critica Marxista* (March-April 1973), pp. 61-72.

COLLIN, C., "Révolution et contre-révolution dans les campagnes portugaises" in *Les Temps Modernes* (Oct. 1975), Vol. 31 (351), pp. 381-409.

COSTA, Joaquim, "Colónias portuguesas nas ilhas de Hawai e America do Norte" in *Boletim da Sociedade de Geografia de Lisboa* (Jun. 1912), 30a série, pp. 233-263.

DA ROSA, Victor M. Pereira, "Migrações humanas: Para uma nova perspectiva teórica baseada no caso açoreano" in *Economia e Sociologia* (1977a), No. 23, pp. 51-57.

DA ROSA, Victor M. Pereira, "Überlieferte Werte und der Unwille zu Veränderungen auf den Azoren" in *Die dritte Welt* (1977b), Vol. 5, No. 4, pp. 468-477.

DA ROSA, Victor M. Pereira, "Die Azoreaner von Montreal" in *Die dritte Welt* (1979), Vol. 7, No. 3, pp. 399-406.

DELACOUR, André, "Le Canada au Radio de Paris" in *Revue Trimestrielle Canadienne* (Dec. 1929), Vol. 15, No. 60, pp. 411-413.

DIAS, António Jorge, "Os Elementos fundamentais da cultura portuguesa" in *Actas do Colóquio Internacional de Estudos Luso-Brasileiros,* Washington, D.C., 1950, pp. 51-65. Nashville, Tenn., 1953.

DIAS, António Jorge, "Algumas considerações acêrca da estrutura social do povo português" in *Revista de Antropologia,* São Paulo (1955), Vol. 3.

DIAS, Eduardo Mayone, "Imigração portuguesa na Califórnia" in *Seara Nova* (Jan. 1972), No. 1515, pp. 11-15.

DIMITRAS, Elie, "Relations entre communautés rurales méditerranéennes et centres urbains des pays industriels européens" in *Contribution to Mediterranean Sociology: Mediterranean Rural Communities and Social Change*, ed., J. G. Péristiany. pp. 235-243. The Hague, Mouton, 1968.

DOUGLASS, W. A., "Peasant Emigrants: Reactors or Actors?" in *Migration and Anthropology*, ed. L. Kasden, pp. 21-35. Seattle, American Ethnological Society, 1970.

ENCYCLOPEDIA CANADIANA, "Portuguese Origin, People of", Vol. 8, pp. 269-270. Toronto, 1966.

ENDRUWEIT, Günter, "Akkulturationstheorien in der Gastarbeiterforschung" in *Die dritte Welt* (1975), Vol. 4, No. 2, pp. 226-258.

ESSER, Hartmut, "Interaktionsstrategien in nicht-definierten Situationen" in *Kölner Zeitschrift für Soziologie und Sozial Psychologie* (1976), Vol. 28.

ESTEP, Gerald A., "Portuguese Assimilation in Hawaii and California" in *Sociology and Social Research* (Sept. 1941), Vol. 26, No. 1, pp. 61-69.

FERRACUTI, F., "Crime et migration" in *Ici l'Europe* (1968), Vol. 5, No. 3, pp. 20-28.

FORGET, Jacques, "Les Portugais de Montréal" in *Dimanche Matin* (Montreal), 24 juin 1973, pp. 3-7.

FOTHERGILL-PAYNE, Peter A., "Portuguese-Canadian Periodical Publications: A Preliminary Check List" in *Canadian Ethnic Studies* (1970), Vol. 2, No. 1, pp. 169-170.

FRANCO, A. de Sousa, "Consequences of Portuguese Emigration" in *Migration News* (1974), Vol. 23, pp. 12-16.

FRIEDL, Ernestine, "Kinship, Class and Selective Migration" in *Family in the Mediterranean*, ed. J. G. Péristiany. London, Cambridge University Press, 1974.

GAGNON, Philéas, "Noms propres au Canada-français" in *Bulletin des Recherches Historiques* (1909), Vol. 15, No. 2, pp. 49-61.

GIESE, Wilhelm, "Zur bauerlichen Kultur der Tierra de Miranda (N.O. Portugal)" in *Zeitschrift für Ethnologie* (1957), 82, pp. 250-256.

GINI, C., "Los efectos demográficos de las migraciones internacionales" in *Revista Internacional de Sociología* (1966), Vol. 4, pp. 351-388.

GONÇALVES, José Júlio, "Os portugueses no continente americano" in *Comunidades Portuguesas* (Jul. 1968), Vol. 3, No. 11, pp. 59-87.

GUINDON, Hubert, "La modernisation du Québec et la légitimité de l'État canadien" in *Recherches sociographiques* (1977), Vol. 18, No. 3, pp. 337-366.

HAWKINS, Freda, "Canadian Immigration Policy and Management" in *International Migration Review* (1974), Vol. 8, No. 2, pp. 141-153.

HEBERLY, R., "Types of Migration" in *Southwest Social Science Quarterly* (1955), Vol. 36, pp. 65-70.

HERCULANO, Alexandre, "Emigração" in *Opúsculos,* Vol. 4. Lisboa, Bertrand, 1882.

HUMBLET, Jean-E., "Problématique de l'adaptation des immigrants au Québec" in *Revue de l'Institut de Sociologie* (1976), Nos. 1-2, pp. 119-147.

JENSEN, John B., "The Portuguese Immigrant Community of New England; A Current Look" in *Studia* (June 1972), Vol. 34, pp. 111-151.

JOST, T. P., "Portuguese Activity Along the Canadian Shore at the Beginning of Modern Times" in *Congresso Internacional de História dos Descobrimentos, Actas.* Vol. 3, pp. 271-284.

KADE, Gerhard et SCHILLER, Günther, "Gastarbeiterwanderungen, ein neues Element in der Wirtschaftspolitik der Mittelmeerländer" in *Weltwirtschaftliches Archiv* (1961), Vol. 102, No. 2, pp. 333-355.

KASDAN, Leonard, "Family Structure, Migration and the Entrepreneur" in *Comparative Studies in Society and History* (1965), Vol. 7, No. 4, pp. 345-357.

KAYSER, Bernard, "L'échange inégal des ressources humaines: migrations, croissance et crise en Europe" in *Revue Tiers-Monde* (1977), Vol. 18, No. 69, pp. 7-20.

KEITH, Henry H., "Emigração portuguesa para os Estados Unidos" in *Comunidades Portuguesas* (Jul. 1971), Vol. 6, No. 23, pp. 4-12.

KOLM, Serge-Christophe, "Portugal: Quelle révolution, vers quelle société?" in *Les Temps Modernes* (Dec. 1975), Vol. 31 (353), pp. 881-897.

LANDECKER, W. S., "Types of Integration and their Measurement" in *American Journal of Sociology* (1951), No. 56.

LAROUCHE, Fernand "L'immigration dans une ville minière. Une étude de l'interaction" in *Recherches Sociographiques* (1973), Vol. 14, No. 2, pp. 203-228.

LEE, Everett S., "A Theory of Migration" in *Migration,* ed. J. A. Jackson, pp. 282-297. London, Cambridge University Press, 1969. Also in *Demography* (1965), Vol. 3, No. 1, pp. 47-57.

LELOUP, Yves, "L'émigration portugaise dans le monde et ses conséquences pour le Portugal" in *Revue de Géographie de Lyon* (1972), Vol. 47, No. 1, pp. 59-76.

MANGALAM, J. J. and SCHWARZWELLER, H. K., "Some Theoretical Guidelines Toward a Sociology of Migration" in *International Migration Review* (1970), Vol. 4, No. 2, pp. 5-21.

311

MARTINS, Hermínio, "Portugal" in *Contemporary Europe,* eds. Margaret Archer and Salvador Giner. New York, St. Martin's, 1972.

MARTINS, Luis Augusto, "Emigração portuguesa no Canadá" in *Boletim da Sociedade de Geografia de Lisboa* (Jul.-Sept. 1971), Vol. 89, pp. 219-230.

MASSICOTTE, E.-Z., "Les premiers messagers de la Nouvelle-France" in *Bulletin des Recherches Historiques* (1921), Vol. 27, No. 7, pp. 211-213.

MAZZATENTA, O. Louis, "New England's Little Portugal" in *National Geographic Magazine* (Jan. 1975), Vol. 147, No. 1, pp. 90-109.

MEILLASSOUX, Claude, "L'exploitation des travailleurs immigrés en France" in *Qui est responsable du sous-développement?* ed. Union générale des travailleurs sénégalais en France, pp. 13-20. Paris, François Maspero, 1975.

MOREIRA, Adriano, "Emigração portuguesa" in *Estudos Políticos e Sociais* (1969), Vol. 7, No. 3, pp. 621-638.

NIKOLINAKOS, Marios, "Notes Towards a General Theory of Migration in Late Capitalism" in *Race and Class* (1975), Vol. 17, No. 1, pp. 5-17.

NOGUEIRA, Armando, "A emigração portuguesa; demissão ou tomada de consciência?" in *Economia e Sociologia* (1969), No. 6, pp. 27-73.

ODORIC, M., "Étude historique et critique sur les actes du Frère Didace Pelletier, Récollet" in *Bulletin des Recherches Historiques* (1911), Vol. 17, No. 4, pp. 118-128.

PAQUET, Gilles, "L'émigration des Canadiens français vers la Nouvelle-Angleterre (1870-1960)" in *Recherches Sociographiques* (1964), Vol. 5, No. 3, pp. 319-370.

PATTERSON, George, "The Portuguese on the North-East Coast of America, and the First European Attempt at Colonization There. A Lost Chapter in American History" in *Proceedings and Transactions of the Royal Society of Canada* (1890), Vol. 8, pp. 127-173.

PEREIRA, Gil, "A emigração portuguesa no decénio de 1951-1960" in *Estudos Políticos e Sociais* (1964), Vol. 11, No. 1, pp. 205-245.

PETERSEN, William, "A General Typology of Migration" in *American Sociological Review* (1958), Vol. 23, No. 3, pp. 256-266.

PETERSEN, William, "The General Determinants of Migration" in *Population* (1961), Vol. 16, pp. 592-621.

PETERSEN, William, "Migration: Social Aspects" in *International Encyclopedia of the Social Sciences,* Vol. 10, pp. 286-292. New York, MacMillan, 1968.

PHILPOTT, Stuart B., "The Implications of Migration for Sending Societies: Some Theoretical Considerations" in *Migration and Anthropology,* ed. L. Kasdan, pp. 9-20. Seattle, American Ethnological Society, 1970.

POINARD, Michel, "L'émigration portugaise de 1960 à 1969" in *Revue Géographique des Pyrénées et du Sud-Ouest* (1971), Vol. 42, No. 3, pp. 293-304.

POINARD, Michel and ROUX, Michel, "L'émigration contre le développement: les cas portugais et yougoslave" in *Revue Tiers-Monde* (1977), Vol. 18, No. 69, pp. 21-53.

POULAIN, Jean, "Le Québec a perdu 317 000 de ses citoyens depuis 67" in *La Presse* (Montréal), 30 octobre 1976, p. A-18.

POWER, Jonathan, "The New Proletariat" in *Encounter* (Sept. 1974), Vol. 43, No. 3, pp. 8-22.

PRICE, Charles, "The Study of Assimilation" in *Migration,* ed. J. A. Jackson, pp. 181-237. London, Cambridge University Press, 1969.

RAVENSTEIN, E. G., "The Laws of Migration" in *Journal of the Royal Statistical Society* (1885), Vol. 48, pp. 167-235.

REDFIELD, Robert, LINTON, Ralph and HERSKOVITS, Melville J., "Outline for the Study of Acculturation" in *American Anthropologist* (1936), Vol. 38, pp. 149-152.

RHOADES, Robert E., "Intra-European Migration and Development in the Mediterranean Basin" in *Current Anthropology* (1977), Vol. 18, No. 3, pp. 539-540.

RIBEIRO, Orlando, "Portugal" in *Geografía de España y Portugal,* ed. Manuel de Teran. Barcelona, Montaner y Simon, 1955.

RICHMOND, Anthony H., "Immigration and Pluralism in Canada" in *International Migration Review* (1969a), Vol. 4, No. 1, pp. 5-24.

RICHMOND, Anthony H., "Sociology of Migration in Industrial and Post-Industrial Societies" in *Migration,* ed. J. A. Jackson, pp. 238-281. Cambridge, Cambridge University Press, 1969b.

RIEGELHAUPT, Joyce, "Saloio Women: An Analysis of Informal and Formal Political and Economic Roles of Portuguese Peasant Women" in *Anthropological Quarterly* (Jul. 1967), Vol. 40, pp. 109-126.

RIEGELHAUPT, Joyce, "Festas and Padres: The Organization of Religious Action in a Portuguese Parish" in *American Anthropologist* (1973), Vol. 75, pp. 835-852.

ROCHER, Guy, "Le multiculturalisme en question; Réponse à Dale Thomson" in *Le Devoir* (Montreal), 12 mars 1976, p. 5.

RONCEK, Joseph S., "Portuguese Americans" in *One America: The History, Contributions and Present Problems of our Racial and National Minorities,* eds. Francis Brown and Joseph Roncek. New York, Prentice-Hall, 1945.

SABISIAK, Walerian, "Probleme der Emigrationskultur" in *Ethnologia Europaea* (1974), Vol. 7, No. 2, pp. 246-257.

SANTOS, Antero Marques dos, "Les émigrants portugais et le retour au pays", in *Options méditéranéennes* (Dec. 1973), Vol. 22, numéro spécial, pp. 67-73.

SANTOS, Benedicta Quirino dos, "Portuguese Yankees" in *Americas* (Aug. 1953), Vol. 5, pp. 20-23.

SAUVY, Alfred, "Le renversement du courant séculaire migratoire" in *Population* (1962), Vol. 17, No. 1, pp. 51-59.

SERGE, J., "Portuguese With Problems Ask This Girl to Solve Them" in *Toronto Daily Star,* March 2, 1970.

SERRÃO, Joel, "Emigração" in *Dicionário da História de Portugal,* ed. Joel Serrão, Vol. II, pp. 19-29. Lisboa, Iniciativas Editoriais, 1965.

SERRÃO, Joel, "Conspecto histórico da emigração portuguesa" in *Análise Social* (1970), No. 32 (VIII), pp. 597-617.

SILVA, Augusto da, "Eleições 75: Fenómeno socio-cultural" in *Economia e Sociologia* (1976), Vol. 19-20, pp. 59-134.

SLINGER, John, "Dreams of Eldorado Fade for Portuguese" in *The Globe and Mail* (Toronto), August 26, 1971, p. 35.

SLINGER, John, "Portuguese Unity Hard to Achieve" in *The Globe and Mail* (Toronto), August 27, 1971, p. 5.

SLINGER, John, "Children of Portuguese Caught Between Two Worlds" in *The Globe and Mail* (Toronto), August 30, 1971, p. 5.

SMITH, M. Estellie, "Portuguese Enclaves: The Invisible Minority" in *Social and Cultural Identity: Problems of Persistence and Change,* pp. 81-91, Athens, Geo., University of Georgia Press, 1974.

SMITH, M. Estellie, "Networks and Migration Resettlement: Cherchez la femme" in *Anthropological Quarterly* (1976), Vol. 49, No. 1, pp. 20-27.

THOMAS, Brinley, "International Migration" in *The Study of Population,* eds. P. H. Hauser and O. D. Duncan, pp. 510-543. Chicago, Chicago University Press, 1959.

TRINDADE, Maria Beatriz Rocha, "Sobrevivência e progresso de uma aldeia despovoada" in *Geographica* (Revista da Sociedade de Geografia de Lisboa) (Jul. 1973a), Ano IX, No. 35, pp. 3-25.

TRINDADE, Maria Beatriz Rocha, "Portuguese Rural Migrants in Industrialised Europe" in *Iberian Studies* (Spring 1975), Vol. 4, No. 1, pp. 9-14.

TRINDADE, Maria Beatriz Rocha, "Structure sociale et familiale d'origine dans l'émigration au Portugal" in *Ethnologie Française* (1977). Vol. 7, No. 3, pp. 277-286.

TRUEBLOOD, Marilyn, "The Melting Pot and Ethnic Revitalization" in *Ethnic Encounters; Identity and Contexts,* eds. George L. Hicks and Philip E. Leis, pp. 153-167. North Scituate, Massachusetts, Duxbury Press, 1977.

VARÃO, A. Proença, "Sistema económico e política regional" in *Seara Nova* (1973), Nos. 1535-1536, pp. 3-8 et pp. 2-8.

VIGNERAS, L.-A., "Corte-Real, Gaspar" in *Dictionnaire Bibliographique du Canada,* ed. George W. Brown, Vol. 1, pp. 241-242. Québec, Les Presses de l'Université Laval, 1967a.

VIGNERAS, L.-A., "Corte-Real, Miguel" in *Dictionnaire Bibliographique du Canada,* ed. George W. Brown, Vol. 1, pp. 242-243. Québec, Les Presses de l'Université Laval, 1967b.

VILLIERS, Alan, "I sailed with Portugal's Captains Courageous" in *National Geographic Magazine* (May 1952), Vol. 51, No. 5, pp. 565-596.

YOUNG, Scott, "New Canadians: Payday Road Gang Heyday" in *The Globe and Mail* (Toronto), June 4, 1957.

WERNER, Heinz, "Freizügigkeit der Arbeitskräfte und die Wanderugsbewegungen in den Ländern der Europäischen Gemeinschaft" in *Mitteilungen aus der Arbeitsmarkt — und Berufsforschung* (Feb. 1974), No. 4/73, pp. 326-371.

WILLEMS, Emílio J., "A família portuguesa contemporânea" in *Sociologia* (1955), Vol. 17, pp. 3-55.

WILLEMS, Emílio J., "On Portuguese Family Structure" in *The Sociology of the Family: An Interdisciplinary Approach,* ed. Mahfooz A. Kanwar, pp. 222-240. Hamden, Conn., Linnet Books, 1971.

OFFICIAL DOCUMENTS

CANADA. Comité spécial mixte du Sénat et de la Chambre des communes sur la politique de l'immigration, *Rapport au Parlement.* Ottawa, Information Canada, 1975.

CANADA. Department of Manpower and Immigration, *Immigration and Population Statistics.* Ottawa, Information Canada, 1974a.

CANADA. Department of Manpower and Immigration, *Immigration Policy Perspectives.* Ottawa, Information Canada, 1974b.

CANADA. Department of Manpower and Immigration, *The Immigration Program.* Ottawa, Information Canada, 1974c.

CANADA. Department of Manpower and Immigration, *Three Years in Canada; First Report of the Longitudinal Survey on the Economic and Social Adaptation of Immigrants.* Ottawa, Information Canada, 1974d.

CANADA. Department of National Health and Welfare, *A Survey and an Action Plan for "Projet Communautaire Pilote A".* n.p., 1976.

CANADA. Ministère de la Citoyenneté et de l'Immigration. Section de la Statistique, *Origine ethnique des immigrants par province de destination: années civiles 1946-1955.* Ottawa, Ministère de la Citoyenneté et de l'Immigration, 1956.

CANADA. Ministère de la Main-d'oeuvre et de l'Immigration. Région du Québec, *Immigration et groupes ethniques: Bibliographie,* Oct. 1976.

CANADA. Ministère de la Main-d'oeuvre et de l'Immigration. Service de l'Information, *Fiche d'information de l'immigration canadienne,* 1974.

CANADA. Secrétariat d'État. Direction de la Citoyenneté canadienne, "Les Portugais" in *Les rameaux de la famille canadienne,* pp. 295-299. Ottawa, L'Imprimeur de la Reine, 1967.

PORTUGAL. Instituto Nacional de Estatística. Serviços Centrais, *Estatísticas Demográficas: Continente e Ilhas Adjacentes,* 1975.

PORTUGAL. Secretaria de Estado da Emigração, *Boletim Anual,* 1975.

PORTUGAL. Secretariado Nacional da Emigração, *Boletim Anual,* 1971, 1972.

QUÉBEC. Ministère de l'Immigration, *Une problématique des ressources humaines au Québec. (Document de travail et de réflexion)*. Montreal, 1974.

QUÉBEC. Ministère de l'Immigration, *Rapport annuel* 1975/1976.

QUÉBEC. Ministère de l'Immigration. Centre de Documentation, *Bibliographie sélective sur le groupe ethnique portugais établi au Québec et au Canada,* Dec. 1975.

QUÉBEC. Ministère de l'Immigration. Comité consultatif de l'immigration du Québec, *L'immigration québécoise et les communautés ethniques.* Synthèse du Colloque tenu les 4 et 5 juin 1977.

QUÉBEC. Ministère de l'Immigration. Direction de la Recherche, *L'immigration au Québec — Bulletin statistique annuel,* Vol. 1, 1973.

QUÉBEC. Ministère de l'Immigration. Direction de la Recherche, *Québec Immigration — Langues 1969-1974; Bulletin Spécial,* No. 4, 1975.

QUÉBEC. Ministère de l'Immigration. Direction de la Recherche, *L'immigration au Québec — Bulletin Spécial No. 3; Catégorie réglementaire d'admission, 1968-1974,* (1975).

QUÉBEC. Ministère de l'Immigration. Direction des Communications, "Les Portugais et la renaissance du quartier Saint-Louis" in *Québec-Monde,* (Nov. 1976), No. 12, pp. 1, 4-5.

QUÉBEC. Ministère de l'Immigration. Direction des Communications. *L'immigration: Rapport annuel 1977-78.* Québec, Éditeur officiel, 1978.

SUBJECT INDEX

NAME INDEX

Corte-Real, João Vaz, 48, 56, 57

Corte-Real, Miguel, 50, 51, 54, 55, 58

Cortesão, Jaime, 56

Côté, Françoise, 42, 180, 203, 206

Couture, Jacques, 282, 286

Cronin, Constance, 116

Cruz, João and Suzana da, 67

Cutileiro, José, 36, 134, 138, 140, 147, 224

D

Da Costa, Mateus, 64

Da Silva, Pedro, 65, 66, 67

Dejean, Paul, 203, 211

Delabarre, Edmund, 50, 54

Delacour, André, 99

Demourache, Joseph, 68

Descamps, Paul, 62, 63

Descôteaux, Bernard, 194

D'Espera, 59

Déziel, Julien, 66

Dias, António Jorge, 36, 87, 96, 98, 122, 130, 204, 238

Dias, Bartolomeu, 48

Drapeau, Jean, 77

Durkheim, Émile, 152

E

Eidheim, Harald, 116

Eisenstadt, S.N., 14

Eldorado, 63

Elkin, F., 93, 118

Éloi-Gérard, 65, 66, 67

Elvas, 51

Engels, F., 36

England, 25, 36, 56, 62, 63, 98, 110, 213

Europe, 21, 38, 47, 48, 86, 88, 93, 105, 117, 198, 213

F

Fagundes, João Alvares, 55, 60

Faial, 52, 79

Fall River, 52

Fermuse, 59

Fernandes, Alvaro, 51

Fernandes, João, 56, 57

Fernández, Ronald, 76

New Brunswick, 70, 85, 108

New England, 50, 52, 60, 113

Newfoundland, 48, 50, 54, 55, 56, 57, 58, 70, 108, 240

New France, 65

New Guinea, 49

New Jersey, 53

New York, 52, 53, 85, 113, 252

Nicholas V, 222

Nicolet, 81

Nikolinakos, Marios, 16

Nogueira, Armando, 41

North Africa, 50

North America, 21, 40, 47, 50, 51, 54, 55, 58, 62

Noury, 67

Nova Scotia, 55, 57, 58, 70, 108

Nunes, Sedas, 105

O

Ontario, 18, 70, 72, 85, 108, 113

Oporto, see *Porto*

Orient, 49, 50, 96, 97

Ottawa, 77, 78, 240

P

Pacific Ocean, 52

Pap, Leo, 50, 54, 153

Paproski, Steve, 15

Paquet, Gilles, 113

Parai, Louis, 193

Paris, 67

Paspébiac, 240

Pasqualigo, Pietro, 58

Patterson, George, 49, 51, 55, 58, 63

Paul VI, 231, 233, 237

Peres, Damião, 55

Perestrelo, Bartolomeu, 51

Pescadero, 52

Pickersgill, J.W., 212

Pico, 52

P.I.D.E., 22, 29

Pire, see *Henne*

Placentia Bay, 54

Poinard and Roux, 106

Point Conception, 52

Ponta Delgada, 73, 86

Port-au-Prince, 240

Port-Cartier, 82

PRINTED BY
L'IMPRIMERIE DES FRANCISCAINS
2010 DORCHESTER BLVD. W., MONTREAL, QUE. H3H 1R6
FOR THE UNIVERSITY OF OTTAWA PRESS
65, HASTEY AVE., OTTAWA, ONT. K1N 6N5
CANADA

Imprimé au Canada   *Printed in Canada*